How to Live an Artful Life

366 Inspirations from Artists on How to Bring Creativity to Your Everyday

Katy Hessel

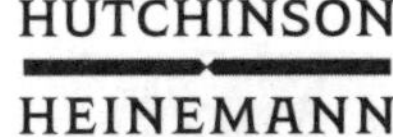

HUTCHINSON
HEINEMANN

HUTCHINSON HEINEMANN

UK | USA | Canada | Ireland | Australia
India | New Zealand | South Africa

Hutchinson Heinemann is part of the Penguin Random House group of companies
whose addresses can be found at global.penguinrandomhouse.com

Penguin Random House UK,
One Embassy Gardens, 8 Viaduct Gardens, London SW11 7BW

penguin.co.uk

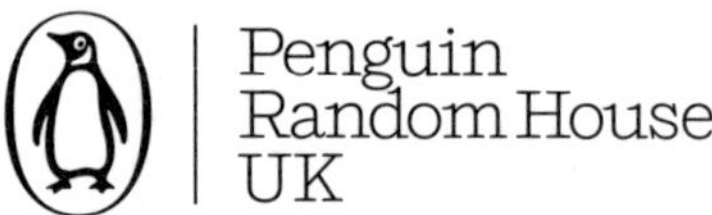

Penguin
Random House
UK

First published 2025
007

Copyright © Katy Hessel, 2025

The moral right of the author has been asserted

Text design by Francisca Monteiro

Set in Adobe Garamond Pro 11/14
Typeset by Six Red Marbles UK, Thetford, Norfolk
Printed and bound in Great Britain by Clays Ltd, Elcograf S.p.A.

The authorised representative in the EEA is Penguin Random House Ireland,
Morrison Chambers, 32 Nassau Street, Dublin D02 YH68

A CIP catalogue record for this book is available from the British Library

ISBN: 978–1–529–15520–4

Penguin Random House is committed to a sustainable future
for our business, our readers and our planet. This book is made
from Forest Stewardship Council® certified paper.

How to Live an Artful Life

A Call to Arms

What is an artful life? Living 'artfully' is not about optimising every moment of everyday life. It's about connecting to the world inside ourselves by consciously taking the time to pause and reflect on the world *outside*. In practice, living an artful life can heighten your sense of joy and expand your sense of beauty.

It's never been more important to turn to those who can help us lead creative lives. The world may be trying to turn us into machines, with creativity outsourced to the likes of AI, but we can still look, read, think, exist for ourselves.

That is where this book comes in.

To live artfully does not mean to be an artist full time, or to be an artist at all, or to always be going to museums or galleries. Although, of course, it can mean that. More expansively, it's a way of thinking and living which we can learn from artists and apply to our day-to-day existence, whatever and whoever we are. It can exist alongside our day jobs – and even enhance those day jobs.

This book is also the story of a year: a way to take time for yourself and your creativity every day. The intention is to build this way of seeing and living artfully over the course of twelve months, though you can begin anywhere in these pages and at any time of the year. Each entry will take about five minutes of your time to read and think about, encouraging you to slow down, go deeper, and notice the small details in the world around us. Together, the suggestions in this book work against the idea of busyness and unwanted distraction.

What follows is an entry for every day of the year, loosely gathered by themes for each month, from how to start, to love and passion, beauty, memory and joy. Each offers an inspiration from an artist alongside a short thought or exercise from me, and a note about the artist in case you feel inclined to learn more and discover their work for yourself.

I've been meeting with, speaking to and interviewing artists across the globe for over a decade, sitting down with them in their studio spaces and hearing first-hand how they see the world. Many of the thoughts that follow have been gifted by those artists specially to this book, or have come from our conversations over the years. The rest are gathered from interviews, books, films and lectures that I have always cherished and kept close to me.

Sometimes there is an image of an artwork, or a story about 'art', because there's an energy to art – a spirit that lives inside of it that can enrich you when you bear witness to it. To train yourself to look carefully at an artwork is a way of training yourself to look at the world. As the novelist and writer Iris Murdoch said, 'Great art is liberating, it enables us to see and take pleasure in what is not ourselves.'

In a world built to distract us, let's find the time and space to pay attention and live artfully, day by day.

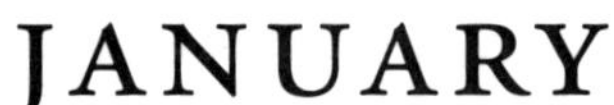

JANUARY

How to Start

January: a quest for clarity and discovery, a time for thinking about beginnings and fresh starts. A perfect moment to seek out and nurture new ideas, which can hatch when they are ready.

As the natural world teaches us, winter can be an important time for growth that is most likely invisible. While this work can be difficult, slow or even painful, do not despair. The year ahead is a great unknown. Time to embrace its energy and ideas.

The power of art

'Art is a material act of culture, but its greatest value is its spiritual role, and that influences society, because it's the greatest contribution to the intellectual and moral development of humanity that can be made.' —Ana Mendieta

Art can come in all different forms: it can be tangible or ephemeral – a solid object or a fleeting performance; it can exist in the physical world, or in our memory. But its power lies in its spirit – it's this that can move us, offer us transcendence, and speak across time and cultures as a universal language.

When you experience an artwork, you don't just see it, but you feel it. That, for me, is where its greatness lies. The best thing we can do is take time with it. There is no right or wrong way to look at or engage with it. Great art keeps being surprising. If you are alive to it, the possibilities it will show you are endless.

Today, think about an artwork that moves you. What does it look like? Why did it remain imprinted in your mind? Take a moment to reflect on what made/makes it special to you. Where did you see it? How old were you then, and how old are you now?

I like to start the year with Ana Mendieta's *Silueta* series, which highlighted the artist's body – and later the absence of the body – in the earth across the United States, Mexico and Cuba, entwining it with nature, and connecting it to all of humanity.

Ana Mendieta (1948–85), born in Havana, Cuba, was an interdisciplinary artist and sculptor, known for her ephemeral 'earth-body' works.

Source: 'Art and Politics', a series of dialogues at The New Museum, NYC, 1983.

What is an artist?

'An artist is someone who goes to a place where no one's been before, and brings back something we/you have never seen before but instantly recognise.' —Nick Willing, recalling a conversation with his parents, artists Paula Rego and Victor Willing

Why do so many of us all around the world take the time to look at art? What is the point?

Whenever people ask me why I pay attention to art I quote the definition above from Nick Willing.

Artists can make the unfamiliar familiar (and vice versa). They can show us something that we instantly recognise, despite it being made in a completely different world and context to our own. Using just twelve musical notes, musicians can express the human experience through melody; using tones and colours, visual artists can hold up a picture that can make our heart pound; through words and sentences, writers can connect us to the great web of humanity, stretching through time and place.

While we can never get inside someone's head, we can attempt to understand the perspective of others through their creations. Whose work will you look at today? How will expand your understanding?

I like to look at Paula Rego's *The Dance*, 1988 (overleaf). Set under a moonlit sky, this painting shows the different stages of a woman's life. We see her dancing as a child, holding hands with her middle- and old-aged self (or perhaps her mother and grandmother). We see her pregnant, with her partner; with her back turned towards us as her lover's gaze suspiciously meets ours – as if he is telling us something she doesn't know. And finally, on the left, alone, bigger and stronger than the rest.

Nick Willing (b. 1961) is a British-Portuguese filmmaker, who, among other titles, made *Paula Rego: Secrets and Stories* (2017), a documentary about his mother.

Source: The Great Women Artists Podcast, *2021*

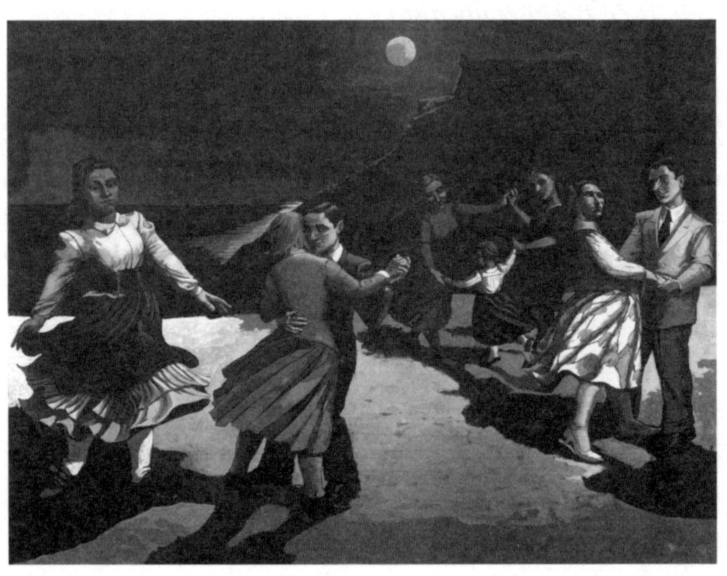

Paula Rego, *The Dance*, 1988

Why should we look to art and artists?

'[Artists] help you make sense. And they help you make senses, your senses, and they give you back, at every level, your senses alive again, to yourself. Whenever you stand in front of or are present with . . . anything that is a piece of art, you attend, you're there, you're actually there and you're attentive, and something in you has been awakened to it. Even if you're having an argument with it, even if you really dislike it, even if you're in the presence of something that has made you furious . . . So we have in it a dialogue immediately where we are present to it and it is present to us. And there's something in the air, which is wordless. And at the same time asks for articulation. So all those things happen. As soon as you're present to art, all the thinking, all the renewing of our senses happens immediately.' —Ali Smith

Think of your favourite artwork. You might have seen it in a gallery, book or online. Show it someone else. Talk about it; debate it; articulate it; be present to it. Ask someone: what's that supposed to be?

If you don't have someone with you, have the conversation with yourself. When I'm in front of an artwork, I've developed a practice of downloading everything I see, think and feel in that moment. (I like to use the notes application on my phone, but handwritten or voice-recorded notes might be more suited to you.) I start by describing what I see, and go from there.

Ali Smith (b. 1962) is an acclaimed Scottish writer of fiction and non-fiction. Between 2016 and 2020, she completed a series of four stand-alone novels, grouped as the Seasonal Quartet, which track unprecedented events in living history. At the spine of each book is an artist: Pauline Boty in *Autumn*, Barbara Hepworth in *Winter*, Tacita Dean in *Spring*, and filmmaker Lorenza Mazzetti in *Summer*.

Source: The Great Women Artists Podcast, *2021*

How art can help us focus

'I like getting stuff out of the way so you can see something clearly, see it sharply, have it be new again. I think making things that appear simple is incredibly hard.

Something about photography is tied to a very specific relationship with the material world. It doesn't have to be, but the way I practice it, it is. So there's an act of observation, but it's not an act of objective recording. It's about framing something and seeing it and understanding that it's relational. It's how you're looking as much as what you're looking at.' —Zoe Leonard

How can you block out the noise in an overwhelming world?

'It's how you're looking as much as what you're looking at.'

Leonard shows us that we can use tools – like the camera – to find clarity in what it is that we are seeking to observe; to help us to look closer, and give our attention to the things that give us life.

It might take only a minute, but art can help us focus. What will you pay attention to, and how will you record what you have noticed?

Zoe Leonard (b. 1961) is an American artist, based in New York City, working across installation, photography and sculpture. She often uses repetition and sequencing to trace – and focus on – an image or object through time, and to see meaning in what might at first seem familiar. This can include photographing the same place or entity, whether it be a riverbank damaged by climate change, clouds out of a window, buildings or people. By using subtle shifts in perspective, or the changing of scale, she gets us to look closer and deeper – away from the overwhelming world around us; and to think about the transient nature of our own reality.

Source: Leonard, Zoe, 'Aerials', via Studio International, 2018. Amended in a note to the author, 2025

Keep a diary

'You can stand anything if you write it down . . .'
—Louise Bourgeois

Louise Bourgeois wrote her first diary entry when she was eleven years old, and never stopped. She had three types – 'the written, the spoken (into a tape recorder), and [her] drawing diary'.

Writing helped her to confront and process her trauma and anxiety – she felt that 'you can stand anything if you write it down'.

Bourgeois's compulsive diary writing was crucial for her creative output, as she turned to it again and again to help inform her artworks.

Sometimes writing a diary, or drawing – sketching doodles in whatever way works for you – can be the truest record of ourselves. It can document our deepest emotions, desires and fears, allowing us to access them even as the feelings pass.

Write it down, then lock it away or use it if you wish. But start now. You will never have this moment or this feeling back, and you never know what it will lead to.

The French-American artist **Louise Bourgeois** (1911–2010) was best known for her sculptures, prints, installations and fabric works, featuring motifs such as the spiral and the spider.

Source, quote 1: Wye, Deborah, ed., Louise Bourgeois: The Complete Prints & Books, *online catalogue raisonné (New York: Museum of Modern Art, 2018), cat. no. 1228–9,* He Disappeared into Complete Silence, *first and second editions, 1947 and 2005; quote 2: Bourgeois, Louise, 'Tender Compulsions', World Art, no. 2, February 1995, reprinted in Bernadac, Marie-Laure and Hans Ulrich Obrist, (eds.),* Louise Bourgeois: Destruction of the Father, Reconstruction of the Father: Writings and Interviews 1923–1997, *London: Violette Editions, 1998*

Put down your phone

'My advice to young people is to put down their phones. That's my advice. Don't think that it's okay to live in your phone. You have a lot more to say than Instagram. And a lot to experience in the real world. The most important thing is to stand in front of another person and breathe the same air. That's real knowledge that can't be found in your phone.' —Nan Goldin

While machines can be categorised as digits, humans can't. While machines can spark emotions in us, they can't show us love. While they can think, they can't feel. That's the job of the human, who has a limitless ability (or superpower) to recognise every emotion.

Be in the world. Talk to people. Go to places, even if it's not far. Look up into the expanse of the skies rather than into our tech-filtered selves. Revolutions won't happen on your phone. Take back your attention and give it to each other.

Nan Goldin (b. 1953) is an American artist who has transformed photography in contemporary art. Her work addresses the human experience with themes of love, loss, sexuality, violence, beauty, addiction and mortality. As an activist, Goldin continues to stand up to injustices committed by governments and global conglomerates.

Source: Nan Goldin's Advice to the Young, *Louisiana Channel, 2023 (video); amended in a note to the author, 2025*

Experiment

'This feeling of experiment, like when you're young, you begin to write, you begin to fill up a page and you're just going to see where it leads you. You don't necessarily understand it, thank God. What would be the point in continuing if you knew everything about it?' —Deborah Levy

Practise forgetting to be self-conscious. See where it leads. Start to notice what happens as you just do it, write it, paint it, draw it. Remember that excitement is in the discovery of the unknown and joy is in the act of experimentation. What would be the point if we always knew the answer?

Deborah Levy (b. 1959) is a South African-born, British writer and the author of several critically acclaimed novels and non-fiction works including her 'living autobiographies' on writing, gender politics and philosophy: *Things I Don't Want to Know*, *The Cost of Living* and *Real Estate*. She has been shortlisted twice for both the Goldsmiths Prize and the Booker Prize.

Source: The Great Women Artists Podcast, *2021*

Where do ideas come from?

'Most artists . . . their work comes from the most simple things because what artists do is just reinterpret the world, and the world is of a certain thing: it is what it is. What we do is sort of search out the strangeness within that and that's what I've done . . . I've looked for something and tried to unfold it and made a deeper way of looking at it – and hopefully a more profound way of looking at yourself.' —Rachel Whiteread

As a child, the sculptor Rachel Whiteread was fascinated by cardboard boxes that stored items like Christmas lights. While at first glance these boxes might seem mundane – often scruffily taped together due to reuse – they can also be seen as representing something meaningful. A memory of Christmases past; the container of an entity that could adorn something as enchanting as an indoor tree; a box that has the power to transport you back to your childhood self.

Whiteread holds on to these memories by casting boxes and household items – like spoons and hot water bottles – in resin or concrete, to preserve the significance of what they once contained.

Art doesn't need to draw from a grand place, it can come from the most ordinary things. Look closely at everyday objects, and show us something anew.

Rachel Whiteread (b. 1963) is a British artist who works across sculpture and drawing, in mediums ranging from concrete to resin, and in scales from minuscule to colossal. Discussing how her work gives, in her words, 'authority to forgotten things', Whiteread transforms familiar objects and buildings into ghostly replicas in the form of casts. Her sculptures have provided a commentary on social and political changes, reflecting a sense of impermanence and loss.

Source: The Great Women Artists Podcast, *2023*

Where do you make art?
How can you make the best of what you have?

'In Chile, I painted in the closet because I didn't have a studio. In one painting you can see the beam of light coming through the door . . .'—Luchita Hurtado

An enduring myth of what an 'artist' looks like and where and how they work might be a large studio, canvases or sculptures everywhere, and a swarm of studio assistants. But the reality for most artists is the opposite – a small corner in a busy room, drawing in a sketchpad on a train, or using the streets as their stage.

The Venezuelan-born painter Luchita Hurtado had her closet, so she used that. But she made the most of it. Maybe her painting, *Untitled* (overleaf), wouldn't have become what it was had that crack of light not come through.

Making the best of what you have is your greatest advantage.

Luchita Hurtado (1920–2020) was a Venezuelan artist who was based in Los Angeles, USA, for much of her life. Constantly experimenting with different art forms, scales and subject matters, which created unexpected perspectives – from looking down at her body to straight up at the sky – Hurtado, through cosmic motifs and geometric abstraction, investigated universality and transcendence.

Source: Lewin, Rebecca and Constable, Joseph (eds.), Luchita Hurtado: I Live, I Die, I Will Be Reborn, *Serpentine Galleries & Koenig Books, 2019*

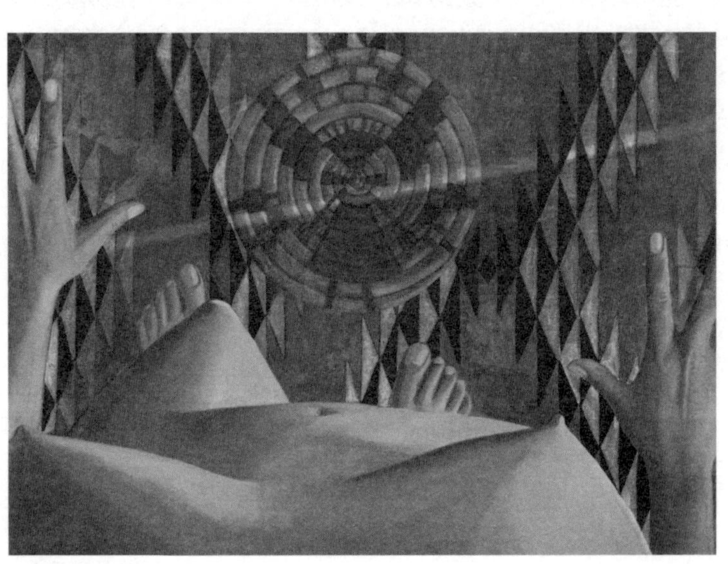

Luchita Hurtado, *Untitled*, 1969

How do you find your language?

'How do we choose our specific material, our means of communication? "Accidentally." Something speaks to us, a sound, a touch, hardness or softness, it catches us and asks us to be formed. We are finding our language, and as we go along we learn to obey their rules and their limits. We have to obey, and adjust to those demands. Ideas flow from it to us and though we feel to be the creator we are involved in a dialogue with our medium. The more subtly we are tuned to our medium, the more inventive our actions will become. Not listening to it ends in failure. (Years ago, I once asked John Cage how he had started to find his way. He will not remember it. "By chance" was the answer.)

Students worry about choosing their way. I always tell them, "You can go anywhere from anywhere".' —Anni Albers

Look around you. Let ideas come to you. Whatever you choose now does not have to determine what you do for the rest of your life. Catch some ideas, let go of others, and remember no work is ever 'finished'. Embrace the knowledge that every sketch, play, idea, sentence, can lead to something else.

Anni Albers (1899–1994), who was born in Germany and died in the USA, was one of the foremost artists working in fibre in the twentieth century. She was also a great educator, as a teacher at the Bauhaus (Germany) and Black Mountain College (USA).

Source: Albers, Anni, 'Material as Metaphor', statement on panel 'The Art/Craft Connection: Grass Roots or Glass Houses' at the College Art Association's 1982 annual meeting, New York, 25 February 1982

Look out for the small details

'To me, lots of things come and go quicker than I can catch them. I mean, they have such clarity and at the same time they're moving faster than I can catch. And sometimes they will come back again. [. . .] Things are given to everyone all the time. I think artists just pay attention to what they're given. And then they run with it, see where it takes them – but it's about having trust in what you're given.'—Kiki Smith

Every second of every day we are confronted with so many small details, from plants to trees, the many people we pass, to the cloud formations in the skies. While we miss most things, it's important to try and 'catch' those that enter into our surroundings while we can.

Look up from where you are reading: what do you see? Is it a detail you have noticed before? Does it surprise you? What do you know of where it comes from? Be attuned to the world, and see what it gives you back. Trust that you can make something from what you see.

Kiki Smith (b. 1954) is an American multidisciplinary artist known for her tapestries and sculptures that often address themes of mortality and decay, the body and the earth, what it means to be human, and our relationship to nature.

Source: The Great Women Artists Podcast, *2023*

Why ideas are best when they change

'What's very, very important is allowing yourself to not be fixed by your original idea. I'm definitely an artist that enjoys the journey. I'm not particularly attracted to work that is an idea that is just made. I actually like art that has evolved and become something that the artist wasn't intending to make . . . For me, that's a much more interesting artwork.' —*Tacita Dean*

Dean often works in analogue film. She uses a photochemical camera, which, by its very nature, prevents you from seeing what you are initially making – unlike a digital one. Only when you process and print, when you turn the lights on, can you uncover it – with the image or moving image revealing itself.

This is a reminder that ideas can't be fixed in advance. As with anything in life, you have to let an idea become its own thing.

Tacita Dean (b. 1965) is a British European artist who works with drawing, photography, installation and found objects, but is best known for film. She is interested in capturing the 'truth of the moment, the film as a medium, and the sensibilities of the individual'. Her analogue films – painterly and unpredictable – at times become portraits of the medium itself.

Source: The Great Women Artists Podcast, *2021*

Get out

'First of all. I hate the studio. I think the studio is a trap for me.'
—Marina Abramović

There is no right or wrong way to live artfully. But if there's one thing: don't stay trapped in your space. Go out and look, observe, engage. Ideas can come from anywhere: from walking a few steps outside your front door to visiting far corners of the world, or even travelling through time with objects in museums, or empathetically through books. Where will you visit today?

Marina Abramović (b. 1946), born in Yugoslavia (now Serbia), is considered as a pioneer and 'warrior' of performance art. Since the beginning of her career, Abramović has stretched the limits of the body. Early works include *Rhythm 0* (1974), which saw her declare herself as the object, and instruct the audience to use props on her as they wished. She has continued to break boundaries for the last five decades and counting.

Source: The Great Women Artists Podcast, *2022*

See the extraordinary in the ordinary

'An artist is not special. An artist is an ordinary person who can take ordinary things and make them special.' —*Ruth Asawa*

American artist Ruth Asawa is known for her cocoon-like sculptures made from looped metal wires. They typically hang from the ceiling and, when lit, they create shadows and unexpected shapes and lines (see overleaf).

But at the root of these sculptures is a single, simple entity: wire.

The artist's job is to see the potential in something. From a single word that can be joined up into a sentence that can grow into a paragraph, speech or book; to a tube of paint that can be used to create an image that might shape the way someone sees the world.

Don't idolise the rare, enjoy the familiar. How will/can you transform something ordinary?

Ruth Asawa (1926–2013) was an American artist recognised for her wire sculptures and public commissions, and as an influential educator and arts advocate in the San Francisco Bay Area.

Source: Nathan, Harriet, 'Oral history transcript/Ruth Asawa', Bancroft Library, 1974 and 1976

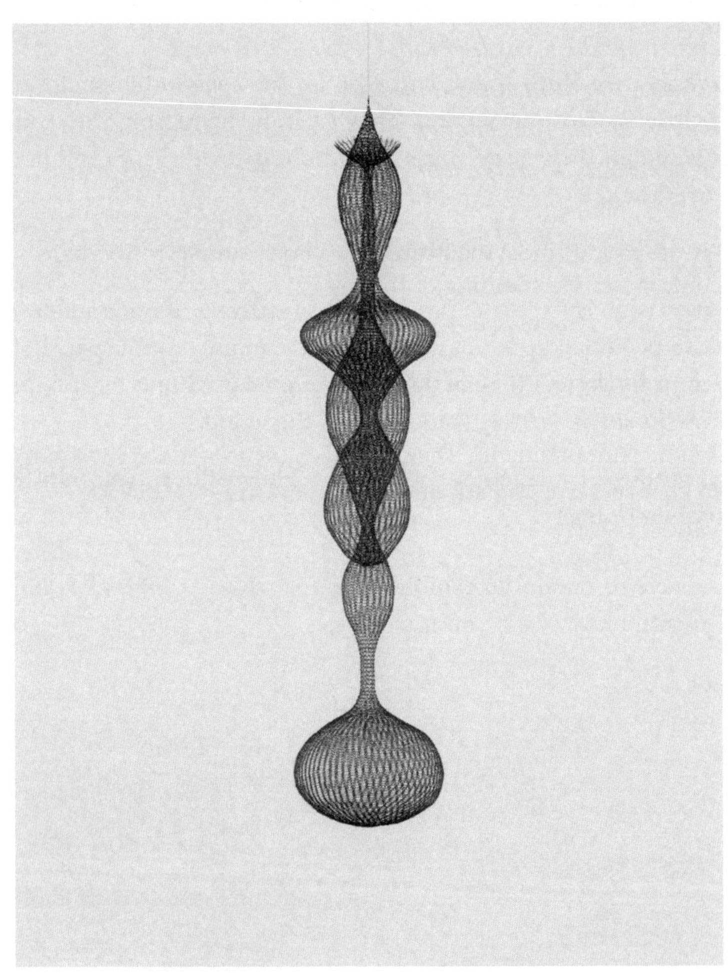

Ruth Asawa, *Untitled* (S.237, Hanging Six-Lobed, Interlocking Continuous Form), c. 1958

Be porous

'One of the more important things that we can do as thinkers is to remain porous to the ideas that the artist is conveying, as opposed to what I would want them to do. It doesn't mean being a supplicant, but it means submitting to this experience, that they have been so generous enough to share with us. Because it's a great act of generosity to make work, I think.' —*Hilton Als*

When we are porous to the ideas of artists and writers, we can gain a much deeper understanding of their craft, leaving us with new ways of thinking about them.

Als, an acclaimed writer and critic, is also a curator. Some of my favourite exhibitions curated by him are 'portraits' of writers, such as Joan Didion or James Baldwin. They feature existing artwork by a range of artists that speak to and ask questions about the subject's life and work.

If you were to 'curate' an exhibition of an artist or writer, what objects, images and films would you use?

Hilton Als (b. 1960) is an American writer, critic and curator, known for his non-fiction books and contributions to *The New Yorker*.

Source: The Great Women Artists Podcast, *2023*

Keep looking

'It is a very interesting exercise. I think you go through different phases as you're observing, and certainly, many of the phases involve extreme resistance to the exercise.

You're sitting there in front of the mirror, or an artwork, and just really resenting the whole idea. But then eventually that resentment fades, and you start to look at something else. So part of the experience is observing the ebb and flow of your own resentment and resistance to that kind of deep observation.

But then there are moments where you suddenly realise, "Wow, I just noticed something that I would never have noticed had I not been doing this." And that leads to a whole new area of inquiry with that object, whatever it might be.' —Ruth Ozeki

In 2022, Ozeki published a part-experiment, part-memoir titled *Timecode of a Face*, which follows a time log of her findings when she took a mirror, placed it on her Zen altar, and looked at herself for three hours. Observing closely the lines on her face, she was reminded of her own memories and even connections to ancestors. From this, she wrote the story of her life.

Ozeki was influenced by the essay 'The Power of Patience' by art historian Professor Jennifer Roberts.

Today's entry is an exercise. Can you look at something – an artwork, a photograph, your reflection – for ten minutes, thirty minutes, an hour, or more, keeping a time log as you go? What will you find?

Ruth Ozeki (b. 1956) is an American-Canadian Zen Buddhist priest, and author of the novel *A Tale for the Time Being*, as well as several other fiction and non-fiction books.

Source: The Great Women Artists Podcast, *2023*

Get into the right frame of mind

'[Patricia Highsmith's] favourite technique to ease herself into the right frame of mind for work was to sit on her bed surrounded by cigarettes, ashtray, matches, a mug of coffee, a doughnut and an accompanying saucer of sugar. She had to avoid any sense of discipline and make the act of writing as pleasurable as possible. Her position, she noted, would be almost foetal and, indeed, her intention was to create, she said, "a womb of her own".' —Andrew Wilson on Patricia Highsmith

Where do you feel most comfortable? What makes you feel good? Sometimes it's not the 'making' that can be the hardest part, but getting going – and being in the right frame of mind. What does that look like for you?

Patricia Highsmith (1921–95) was an American author of novels and short stories, famously known for creating the character Tom Ripley.

Source: Wilson, Andrew, Beautiful Shadow: A Life of Patricia Highsmith, *Bloomsbury, 2003, quoted in Currey, Mason,* Daily Rituals: How Artists Work, *Alfred A. Knopf, 2013*

Question authority, find out yourself

'During the seventies, and into the eighties, I was very much questioning what happens to art. . . . What [does] art have to be for, in perpetuity, longevity? What happens if it's not [long-lasting]? Is it such a terrible thing?

Those things made me question how art becomes institutionalised. That then requires certain aspects of authority to say "this art is good", and "this art is bad". I think that's what I was really trying to look at. Why is bad art bad? You know, who says so?'
—Phyllida Barlow

Who gets to decides what is good, and what is bad? What 'should' or 'shouldn't' art be? Should it hold our attention indefinitely, or for only a moment? Who has historically been able to decide what we can and can't see?

Ask yourself today: what do you find to be good? That is all that matters.

Phyllida Barlow (1944–2023) was a celebrated British artist, mostly known for her work in sculpture that could be simultaneously colossal and intimate, precarious and triumphant, made from cement, cardboard, fabric and chicken wire. An influential educator at the Slade School of Art, London, for four decades until 2009, Barlow represented Britain at the Venice Biennale in 2017.

Source: The Great Women Artists Podcast, *2021*

Find your own rules

'I had actually come up with this different technique, because I hadn't known the rules. So I think that's what most of my work is. Because I don't know the rules. I just make some up.'
—Cornelia Parker

Were some of the greatest artworks made according to a formula, or were they made with a pioneering spirit? Did they show us something we already knew, or something that nobody had ever seen before?

Let's take Cornelia Parker and her fractured installation *Cold Dark Matter: An Exploded View* (1991; overleaf), which saw her blow up a garden shed (and its contents, such as bicycle wheels, hair curlers, old coke cans) and suspend the remains from the ceiling. She hung them on metal wires and added a light bulb in the centre of the fragmented items.

See the work in person, and it will distort everything you think you are looking at.

When it comes to making art, there is no textbook or manual. If you're abiding by that, then you're probably making a picture, not art. Art is about invention, possibility, rule-breaking. What will you do today that no one has done before?

Cornelia Parker (b. 1956) is a British artist who works across a spectrum of mediums, from sculpture to installation, reconfiguring, resurrecting and transforming familiar objects and materials.

Source: The Great Women Artists Podcast, *2020*

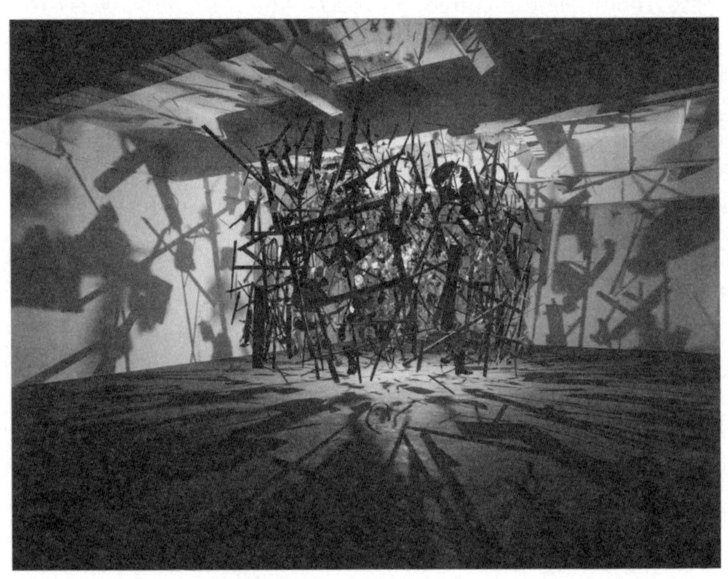

Installation view of Cornelia Parker, *Cold Dark Matter: An Exploded View*, 1991

What is the role and responsibility of an artist today?

'I believe that the new role of the artist is to create an art that is more than decoration, commodity or political tool – an art that questions the status quo . . . Making art today is synonymous with assuming responsibility for our fellow human beings.' —*Agnes Denes*

In 1982, Agnes Denes planted, grew and harvested a two-acre farm of wheat at the tip of Manhattan, for a work she called *Wheatfield: A Confrontation* (overleaf).

'Confronting' how people were mistreating and mismanaging the land, the work responded to the ever-evolving climate crisis and ongoing damage of land by capitalist structures for financial gain. It is a work made all the more powerful because it could not be made today: there is not a two-acre space available on the tip of Manhattan.

What can you make that holds up a mirror to the truths of what is happening in the world?

Agnes Denes (b. 1931) is recognised as a pioneer of ecological and land art, as well as other art forms. Often working on a monumental scale, her visionary work deals with environmental, cultural and social issues, and is immersed in science, philosophy, history and psychology, addressing the challenges of global survival.

Source: A note to the author; quote date 1978

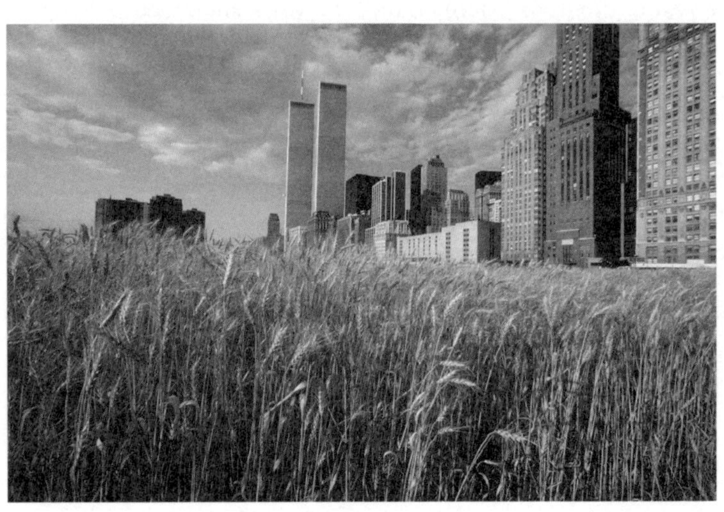

Agnes Denes, *Wheatfield – A Confrontation: Battery Park Landfill, Downtown Manhattan –
With New York Financial Center, 1982*

You can use anything

'I started painting clouds – I was always looking at the sky. One day, I was lying in the field . . . Totally no clouds – blue sky – and out of nowhere twelve military planes arrive. They crossed like ultrasonic: "Vroom!" When they crossed, you have this incredible drawing from what they made in the air. I was looking, absolutely mesmerised, at this drawing . . . and I got this realisation. I could make drawings with the planes. I could use fire, water, earth, whatever . . . I could use my body.' —Marina Abramović

We're back to Abramović again. She's good to think about at the start of the year; she shows us that there are so many possibilities. Use whatever you have around you – from the clouds to jets that fill up the sky – but also what is stored inside you: love, anger, pain, humour, fear, sadness, loneliness, happiness, joy. The list is endless.

Marina Abramović (b. 1946), was born in Yugoslavia (now Serbia) and is considered as a pioneer and 'warrior' of performance art. Since the beginning of her career in the 1970s, Abramović has stretched the limits of the body. Early works include *Rhythm 0* (1974), which saw her declare herself as the object, and instruct the audience to use props on her as they wished. She has continued to break boundaries for the last five decades and counting.

Source: Abramović, Marina; Warsh, Larry (ed.), Abramović-isms, *Princeton University Press, 2024*

You can't go wrong doing you

'My mother used to say: "Take what you have to make what you need." In essence, you don't have to buy pieces, you can use what you have. Instead of going out there trying to get what other people have and what other people do – do you! You know that you can't go wrong doing you.' —Loretta Pettway Bennett, *Gee's Bend Quiltmakers*

When I was younger, I was terrified of writing 'about art' because I was too worried about getting it 'right' – too scared to say what I thought. As a result, my essays had barely any original ideas.

My life as a writer changed when I read a book called *The Lonely City* by Olivia Laing, which explores loneliness through the eyes of artists in New York City (Laing had just moved there). The book made me *feel* how exciting art writing can be, how it can be written about through any lens.

Choose your lens and say what you think. As Loretta Pettway Bennett says, you can't go wrong doing you.

Loretta Pettway Bennett (b. 1960) is part of the Gee's Bend Quiltmakers, an all-female, Black American community based in Alabama, USA, made up of more than four generations of women. They make their colourful and jazzy quilts for a multitude of reasons.

Source: The Great Women Artists Podcast, *2021*

Smash it

'If you can't open the door, smash it down!' —*Tracey Emin*

How do you think Tracey Emin became Dame Tracey Emin? Smash it!

Tracey Emin (b. 1963) is one of the most influential British artists, looking to her life for primary material, and creating work across painting, sculpture, installation, drawing and more.

Source: The Great Women Artists Podcast, *2022*

You have not a moment to lose!

'Seventeen years wasted in eating, dawdling and frittering time away . . . Art is eternal, but life is short . . . I will make up for it now, I have not a moment to lose.' —*Evelyn de Morgan*

Nineteenth-century artist Evelyn de Morgan wrote this in a diary entry on the eve of her seventeenth birthday. She was one of the first women offered a state-funded art education in the UK, after the Slade School of Art opened its doors to male and female students in 1871.

Finally given an artistic opportunity equal to her male counterparts, it's not surprising that she felt she wanted to seize the moment. What would you like to seize? Write it down.

Evelyn de Morgan (1855–1919) was a British artist, often associated with the Pre-Raphaelites. She is known for her meticulously rendered and often vividly coloured paintings of Biblical and mythological characters.

Source: via De Morgan Foundation archives

Power of experience

'Well, what is education? Education is your whole life. Everything is education. Good, bad or indifferent, all are important.' —Leonora Carrington

It can be easy to measure ourselves against those who have multiple degrees, a string of exhibitions or books under their belt – but, as Carrington says, education is your whole life.

You are never starting from ground zero. All experiences are valuable.

Leonora Carrington (1917–2011) was a British-born artist and writer who lived in France and Spain before settling in Mexico during the Second World War. She painted fantastical beings and creatures within scenes that were enigmatic, otherworldly, yet strangely familiar.

Source: Leonora Carrington in conversation with Joanna Moorhead, Roma Norte, Mexico City, 2009

What does success mean?

'Success for me is staying true to who you are and not deviating from a path. I don't think my successes would've come to me as easily had I not committed to making the work in such a way that made me uncomfortable. I could've gotten the job teaching or could've made myself comfortable, but I didn't. I did a job that I didn't want to do, so I could do a job that I wanted to do.' —*Amy Sherald*

What do you want? What are you trying to convey? How can you go about making it happen?

Tomorrow's entry can help with the first steps.

Amy Sherald (b. 1973) is an American painter of people known for intimate portraits that explore Black American life and challenge traditional narratives of race and representation.

Source: Interview with Samra Khawaja, 2016, via the National Endowment for the Arts

The first steps can be small

'What is success? I think success is getting up each day and making a decision to create something, expressive or imaginative or innovative. I've taken that choice and stayed focused.' —Barbara Walker

Starting on a small scale can lead to the greatest work. How can we commit to doing something creative every day? Is it something artistic, such as drawing, that will leave you with hundreds of sketches at the end of the year? Writing something short that will help you amass a body of work over time? Seeking out a new subject, or learning a new language?

In October 2015, my goal was to teach myself about women artists past and present and to share my findings with whoever else wanted to learn along the way. I started my Instagram account, @thegreatwomenartists, and promised myself I would do it every day – and I did, whether by writing on the bus, in bed or at my desk, before or after my office job. By committing to a daily practice, and persisting with it, I have been able to give myself the greatest education possible.

We all need to be creative in order to survive life. What one thing do you want to commit to that you could be able to carry out every day or every week, for the rest of the year? Once you get going, you won't want to stop.

Barbara Walker (b. 1964) is a British artist who creates works on paper, paintings on canvas and large-scale charcoal wall drawings. They are filled with empathy, depth and emotion, and address the state of Black communities, their experiences and histories.

Source: Gentleman, Amelia, ' "I'm pointing a finger": Barbara Walker on her paintings about the Windrush scandal and her son's victimisation', Guardian, 30 September 2024

Catch those moments!

'One of the reasons I painted was to catch life as it goes by, right hot off the griddle.' —Alice Neel

The great American artist Alice Neel used paint as a way to 'catch life'. She painted the people who wandered in and out of her apartment – from journalists and writers to her family and neighbours – no matter their status. As a result, her paintings document the people who lived in and shaped New York City.

If you were to 'catch life', what would it look like? Would it be through paintings, to-do lists, diary entries or doodles? Choose a way to catch it; don't let it pass you by.

Alice Neel (1900–84) described herself as a 'collector of souls'. She was a painter of people, and always worked in her home-based studio in Spanish Harlem, and later the Upper West Side.

Source: Hills, Patricia, Alice Neel, *Harry N. Abrams, 1983, reprint 1995, quoted in Carr, Carolyn Kinder,* Alice Neel's Women, *Rizzoli International Publications, 2002; 'collector of souls' quote: Hills,* Alice Neel

Take a chance

'I want that release. I can't go on a sheer program. At times I thought "the more thought the greater the art", but I wonder about that and do have to admit there's a lot that I'll just let happen and maybe it will come out the better for it. I used to plan a lot and do everything myself and then I started to take a chance . . .' —*Eva Hesse*

We will talk a bit more about 'chance' in September. For now, we can look to the German-born American sculptor Hesse as an example of someone who took chances with material and form. For her sculptures, she mixed machine parts with cord, plaster with industrial materials, and even worked with liquid latex.

She worked innovatively and unconventionally, and let her chance encounters with these materials guide her.

But she prompts us to ask – isn't all art about chance? Isn't all life about chance? From the surprises that arise to the encounters we have with people, Hesse reminds us that we are best off not being too precious. We have to let it happen, as she says, and 'maybe it will come out the better for it'.

Eva Hesse (1936–70) was a German-born, American sculptor who lived and worked mostly in New York City in the 1960s. Despite her brief, only decade-long career, Hesse was a profound experimenter. Always searching for a new material or form, she fused incompatible substances found lying about on her studio floor for her process-based work.

Source: Nemser, Cindy, Art Talk: Conversations with 15 Women Artists, *HarperCollins, 1995*

It's up to you

'You can't sit around and wait for somebody to say who you are. You need to write it and paint it and do it.' —*Faith Ringgold*

We need stories by everyone in the world. You are just as qualified as the next person to tell yours. If you don't, someone else might for you.

Make it yours; tell it for yourself. Be vague, be specific; write down or sketch an experience or a feeling, and go from there.

Faith Ringgold (1930–2024) was a pioneering American artist known for her paintings, sculptures, story-quilts and children's books. Instrumental as an activist in the civil rights and feminist movements – and beyond – Ringgold, through her art, constantly challenged gender and racial inequalities and gave voice to the stories hidden by the media at the time.

Source: Faith Ringgold interviewed by Betsy West, Makers: Women Who Make America, *Kunhardt Film Foundation, 15 July 2001*

Treat life as art

'Because of the routines we follow, we often forget that life is an ongoing adventure. We leave our homes for work, acting and even believing that we will reach our destinations with no unusual event startling us out of our set expectations. The truth is we know nothing . . . Life is pure adventure and the sooner we realise that, the quicker we will be able to treat life as art: to bring all our energies to each encounter, to remain flexible enough to notice and admit when what we expected to happen did not happen. We need to remember that we are created creative . . .'—Maya Angelou

You got here. The end of January. Take a moment to reflect on what you've learnt this month. Where do ideas come from? How can you seek out the details? Where can you go to 'make' art, and what can you use, that is entirely yours, to your advantage? The year has just started. We have eleven months to go. Use it wisely, but freely. As Angelou remarks, it is an ongoing adventure.

Maya Angelou (1928–2014) was a great American writer, editor, essayist, playwright, poet, educator and civil rights activist.

Source: Angelou, Maya, Wouldn't Take Nothing for My Journey Now, *1994, Virago*

FEBRUARY

Love and Passion

February, the month of love and passion. A time to think about how we can use love in our life and our work – both emotionally and intellectually – and reflect on art's enduring appeal.

What is it about art that is so enrapturing that temples have been built across the globe to house and preserve it?

I find it miraculous that despite the fact humans have used similar foundational materials for thousands of years – like paint, clay, stone or pencil – they always find new things to say.

This month we will look at making art with and from love; how to encompass pain and grief; art as companionship, a place or thing to which to return – and to know that it is always there; and how artists can get us to fall in love with it day after day, year after year . . .

I like to find solace in art. Its power is its ability to speak to any of us at any time. Look to art for the answers because across the years, decades or centuries, in work by someone who lived a completely different existence to you, you'll find something you instantly recognise. And when you do, pass it on to someone else who might need it, too.

Let's explore art through the lens of love.

Love as religion

'I have my own religion. It suits me. I made it up myself. I read all about everybody else's religion before I settled on mine. It's a secret religion. You don't go out looking for converts or anything like that. Well, I guess I can tell you. It's about love, not God. There's no God but just love. That's all I'm going to tell you.' —*Agnes Martin*

If love was your religion, what would your temple look like, where would it be, who would your icon be? What can represent this force that is so powerful yet invisible?

While there might only be one word for love in the English language (in Arabic, there are eleven), you can look to art – to an infinite number of pictures, songs, objects, entities – to represent it. What captures 'love' (and the many different kinds of love) for you?

Agnes Martin (1912–2004) was a Canadian-born artist who lived mostly in Taos, New Mexico. She was known for her six-foot-square canvases made with subtle pencil marks, or serene bands of diluted colour.

Source: Agnes Martin: Between the Lines, *directed by Leon d'Avigdor, Leon d'Avigdor Film, 2002/2016*

Love as an intellectual subject

'Why are we so afraid of love and emotionality? Why is that not interesting? Why is that not intellectual? These are parts of the human experience that in visual art we've been led to believe we're not supposed to talk about.' —Jenna Gribbon

It was reading *All About Love* by the American author bell hooks that made me think: why do we not view love as an intellectual subject? Why is this entity that connects us all not studied at school or university? Is it not the thing we need to understand most in the world? Why is it not analysed and worked through?

So use it and, as Gribbon says, talk about it: intellectually and emotionally.

Jenna Gribbon (b. 1978) is a painter who draws from memory, art history and contemporary life, often depicting her wife, Mackenzie Scott, in everyday scenes.

Source: The Great Women Artists Podcast, *2022*

Make from love

'Nothing I had drawn or painted in my one previous year of art study was any good, but these drawings were. [. . .] Need and yearning drove them. They were all I would have of him. It may sound trite, but I would say that love made those searching, tentative lines on the paper.' —*Mary Husted*

In 1962, when Husted was seventeen years old, she became pregnant. But because she wasn't married to the father, she was forced to give up her child for adoption. When her baby boy, Luke, was born, she was allowed ten days with him and sketched him, capturing every detail: his hair, brow, eyelash, how he slept, and clenched his fist.

On returning to art decades later she used these sketches as inspirations for her golden collage *Dreams, Oracles, Icons*, 1991. It's of a newborn cradled in a nest-like form, and a mother setting a bird free. She gave it to the Women's Art Collection at Murray Edwards College, Cambridge University.

In 2007, Luke, now aged forty-four and married with two sons, went looking for his mother and was able to track her down. Alongside Husted's name on the college's website was *Dreams, Oracles, Icons*. Mother and son soon met, and have been in daily contact ever since.

From these drawings – this act of love – we can take away the power of art as a tool to retain the most meaningful memories. While a camera phone can be useful for recording moments, taking time to look, feel and physically record what is in front of us can transport us to a place that we can hold on to forever.

What precious memory will you hold on to?

Mary Husted (b. 1944) is a British artist, based in South Wales, who works across painting, drawing and collage, often incorporating her personal experiences.

Source: A note to the author, 2024

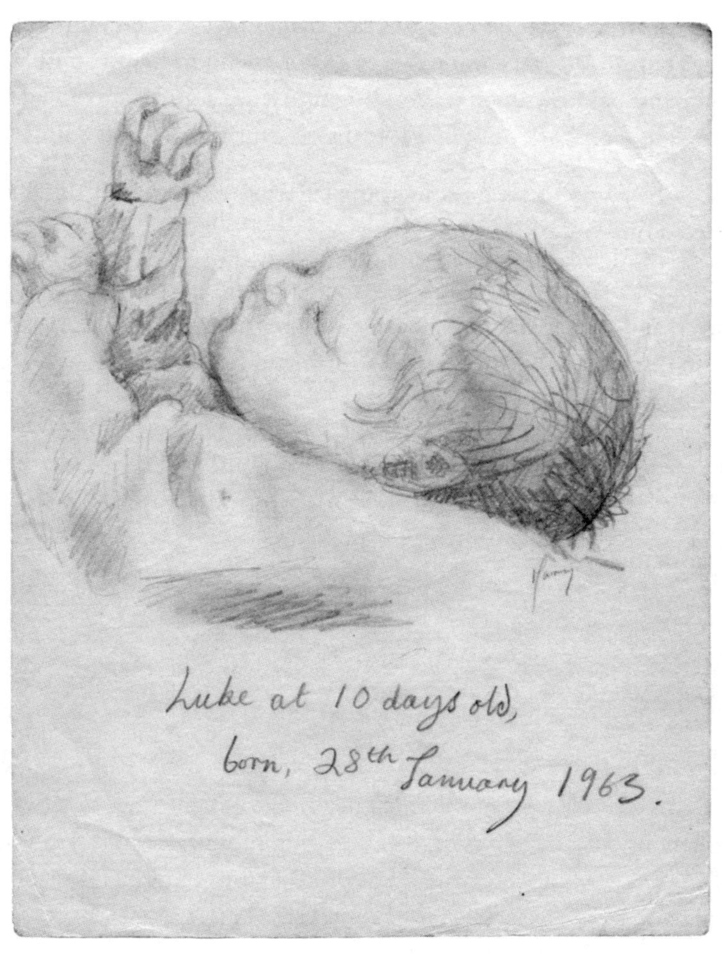

Mary Husted, *Luke at 10 Days Old, Born 28 January 1963*, 1963

Paint your way through pain

'Paint that pain.' —Antonia Showering

We all know love can be hard. It's not always rosy and endings aren't always happy. But art can be there as your friend to help you draw, sketch and paint through it. You might just see something else on the other side – or work out what it is that is causing you that pain.

Art can be a way to create something external, and for that thing to be reflected on.

The poet Emily Dickinson once wrote, 'Tell all the truth but tell it slant' – and that is what art does. It is something we can create from within ourselves, and then use as a mirror to hold up to us, and look at from a different angle.

Think about what's painful for you; what could you put down in images or words? Take your pain and gather what you have from within.

Antonia Showering (b. 1991) is a British artist known for her richly textural and layered paintings of figures that meld with landscapes. Showering's paintings pay homage to the significant places and people in her life, from her Chinese grandfather who taught the young artist how to draw to the mountain ranges near where her Swiss grandmother grew up.

Source: A note to the author, 2024

But remember to bring the lightness in

'There is nothing more precious than laughter – it is strength to laugh and lose oneself, to be light.' —Frida Kahlo

The days are still long and dark. What can you find today that will make you laugh? Bring that preciousness, love and laughter into your life, and into your work.

Frida Kahlo (1907–54) was a Mexican artist remembered for her self-portraits imbued with vibrant colours that address every emotion. Although spending much of her life in physical and emotional agony – as a child she had polio; in her teens she was involved in a bus crash that left her body shattered; as an adult she was in a tumultuous relationship with the artist Diego Rivera – Kahlo, through art, transformed pain into beauty, from painting tears like white crystals, to depicting a fluted column that thrusts through her body as a stand-in for a spine, keeping her head held high, queen-like and alive.

Source: Kahlo, Frida, The Diary of Frida Kahlo: An Intimate Self-portrait, Harry N. Abrams, 1995

Make acts of love

'[Portrait painting] is just like a love affair, in that it's a very intimate thing, and at the end of it, you hope there's a decent painting and not a broken heart. And so I wouldn't paint somebody I had no kind of fellow feeling, understanding or rapport with . . . It would be pointless because, above all, any work of art has to be a work of love.' —Maggi Hambling

Hambling reminds us of the important role of feeling love in all that we do, whether work or play, artistic or non-artistic. To not make with love, as Hambling says, is to miss the point. What can you make with love today?

Maggi Hambling (b. 1945) is a British artist hailed both for her public sculpture, such as the four-metre-high *Scallop* on Aldeburgh beach for the composer Benjamin Britten, the first memorial in London for Oscar Wilde, or her *A Sculpture for Mary Wollstonecraft* at Newington Green, and paintings of people and the natural world that are held in multiple important museum collections. Hambling's work responds to the essence of human life and emotion: the simultaneous presence of chaos and control, life and death.

Source: The Great Women Artists Podcast, *2019*

What is the reality vs the fantasy of love?

'I've had couples lie down for me on the bed . . . You have these ideas about how love would look . . . You can set something up, or you can arrange a couple, you can do all that. But what comes out in a painting on the day or the time that you make it – that's always other.' —*Chantal Joffe*

What is your idea, or fantasy, of love? And what does the reality look like?

Love is what and who we dedicate our time to. For me, that is where the reality lies – not the fantastical ideas, although they can be fun too. To who or what do you want to dedicate your time?

Chantal Joffe (b. 1969) is an American-born British painter. She paints those close to her, mostly from life in her London studio. Painting someone from 'life' means the subject is present in the room, and allows for the painter to capture the conversation that might have played out, how the sitter seemed in that moment, and the energy of the space.

Source: A conversation with the author, 2024

Falling in love

'I've found getting older has made my life simpler. It was probably that there was just room because it was almost like falling in love. And you have to have space in your head to be able to do that. So [painting] was like falling in love. It's been like a lover. A mad lover.' —*Unskilled Worker*

Is there something you've always wanted to do, and yet have never found the time or space? Is there a way that you could begin to make it happen, even in the smallest of ways?

The artist who goes under the moniker of Unskilled Worker turned to painting in 2013 at the age of forty-eight. She told me: 'A few months earlier, at a party, I found myself talking with a much older, fascinating woman. I asked her, "How do I grow old?" She replied, "You become so obsessed with doing something new that you forget yourself." I'm certain this conversation triggered me to begin painting.'

No matter what age you are, you can still fulfil that dream.

Go out there and fall in love again.

Helen Downie (b. 1965), known as Unskilled Worker, is a self-taught British artist who paints fantastical images of people in her present and past life, or literary heroes, such as Radclyffe Hall, in colourful, refined interiors or landscapes, but always with a darker undertone, and intense sensibility.

Source: The Great Women Artists Podcast, *2019*

Invite silence in

'Make friends with silence.' —*Catherine Goodman*

In a technologically fuelled world that has the potential to never bore us, or allow us to hear silence, try – as the painter Catherine Goodman says – to actively befriend it.

She continues: 'It has been fed by my daily meditation practice, and is of course difficult and paradoxically easy . . . In silence, ideas grow and gain reality. Somehow it also teaches me to be brave, and, most importantly, to try to pursue beauty and feelings in all their elusiveness.'

Try listening to silence. What will you hear? What ideas will grow from it? How will it keep your attention?

Catherine Goodman (b. 1961) is a British artist hailed for her intensely expressive and atmospheric paintings that explore both figuration and abstraction through her unique employment of oil paint and oil stick. She has been a pioneering educator as the co-founder of the Royal Drawing School, London.

Source: A note to the author, 2025

How do we deal with that lover taking over?

'My secret jealous Lover (my work) is always there waiting for me. He is tall and elegant and like Count Dracula wears a black cape. He whispers in my ear that there is not much time left for what I am meant to do. He is jealous of every moment I spend away from him. He is even jealous of my locked bedroom door. Sometimes at night he [flies] through the open window of my room in the form of a huge bat. I shiver as he takes me in his wings. I struggle for an instant in my long white nightdress. His teeth sink into my soul. I am his.' —Niki de Saint Phalle

Have you ever felt so in love with what you are doing that it's inescapable? Niki de Saint Phalle reminds us that we are not alone when we feel like those things we want to build and grow are like a jealous lover taking us over.

Niki de Saint Phalle (1930–2002) was a French-American artist, working across sculpture, painting and film. She was a pioneer in performance and conceptual art in Paris in the 1960s, and went on to explore large-scale immersive environments through her joyous, bulbous and sometimes glittering 'Nana' sculptures. These include the Tarot Garden in Tuscany (1970s–1990s) and *Hon – en Katedral* (1966) at the Moderna Museet in Stockholm, where visitors entered through the giant open legs of one of her Nanas, only to unveil a twelve-seat cinema, a bar, a playground for kids, a fish pond and sandwich vending machine.

Source: de Saint Phalle, Niki, drawing in Niki de Saint Phalle, Bilder – Figuren – Phantastische Gärten, *Munich: Prestel Publishing, 1987*

The magic of alchemy

'Art[making] is a magic which makes the hours melt away and even days dissolve into seconds . . .'—*Leonora Carrington*

How can we continue to be mesmerised by the magical powers of artmaking?

One way to do this is to recognise paint as 'alchemy' – as Carrington, along with her best friend and fellow artist, Remedios Varo, did.

Let's think about it. One the one hand, pigments come from coloured rock (the earth) which are ground and processed to create paint, something liquid. Then it is used by an artist to make something solid again: a painting. But isn't it incredible that the very entity that was once solid, then liquid, and then solid again, can also picture something that is liquid (like water) or solid (a rocky landscape)? Or even both in one image – reflecting the life cycle of the very medium that made it?

More literally, you can consider the hidden alchemy of Carrington's painting, *The Giantess (The Guardian of the Egg)*, 1947 (overleaf) – made from egg tempera – which shows the egg as the source of all creation.

Look closely at the hands of the colossal female figure – with her lunar face and frizzy yellow hair – and you'll see she's clutching a golden egg. It's as if she's the keeper of the very thing that made her and her image, holding the power of both life and painting in her tiny hands.

How can you be mesmerised by alchemy?

Leonora Carrington (1917–2011) was a British-born artist and writer who lived in France and Spain before settling in Mexico during the Second World War. She painted fantastical beings and creatures within scenes that were enigmatic, otherworldly, yet strangely familiar.

Source: Carrington, Leonora, The Seventh Horse and Other Tales, *Penguin, 1988*

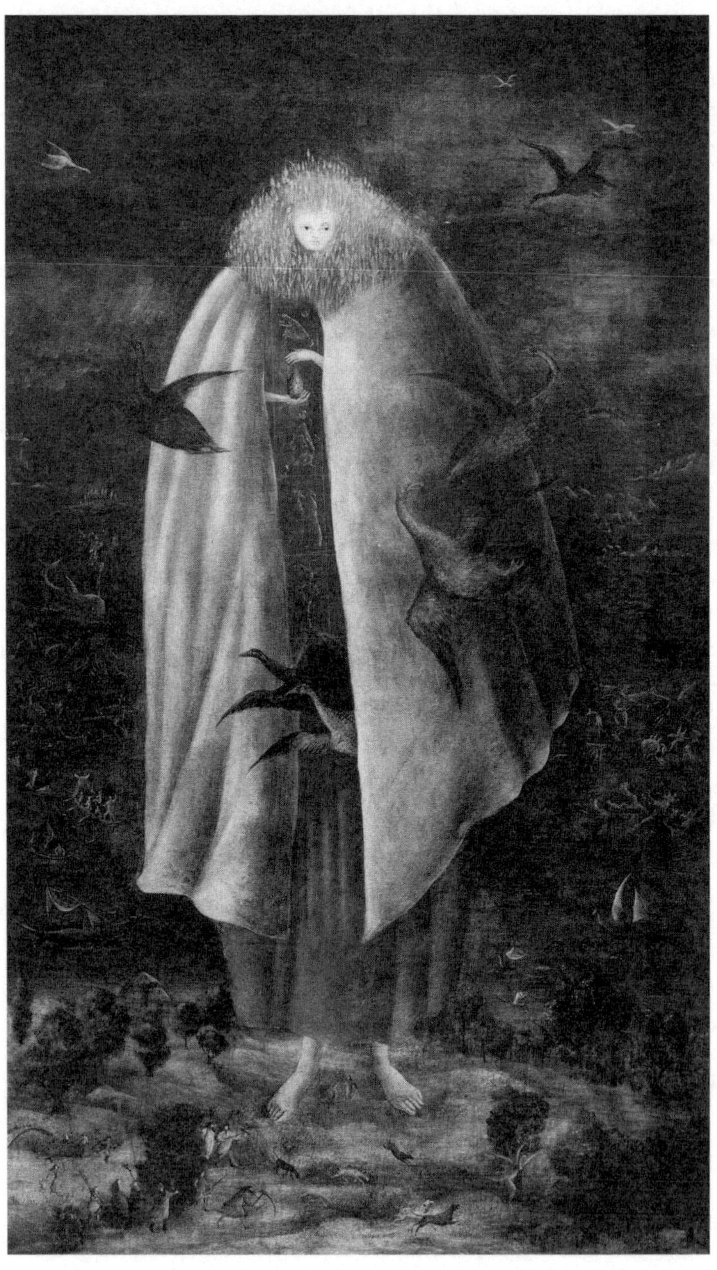

Leonora Carrington, *The Giantess (The Guardian of the Egg)*, c. 1947

Why is oil paint so continually compelling?

*'I think that there's some kind of magical quality in oil paint. [. . .]
Because when you're painting, I get it around three or four in
the morning, in that delirium of tiredness and knowing that it's
probably time to go home, but just giving it that extra few hours'
push, and then you go into this trance-like state. And because oil
takes a long time to dry, you're allowed time to sit with decisions.'
—Antonia Showering*

Artists have chosen all kinds of ways to employ paint – and yet
they are still awestruck by its potential. What are its magical
qualities? What can we learn by paying attention to something used
in a craft? I discussed these questions with Showering, who told me:

> *It's the smell of it, and its physical quality. [. . .] But it's also the
> differences in – and individuality of – each colour. Some take
> longer to dry than others. Some are opaque, whereas others are
> more translucent . . . Some stem from the minerals in nature –
> for example, the original dye of Sap Green came from the sap of
> the buckthorn berry [. . .] The mice in my studio always eat
> the cadmium yellow or red!*
>
> *[. . .] You don't have to paint straight from the tube. You can
> leave the paint drying on the palette for a few days. When you go
> back to it, you can get an entirely different mark. Add turpentine to
> thin it down; beeswax to thicken it.*

What medium or artform do you find continually compelling?

Antonia Showering (b. 1991) is a British artist known for her richly textural and layered
paintings of figures that meld with landscapes. Showering's paintings pay homage to the
significant places and people in her life, like her Chinese grandfather who taught the
young artist how to draw to the mountain ranges near where her Swiss grandmother
grew up.

Source: The Great Women Artists Podcast, 2022, and a conversation with the author, 2025

Find your possibilities

'I mean, obviously, there are days where you really don't feel like painting. But the longer you do it, the deeper you are into it and the more compelling it becomes, because there's always something else to do, there's always a different direction you can take.

Colours always behave differently next to other colours. So in a way, you're just never done. But that's also the exciting thing about it. And the fact that you're never done means you can hope to live a very long life and not worry that you're going to get bored.' —Cecily Brown

Even if we don't work in a studio every day – I don't – Brown's words about not feeling like doing something gets me to think about the many things we don't initially feel like doing. Yet, the more we do them, and the deeper we dig into them, the more compelling they become. When we commit, we get better. So do that thing. It will be worth it. Revel in the repetition – love is built through it.

Cecily Brown (b. 1969) is a British-born artist, based in New York, known for her fleshy oil paintings that meld the grand themes and scale of the European Old Masters with the action-like strokes of the Abstract Expressionists.

Source: The Great Women Artists Podcast, *2020*

Find companionship in art

'I think that art is companionship . . . it has always made me feel less lonely when I'm alone.' —Anna Weyant

People come and go, but art is a constant; it is always there, whether you are making it or viewing it. Whenever I am stuck, I take myself off to look at art and I have a conversation with it. Some of the loneliest times of my life, I've forced myself to get out and just 'be' with a work of art.

Somehow it will speak to me, surprise me, teach me something, and, like Weyant says, make me feel less alone. It's a perfect reminder on a day like this: a day of love, which can also be just as much about pain.

How can you make art your companion today? Will you be a maker, or spectator?

Take yourself off somewhere, to an exhibition, to your local cinema, or on a walk – with a sketchpad, notepad or camera. Capture one thing. Go on a date with 'art'.

Anna Weyant was born in Calgary, Canada, in 1995. After earning a BFA in painting from the Rhode Island School of Design, she relocated to New York. Weyant is known for her moody, figurative works that blend classical technique with contemporary references.

Source: The Great Women Artists Podcast, *2023*

Write to an artwork

'Rather than writing about artworks, I spend most of my time at exhibitions or galleries writing to them. I write to them about the feelings they solicit, the forms of discomfort they evoke, the emotional work they require and often demand, and the potentially transformative effects they will have when we allow ourselves to inhabit those feelings and responses.' —Tina M. Campt

Following on from yesterday, why not try writing to an artwork, even if it's just in a book or on a screen? What will you say to it, what questions will you ask? Sit with a painting or a sculpture, a piece of music or a poem, and figure out which emotions it elicits in you. How can you use art as a companion in multitudinous ways?

Tina M. Campt (b. 1964) is a feminist theorist of visual culture and contemporary art. She is the Roger S. Berlind '52 Professor of Humanities in the Department of Art and Archaeology and the Lewis Center for the Arts at Princeton University, and is the author of several books.

Source: Campt, Tina M., A Black Gaze: Artists Changing How We See, *MIT Press, 2023*

Trace human history

[On the magic of clay:] *'It's the realisation that it's a material that has an expansiveness that all the other materials don't have. It's attractive because of its materiality. It's pliable, it's intriguing, it's malleable. It has all sorts of facets, from being dust that can be made into a lump of clay. And from that lump of clay, you can mould something with it . . . And when you put it in a fire, it actually strengthens it, modifies it, and makes it into ceramics.*

Clay is pliable when it's not fired. But after it's fired, it becomes this object that has almost eternity. It lives on forever and ever. It's fragile, too, because pots can crack and can break, but they still exist . . . Archaeologists find they can tell a lot about the history of human beings by just having a shard of pottery . . .' —Magdalene Odundo

Today, let's think about what lasts in this world. What can break, but can still exist? What fragment can a story be extracted from – or a world be discovered?

But, in a month about love, I also want to draw on what Odundo said about the fragility of fired clay, and how it can crack, and break – like our hearts – but also, like our hearts, repair. There's a Japanese art called 'kintsugi' which is the act of mending broken pottery by adorning the seams with gold. It highlights where the vessel has broken, rather than concealing it, and in doing so, makes it into something else, which can be all the more beautiful.

Magdalene Odundo (b.1950) is a Kenyan and British artist known for her laboriously produced clay-based sculptures. Created using hand-built techniques, Odundo's work is akin to or reminiscent of the form of a female body. She has said of her medium, 'I have always equated clay with the humanity that is within us, fragile and temperamental like human beings. Vessels made in clay can be precariously balanced, and like human beings if pushed just slightly on the wrong pivot, they can break your heart.'

Source: The Great Women Artists Podcast, *2021*

The importance of making your mark

What and who do you want to preserve? How will you remember, hold on to and treasure the memory of those you love, externalising them so you can see them whole?

The celebrated British classicist Mary Beard once told me a story about a young woman who might just be the first ever portrait artist, male or female. We don't know her name. We only know her as the daughter of Butades of Sicyon (*c.* 600 BC), an ancient Greek potter, who, according to the Roman writer Pliny the Elder, was the first modeller to use clay. In Beard's words:

> *She [Butades's daughter] has a lover who is going away for a long time, and she is sad to see him go. According to various ancient accounts, including Pliny, she wants to remember him when he's away. So, she gets a candle and casts a light in front of his face, so that it throws his shadow onto the wall behind: it's his silhouette. She then traces around it so that she's captured the representation of him. And that is the first portrait in the ancient world that there ever was. Interestingly, it is a portrait which is born out of female passion and desire, and out of her desire to preserve the image of the young man. But typically she herself remains in the shadows. We don't know her name; we only know that she is her father Butades's daughter (some accounts call her Kora, but that just means 'girl'). But also, what's interesting is that her dad takes over and makes a ceramic model out of the tracing that his daughter has done . . . so, it's still rather constrained, not just because they don't give her a name, but also in the end it's Dad who goes one better by taking her tracing, and making a ceramic portrait sculpture of the bloke . . .*

Who do you want to remember?

Mary Beard (b. 1955) is a British classicist who served as Professor of Classics at the University of Cambridge for nearly four decades. One of the most important scholars on her subject, Beard has fronted numerous TV documentaries and authored multiple books including her trailblazing manifesto, *Women & Power*.

Source: The Great Women Artists Podcast, *2022*

Look to the light

'November and February are my favourite months because the sun is low enough, but not too low, for something magical to occur in my north-facing studio with its view onto the forecourt of the British Museum behind which, to the left, looms the strange presence of the BT Tower. On a bright day in either November or February, there is a moment when the sun catches on the glass top of the tower, causing it to emit a refracted beam of light through my window, casting shadows of the branches of "my" plane tree onto my studio wall. For an instant, as if suspended on the wall, I have what appears to be a Japanese ink painting of delicate leaf tracery on a long parchment scroll, before it vanishes. Chance encounters with effects of light can change the way I see, making me pay attention.' —Celia Paul

There's something extraordinary about the end of February, especially where I live, not far from Celia Paul, in London. After a time of darkness, the end of February can be a glimmer of hope, with a hint of the seasons changing: small flowers budding and evenings getting noticeably lighter.

The light can be magical at this time of year: low, quiet, but still harshly bright. How can we make the most of this, and seize the brightening sky?

Look at how the light reflects on your wall at this time of year: how does it appear, what does it accentuate? Turn the page to see how Paul captures it.

Celia Paul (b. 1959) is a British artist, born in India. She paints intimate portrayals of those close to her, from her sisters to past lovers, whom she cloaks in a hazy glow.

Source: A note to the author, 2024

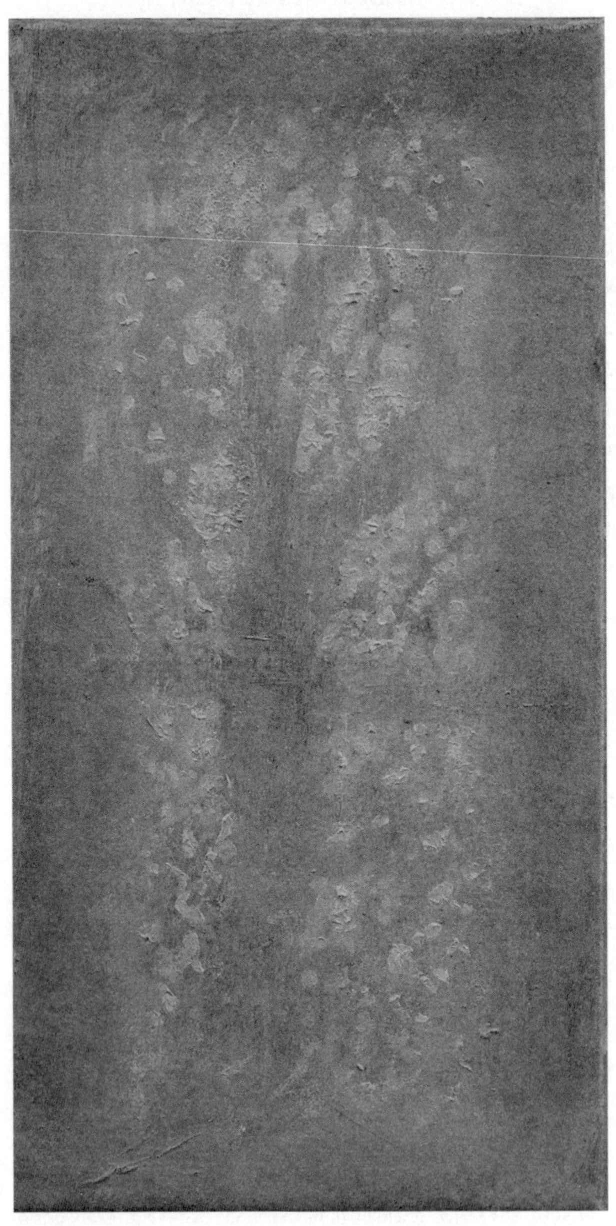

Celia Paul, *Plane Tree Shadow on my Wall*, 2013

The importance of listening

'I love stories. I love language. I love words. I can spend hours thinking about just one line, one sentence. But as much as I'm drawn to words and stories, I'm equally drawn to silences. And there's a part of me that wants to understand.

So there's a part of me that wants to open up conversations. This doesn't mean that I do know the answers. I don't. But it only means that I care about the questions. I care about those silences. And I think it's very important that we be able to talk about them. Because silence is to keep us apart. Keep us fearful, in our own cocoons. It's only when we connect and communicate, and when we hear each other's stories, only then we can emotionally bond, we can start to care. Only then we can demolish those walls of apathy. So empathy requires first of all listening. We have to become good listeners.' —Elif Shafak

Listening is as important as storytelling. What can you listen to today?

Elif Shafak (b. 1971) is a celebrated French-born, Turkish-British author. To date she has written nineteen books, twelve of which are novels, and has been instrumental in her work as an advocate for women's and LGBTQ+ rights and freedom of expression.

Source: The Great Women Artists Podcast, *2023*

Go out alone

'I love being alone and being out in the world and going into difficult places alone and confronting it by myself and doing whatever I need to do to get the photograph. I use a simple tripod and a simple camera and roll film.' —*Carrie Mae Weems*

Being alone can be some of the most magical times of our life. Some of my happiest memories are from solo adventures. Weems's words are a reminder of the possibility to confront the world as a single being, and what can unfold when we go out alone. Sometimes we have to seize moments while we can, and if there's no one around to do it with us, then we must go out and seize them ourselves.

I am reminded of a passage from Tove Jansson's essay, 'The Island', about the beauty of being alone: 'When you've been alone for a very long time, you begin to listen differently, to feel the organic and the unexpected all around, and see the incomprehensible beauty of the material world.' What will you discover?

Carrie Mae Weems (b. 1953) is an American artist who – through photographs, text, fabric, audio, installation, video and more – investigates history, identity and power.

Source: Sollins, Susan, 'Carrie Mae Weems: On Photography', Art21, September 2018

Give someone an entire world

'If you give a child a pen and paper, you give her an entire world.' —Helene Schjerfbeck

Today, let's think about the possibility of one small thing. What one thing changed your world for the better, when you were a child, or more recently? Was it something someone said or gave to you, like a pencil, book, notepad, or a key – literally or hypothetically – to another world? Was it something they showed you, like a place or a film? Was it a song, or an instrument?

I can still remember visiting the vast expanse that is Tate Modern in London as a child. I had no idea what an 'art gallery' was for, and definitely no prescribed notion of how I was meant to think or feel. But seeing one of Louise Bourgeois's colossal steel spiders, I knew I was excited and wanted to find out more.

What can you give – or show – someone, no matter how small? You never know what it will open up for them.

Helene Schjerfbeck (1862–1946) was a Finnish artist. She painted landscapes *(en plein air)*, portraits and expressive self-portraits that showed her confronting herself in the ageing process.

Source: Lahelma, Marja, Helene Schjerfbeck – An Artist's Life, *Finnish National Gallery/ Ateneum Art Museum, Helsinki, 2023*

Keep a list of people who love you

'I used to keep a list on my phone – for when I would feel lonely – of all my friends. Just so I could look at it and remind myself that all these people do love me.' —Michaela Yearwood-Dan

Working, making and/or living alone can be an isolating process. But just because you're not with anyone at a certain time doesn't mean that no one loves you. Remind yourself, as Yearwood-Dan does, by keeping a list of those who love you – even if they're no longer around – for that comforting feeling. In a way, it can set you free, because it's possible to do anything when you know someone is championing your every move, even if they're not right beside you.

Michaela Yearwood-Dan (b. 1994) is a London-based artist working across painting and ceramics. She creates lush, vividly coloured works in the language of abstraction that draw on botanical motifs and are infused with meditations through text.

Source: A conversation with the author, 2025

Rebuild; invent

'I wanted to break down the accepted order and rebuild and make my own order.' —Barbara Hepworth

What is the 'accepted' order? Is it an order that suits you, or is it an order that suppresses you and people like you? Will you, like Hepworth, be forced to invent your own?

What structures are in place for you: how can you rebuild and reconfigure them to work for you? Without realising, you might be paving the way for other people just like you.

Hepworth, in every sense, had to rebuild the idea of being an artist. Not only as an artist-mother in the twentieth century, when it was a taboo subject to discuss both publicly and in one's work, but also when it came to reconfiguring the nature of sculpture itself. Working through the Second World War, she adapted to using the unconventional materials around her, and managed to continue to create when there was scarce available.

Barbara Hepworth (1903–75) was a giant of British sculpture. Born in Wakefield, Yorkshire, she carried with her the rhythms of the Northern hills. From 1939, she was based in St Ives, a fishing village in Cornwall famed for its rocky beaches, and the weathered lines and ocean swirls of her surroundings made their way into her highly textured sculptures. Working in an interior and exterior environment, Hepworth interacted with the natural forms of the landscape, as well as analysing the many forms that the human body can take.

Source: Hepworth, Barbara, Barbara Hepworth: Carvings and Drawings *(introduction by Herbert Read), Lund Humphries, 1952*

Find freedom

'I wanted more freedom in my life . . . I say to myself: look, you wanted a wider experimental kind of life, where you could really free your whole self, especially as a woman . . .'
—Katherine Bradford

Why do we want to live artfully? To live artfully is to live as our whole selves, to enrich and to feel enriched, with a sense of freedom and outside of societal constraints.

We can still have our normal day jobs alongside our lives – it's about using creative ways to help enhance our daily routines.

How can living in this way give us more freedom? I think there's a magic to be found when you are creating – whether you're putting pen to paper, paint to canvas, or making something with your hands. When you use art as an instrument for feeling, it will expand into something you never thought it would be, in ways that will endlessly surprise you, and free you.

Katherine Bradford (b. 1942) is an American artist. Translating the freedom she felt after leaving the life of being a woman in stifling 1960s Connecticut and swapping it to be an artist in New York City, Bradford paints luminous paintings of swimming pools and cosmic skies, ballet dancers and bicycle riders. Looking at Bradford's paintings is like being transported into another world, whether it be outer space or in cosmic waters.

Source: Katherine Bradford: Making Things, *ARCTYPE, 19 April 2024 (video)*

Stay on your path

'Stay true to what you're doing, and try to make the best work you can make – regardless of the fickleness and craziness of the market system around you. Most artists will never be part of that market system.

We all [Kruger's artist friends] had a very critical relationship to the building of careers, and how they happen. That's the most that I could say: don't personalise everything, because when things happen really soon, and then you're abandoned, you have like, thirty years of performance anxiety to go through . . . You just can't personalise it, because the market is just brutal. You have to make your work and make it as strong as possible – and not destroy yourself with comparisons to your peers.' —Barbara Kruger

It can be hard at times, but stay on your own path. Work on not personalising anything exterior, or focusing on the success of others. Embrace the failures; they're inevitable. Make the work and try to be as true to yourself as you can be at that moment. You're the only one who can destroy yourself, pick yourself up again, and discover what something means to you. What will you find?

Barbara Kruger (b. 1945) is an American artist who works within an iconic visual language, made up of words and images, that is graphic, bold and easily identifiable, and borrows from advertising and other media.

Source: The Great Women Artists Podcast, *2024*

What is meaningful to you?

[Speaking about the characters in her novel, *On Beauty*:] '*The Belsey children need to stop worrying about their identity and concern themselves with the people they care about, ideas that matter to them, beliefs they can stand by, tickets they can run on. Intelligent humans make those choices with their brain and hearts and they make them alone. The world does not deliver meaning to you. You have to make it meaningful.*' —*Zadie Smith*

What do you love? What is meaningful to you? How can you find strength in it, and stand by it?

Zadie Smith (b. 1975) is a celebrated British novelist, essayist and short-story writer. Her acclaimed novels include *White Teeth*, *The Autograph Man*, *On Beauty*, *NW* and *Swing Time*.

Source: Zadie Smith, On Beauty, *Penguin, 2005*

Feeling is crucial to understanding a work of art

'Most art historians are similarly queasy about emotion and instead write about form, colour, influences, or historical context. Feeling, however, is not only unavoidable; it is crucial to understanding a work of art. Indeed, an artwork becomes senseless without it. In a letter to a friend, Henry James wrote, "In the arts feeling is always meaning". . .' —Siri Hustvedt

How could you approach something differently, with feeling rather than form or context? From a news story that is full of statistics, or a subject you are learning about, think about the feeling behind it, because once you see that, you will see the humanity.

Whenever I talk to an artist or academic about a piece of art they're interested in, whether it's an eighteenth-century royal portrait or a war photograph, I always start by asking them how it makes them feel. It's easy to riff off information or numbers, but if we don't have any emotion, or empathy, then we can't even begin to look at it.

The writer Siri Hustvedt reminds us that love is crucial in every aspect of our lives. Look with love at the world.

Siri Hustvedt (b. 1955) is an American novelist, essayist and author of eighteen books. From memoir to poetry, non-fiction to fiction, Hustvedt's groundbreaking writing has touched on the topics of psychoanalysis, philosophy, neuroscience, literature and art.

Source: Hustvedt, Siri, A Woman Looking at Men Looking at Women: Essays on Art, Sex, and the Mind, *Simon & Schuster, 2016*

Love is a two-way street

'I think you have to make up your mind, what you love and what loves you. And I think that's a two-way street. And I think you have to be patient with your love.' —*Nikki Giovanni*

What do you love? Write it down. How can you be patient with it? How can you take time with it?

1. ____

2. ____

3. ____

4. ____

5. ____

Yolande Cornelia 'Nikki' Giovanni Jr (1943–2024) was an American poet, writer, commentator, activist and educator. She was one of the leading voices of the 1960s Black Arts movement.

Source: On Being with Krista Tippett, Remembering Nikki Giovanni – 'We Go Forward with a Sanity and a Love' *(The On Being Project), first broadcast 17 March 2016*

Time

'Time is something that scares me . . . or used to. This piece made with the two clocks was the scariest thing I have ever done. I wanted to face it. I wanted those two clocks right in front of me, ticking.' —*Felix Gonzalez-Torres*

On a day that happens once every four years, that I like to think of as stolen time, I want to tell you about *"Untitled" (Perfect Lovers)*, 1987–1990, by Felix Gonzalez-Torres. It's of two clocks, ideally hung above head height, and set to the same time at the beginning of each installation. But, just like in any relationship, one battery will eventually die first. Gonzalez-Torres instructed that when this happens, the clocks are to be immediately reset. Confronting us with the inevitability of death, and the possibility of perpetuation, *"Untitled" (Perfect Lovers)* (overleaf) reminds us of the sacredness of time.

In 1988, Gonzalez-Torres wrote a letter to his long-term partner, Ross Laycock. He told him not to be afraid of the clocks, as time had been so generous to them, and they had conquered fate by meeting at a certain time. And that he loved him.

In 1991, Laycock died of AIDS-related complications; Gonzalez-Torres died of the same disease five years later.

What will you do with this extra, sacred day?

Felix Gonzalez-Torres (1957–96) was an American Cuban-born artist, working mostly in New York City, who was known for his sculptures, photographs and wide-ranging installations that explore transience and loss, equality, power structures and the role of ownership, and they often invite public participation.

Source: Nickas, Roberts, 'Felix Gonzalez-Torres: All the Time in the World', Flash Art International, *Nov–Dec 1991*

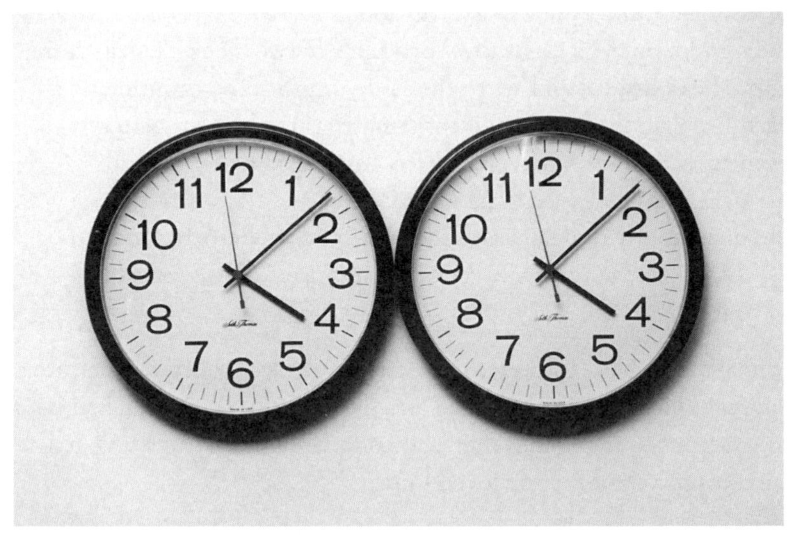

Felix Gonzalez-Torres, *"Untitled" (Perfect Lovers)*, 1987–1990

MARCH

March signals the beginning of spring: a time of rebirth and renewal when the bright green shoots of plants are emerging from hibernation, no longer sleeping under their blankets. The air smells different with the arrival of a new season; more colours appear in the natural world, and more birds, who began to nest in February, start to fill the sky. It's time to come out from concealment.

This month, let's explore how we can shift perspective, literally and emotionally. A new season signals a new time. Be present, carve out time for yourself, involve all your senses, and increase the chance that creativity can happen anywhere, at any time.

Waking up to a new time

'Here was a group who had once made history and now after a long sleep was awaking, gradually unwinding the bandage of its mummied past and looking out on life again, expectant but unafraid and with at least a graceful gesture.' —Meta Vaux Warrick Fuller

Ethiopia (1921), by the great Harlem Renaissance artist Meta Vaux Warrick Fuller, is a statue of a tall, elegant, mummified female figure, turning towards us in a noble, graceful stance. The work was made in response to the period following the Reconstruction era in the early twentieth century, marking a new time for Black American citizens. It's as if Warrick Fuller's *Ethiopia* is waking up, on the dawn of a new time – unafraid and expectant of what life/the world has to offer.

Meta Vaux Warrick Fuller (1877–1968) was an American sculptor, associated with the Harlem Renaissance movement. She is celebrated for her work addressing the Black American experience.

Source: Letter from Fuller to Mrs W. P. Hedden, 5 October 1921, quoted in Ater, Renee, 'Making History: Meta Warrick Fuller's "Ethiopia"', American Art, Vol. 17, No. 3, 2003

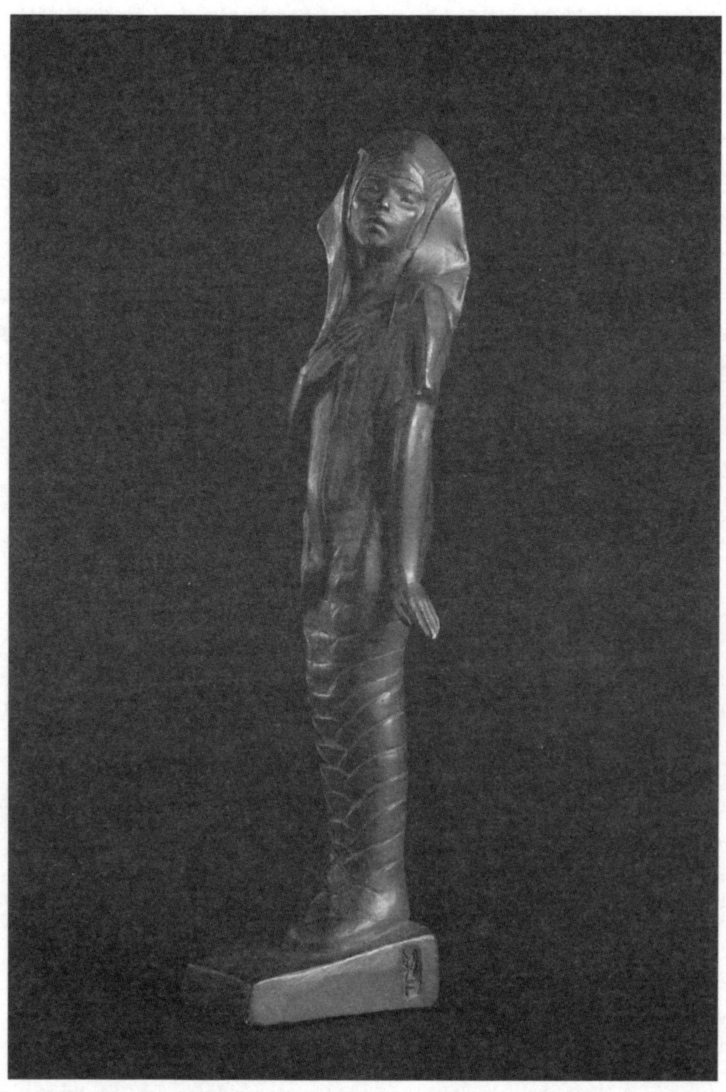

Meta Vaux Warrick Fuller, *Ethiopia*, c. 1921

Look at the world as an artist might, like a child

'I found my artistic language when I was a child. I had a great sense of smell, and one day I smelled a butterfly breaking out of its cocoon. I watched the whole procedure. It was like an instrument for seeing magic. The epiphany of the butterfly. I love the patterns on butterfly wings. In the tropics there are these extraordinary butterflies.' —Luchita Hurtado

In the first days of spring, how can you look to the outside world to revel in the magic of what it has to offer, and remember the way you viewed the world as a child?

What small, early memories shaped how you saw something, like Hurtado's close looking at the mesmeric detail of a butterfly wing? As an adult, do you still honour those viewpoints the way a child might? If not, why is that?

The writer Elif Shafak once told me that when she visits primary schools, she asks those aged five or six, 'Who wants to be a painter? A poet?' and they all put their hands up. But when she asks the same question to those ten years older, hardly any of them raise their hands.

Artists are great instruments to remind us of the importance and value of a child's perspective – from listening to children to remembering what shaped us. Hurtado was in her nineties at the time of this interview. If you could find that childlike sensibility for yourself, how might you see differently?

Luchita Hurtado (1920–2020) was a Venezuelan artist who was based in Los Angeles, USA, for much of her life. Constantly experimenting with different art forms, scales and subject matters, which created unexpected perspectives – from looking down at her body to straight up the sky – Hurtado, through cosmic motifs and geometric abstraction, investigated universality and transcendence.

Source: 'Luchita Hurtado in conversation with Hans Ulrich Obrist', in Lewin, Rebecca and Constable, Joseph (eds.), Luchita Hurtado: I Live, I Die, I Will Be Reborn, *Serpentine Galleries & Koenig Books, 2019; Elif Shafak,* The Great Women Artists Podcast, *2023*

Take time

'I think the time that painting allows is really spectacular. It's beyond us holding our phones and moving from point A to point B. It allows pause, which I think is a very important part of life.' — Jordan Casteel

What, or who, can you pause in front of, and observe today? What will that slow looking allow you to see?

When I was a child, my eldest sister often took me to museums on a Saturday afternoon. She always encouraged me to bring a sketchpad and a pencil, because when you sketch something, it allows you to really look at the thing in front of you as well as the mark you are making on the page. As a result, I still remember the smallest of details in artworks I saw decades ago, like the shape of an eyelid in a painting by the Italian Renaissance artist Sandro Botticelli, or the detail in a dress.

What can you see today? How will you capture it, in words, paint, pencil or clay? A small moment of looking can change the experience of time.

Jordan Casteel (b. 1989) is an American painter known for capturing people through myriad colours and textures – both the wide scope of their personalities and their relationships to one another. Sometimes, as a viewer, it feels as though we are meeting her subject mid-conversation. She is an astute observer of people – she pauses, and takes time.

Source: The Great Women Artists Podcast, *2021*

See the mundane in new ways

'We're so used to picking up a cup and just drinking tea and not actually having time to think about the person who made it, why it was made, where it was made . . . It's very like when you encounter a new person that you've never met: hopefully one is mesmerised into wondering what the person is all about, who the person is from the inside, and for us not to make judgements of the exterior of a person. We all dress up, we all embellish our beings, so that we don't look like who we are. But we give an impression of what everybody else wants or what we think people should make of us.' —Magdalene Odundo

Odundo reminds us to cherish the potential of being amazed. If we notice then we can find what is loveable, admirable and inspirational, perhaps especially in what has been confined to daily familiarity and put away. What can you be amazed by? Being amazed might enrich your life, and give you knowledge too. Notice the people around you, their attributes, their history, what they're like on the inside as well as the outside. Look deeper, beyond, underneath, within, and doing so will help prevent life passing you by.

Magdalene Odundo (b. 1950) is a Kenyan and British artist known for her laboriously produced clay-based sculptures. Created using hand-built techniques, Odundo's work is akin to or reminiscent of the form of a female body. She has said of her medium, 'I have always equated clay with the humanity that is within us, fragile and temperamental like human beings. Vessels made in clay can be precariously balanced, and like human beings if pushed just slightly on the wrong pivot, they can break your heart.'

Source: The Great Women Artists Podcast, *2021*

Look outwards

'For me, in the Global South, starting our history meant that I was in a little corner of a huge world. So we're always looking outwards. We're not looking inward. And I think that was essential to me. That ability not to centre the world in myself. But looking outwards. That was the greatest lesson for me from studying art history.' —Doris Salcedo

How do we get out of ourselves and see the world?

Study a subject totally different to one that you know. Read a book by someone who died before you were alive. Look at a picture made by someone who lives on the opposite side of the planet to you. Art can be a gift in showing you the deepest and intimate parts of a life that is entirely different to yours.

It's why, as Salcedo says, art history can be a great tool. To study art history is to study the history of the world through another individual's lens, working from their particular place and time. It is a way to understand that the world is bigger than our experiences and can be a conversation that can continuously happen and open up through the ages. Where will you look today?

Doris Salcedo (b. 1958) is a Colombian artist who works with public – at times participatory – installation, and found objects, such as chairs, roses, tables. While her work draws on her experiences of Colombia's violent political history, it can also speak to wider and timeless global issues.

Source: The Great Women Artists Podcast, *2024*

Ask the person next to you

'[In a museum] I often turn to the person next to me and go, "What are you thinking about that? What do you think of that flayed skin of Marcius?" And it blows my mind, every time what other people are thinking. So I'm interested in the Greek chorus of voices that sees what the characters can't see. Try to sing it out loud. I'm interested in a community because we are that; losers, pirates, visionaries, needy people like me, all of us on this sort of ship of the beautifully damned.' —Jerry Saltz

Conversation can be the greatest starting point for ideas. How often have you turned to the person next to you, and asked them: what do you think? I think if we all did this once a day, or once a week, we might live in a more harmonious world.

Do as Saltz says, and sing it out loud.

Jerry Saltz (b. 1951) is an influential American art critic and the author of several acclaimed books. Only beginning to write at around forty when he was still a long-haul truck driver, Saltz is now the senior art critic for *New York* magazine and its entertainment site *Vulture*. In 2018, he won the Pulitzer Prize for criticism and was twice nominated when he was the art critic for *The Village Voice* between 1998 and 2007.

Source: The Great Women Artists Podcast, *2022*

Go to books for the answers

'You think your pain and your heartbreak are unprecedented in the history of the world, but then you read. It was Dostoevsky and Dickens who taught me that the things that tormented me most were the very things that connected me with all the people who were alive, or who ever had been alive. Only if we face these open wounds in ourselves can we understand them in other people. An artist is a sort of emotional or spiritual historian.' —James Baldwin

How can we better understand the human condition? Read!

To spend time with a book is to give time to the capabilities and complexities of our species. What are you going through? What is happening in this wounded world that is troubling you? How can you better understand this, from an individual perspective? While books can't give us the answers, they can give voice to experiences, connecting us with the lineage of humanity. As the great Fran Lebowitz once said, 'The closest thing to a human being is a book.'

James Baldwin (1924–87) was one of the most influential American writers of the twentieth century, acclaimed for his essays, novels, plays and poems.

Source: Howard, Jane, 'Telling Talk from a Negro Writer', LIFE magazine, 24 May 1963; Fran Lebowitz quote: Collection in Focus: Fran Lebowitz on the Process of Great Writing, The Morgan Library and Museum, 2024 (video) **LIFE**

Recognise the value of women

'I will show Your Illustrious Lordship what a woman can do.'
—Artemisia Gentileschi

It's International Women's Day. Today, I want to spotlight Artemisia Gentileschi, an artist working in seventeenth-century Rome, famed for her visceral, bold and fiercely strong depictions of Biblical heroines. Working from a distinctly female lens, she showed women as capable, beautiful – as survivors. Her paintings remind me that viewpoints just like ours today existed hundreds of years ago, despite the constant erasure of these voices in history.

Without her perspective, art history would look very different. She gave voice to women who lived 400 years ago. I find it inspiring to think that if she could do it then, we can do it now.

Artemisia Gentileschi (1593– *c.* 1653) was a painter working in the Baroque style, involving theatrical scenes and striking light effects, and often charting Biblical stories. She was one of the most successful women artists working in her era. People were so enamoured by her and her work that they commissioned pictures of her hand: they thought it was so divine.

Source: Letter from Artemisia Gentileschi to Don Antonio Ruffo, 7 August 1649, from Francesco Solinas, Lettere di Artemisia, *De Luca, 2011, Letter 53. Cited in Treves, Letizia et al.,* Artemisia, *National Gallery, 2020*

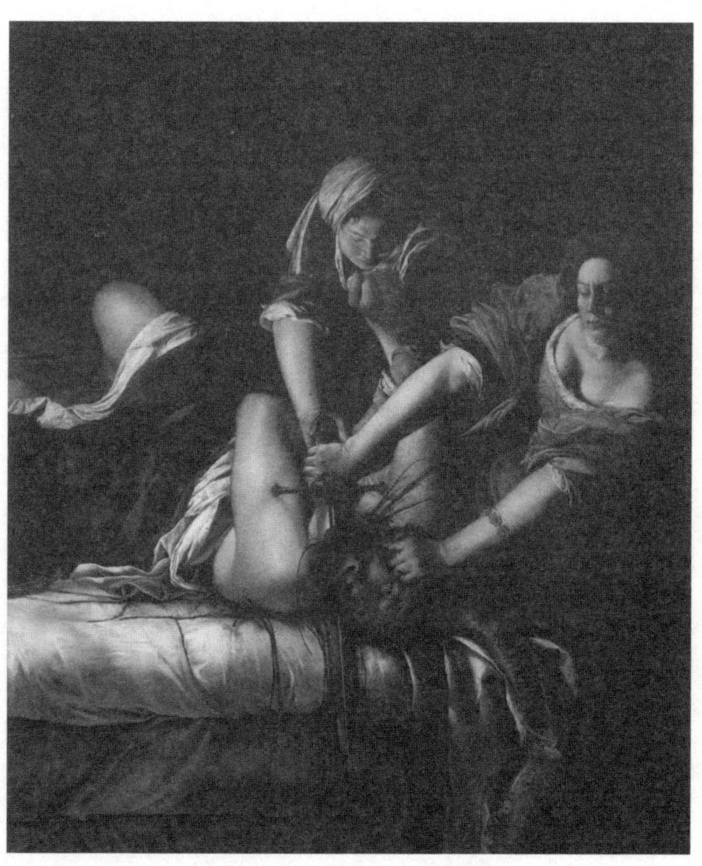

Artemisia Gentileschi, *Judith Slaying Holofernes*, c. 1620

Learning is a secret weapon

'You learn for yourself, not for others, not to show off, not to put the other one down. Learning is your secret. It is all you have. It is the only thing you can call your own. Nobody can take it away.' —*Louise Bourgeois*

The more you learn, the better you'll understand yourself, the world and others around you. Learning is eternal, infinite, and continuously compelling. When we learn, we never fail. Our worlds can only get richer and more expansive. As Bourgeois says, it is always something you will have – for free, and for yourself.

The French-American artist **Louise Bourgeois** (1911–2010) was best known for her sculptures, prints, installations and fabric works, featuring motifs such as the spiral and the spider.

Source: Bourgeois, Louise, The View from the Bottom of the Well, *1996, portfolio with nine drypoints and letterpress text, reprinted in Bernadac, Marie-Laure and Hans Ulrich Obrist (eds.),* Louise Bourgeois: Destruction of the Father, Reconstruction of the Father: Writings and Interviews 1923–1997, *Violette Editions, 1998*

Knowledge – not information

'How can we deal with less information in our daily lives, but with more knowledge, and hopefully, eventually, with more wisdom? I think for knowledge, you need to slow down; knowledge cannot be rushed.' —*Elif Shafak*

The world is moving faster than it is turning, with the proliferation of information and images constantly being fed to us at increasing speed, day by day, hour by hour, minute by minute. How can we process this, and spend time with each thought? How can we slow down to make sure we are acquiring knowledge, not just information?

Spend time with one thing, one story, as opposed to absorbing a great barrage of information that can feel overwhelming. What will you choose today?

Elif Shafak (b. 1971) is a celebrated French-born, Turkish-British author. To date she has written nineteen books, twelve of which are novels, and has been instrumental in her work as an advocate for women's and LGBTQ+ rights and freedom of expression.

Source: The Great Women Artists Podcast, *2023*

How should we use language?

'I feel that it's our duty that if we have language, we can share that language. And by sharing language, we're giving people access to ideas . . . To do that requires language that doesn't – as Toni Morrison used to say – "language that doesn't sweat". One of the great efforts and beauties of being able to write, and care about writing, is: how do we make this information available to all kinds of people, not just people who are involved in the art world? I feel that my job really is in that context, is as a translator. And one of the things that can happen, if you're a translator, is to give people the sense that they're not alone in the discovery.' —Hilton Als

Carrying on from yesterday, if you do have knowledge – and that knowledge comes in the form of language – how can you share it, give it, gift it? How do you make it available to people of all kinds, so that they can pass it on, too?

Hilton Als (b. 1960) is an American writer, critic and curator, known for his non-fiction books and contributions to *The New Yorker*.

Source: The Great Women Artists Podcast, 2023

Keep paying attention

'Whether I'm painting or not, I have this overweening interest in humanity. Even when I'm not working, I'm analysing.' —Alice Neel

Alice Neel had an incredible ability to see people for who they were and, more importantly, their individuality. She painted people across the whole spectrum of society, including those who were rarely recorded in paintings from the 1930s to 1980s: queer people, people of colour, those of a lower socio-economic class.

It's Neel's 'overweening interest' in humanity that makes her work feel so contemporary. And her ability to capture not just humanity as a whole, but the slight differences between us all.

Living an artful life is about looking and being interested; about acquiring a type of knowledge that requires time, perception, awareness and our attention; not seeing people as a group, but noticing the minutiae of their individuality.

If you were to create a portrait of someone close to you, what details would you include? What makes them unique?

Alice Neel (1900–84) described herself as a 'collector of souls'. She was a painter of people, and always worked in her home-based studio in Spanish Harlem, and later the Upper West Side.

Source: Alice Neel *by Andrew Neel, SeeThink Films, 2007*

Look out for unheard stories

'I think, all through time, women have been up against the limitations of their representation. They have been written out of history, their reality "unnamed" and denied meaning. We are so accustomed to this, and it is ingrained in our culture everywhere we look. It is as if women are unrecognisable if unrelated to male desire. Women are always in relation to lack, constantly up against unconscious bias. I wish for women to be at the centre of things . . . to be all things, whole, boundless, perverse, and representative of humanity. I want to give voice to this experience of being alive, now, in this culture, as a woman.' —Prudence Flint

Always question what you are looking at, and ask yourself: where are the women, and how are they represented? And use your voice.

Prudence Flint (b. 1962) is an Australian artist who paints female subjects occupying intimate, everyday, stylised domestic interiors.

Source: Pyatt, Charlotte, 'Prudence Flint: Portrait of the Unnamed', Juxtapoz Magazine, 2020

Searching, and holding on to, identity

'Whatever happens, there is always hope that things can get better. And that you can find yourself . . . I often liken it to young women who perhaps wanted to be an accountant or a dancer, and somehow their lives are slightly derailed, intentionally. They lose the identity of who they really are. Or they're known in relation to their partners, or in relation to their children. But there is still something that is very essentially them, within themselves. The secret of it is to find that again; you don't need to abandon anything, but find what essentially drives you and always drove you.

One retains, bizarrely, even in the depths of trauma, a small kernel that is still you. The secret is to hang on to it and try to nurture it.' —Lubaina Himid

You have what is already inside of you, as Himid says; all it takes is for you to nurture it, or someone to shine a light onto it.

Himid makes works that investigate the history of an object, or the history of a person and their unique identities, which might have been buried for different reasons.

What identities can you hold on to that are uniquely yours? Although someone might be 'known' as something specific, there are many layers inside us all. Hold on to them, nurture them, recognise that they are still within you, whether others see them or not.

Lubaina Himid (b. 1954) is a British artist, born in Zanzibar. She trained as a theatre designer and works across painting, sculpture and installation. She was a pioneer of the British Black Arts movement of the 1980s.

Source: The Great Women Artists Podcast, *2020*

Steal just a moment for yourself

'A woman artist is not deprived by cooking and having children [. . .] – one is in fact nourished by this rich life, provided one always does some work each day; even a single half hour, so that images grow in one's mind.' —Barbara Hepworth

Steal time for yourself today. What will you do with it? How will an idea grow?

Barbara Hepworth (1903–75) was a giant of British sculpture. Born in Wakefield, Yorkshire, she carried with her the rhythms of the Northern hills. From 1939, she was based in St Ives, a fishing village in Cornwall famed for its rocky beaches, and the weathered lines and ocean swirls of her surroundings made their way into her highly textured sculptures. Working in an interior and exterior environment, Hepworth interacted with the natural forms of the landscape, as well as analysing the many forms that the human body can take.

Source: Hepworth, Barbara, A Pictorial Autobiography, *Adams & Dart, 1970; revised 1978 (now published by Tate Publishing)*

How do you make yourself present?

'It is so very hard, I believe, for women to make themselves present, because there's so much to absent ourselves from. Especially for Francesca Woodman's generation – the societal gaze, or you could say, the patriarchal gaze, whatever, is so violent, is on you all the time. So why would you just be totally present to it? You'd want to sort of zone out of it. This is how I talk about absence and presence. It's not an easy thing; it's not a mindfulness thing. To make yourself present in art, for that generation, is a huge triumph, really.' —Deborah Levy

Levy, here, was telling me about the photographer, Francesca Woodman (1958–81), whose small, mostly black-and-white photographs conceal and reveal herself, using blurring effects, or a mirror, to be both there and not there (see overleaf).

Was she running away from the camera, to disappear, or was she trying to be in it? But just by making the work, she was making herself present.

History is full of the presence of some communities, while others are mostly absent. How can we find or create their presence? How will you make yourself present?

Deborah Levy (b. 1959) is a South African-born, British writer, and the author of several critically acclaimed novels and non-fiction works, including her 'living autobiographies' on writing, gender politics and philosophy: *Things I Don't Want to Know*, *The Cost of Living* and *Real Estate*. She has been shortlisted twice for the Goldsmiths Prize and the Booker Prize.

Source: The Great Women Artists Podcast, *2021*

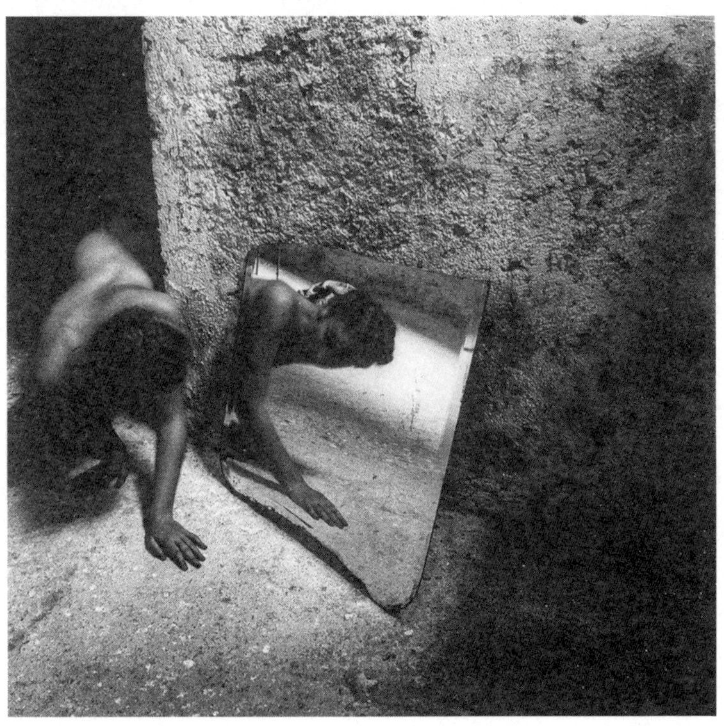

Francesca Woodman, *Self-Deceit #1*, 1978

Write yourself in

'That's what I like, to be able to make something that doesn't otherwise exist. You have to do it yourself, to write it yourself, and you have to write yourself in. That's what I've been doing for a long time: writing myself in, and creating things that I find beautiful at the same time. This kind of work gives me energy.' —Frida Orupabo

Orupabo's artistic language is collage (see overleaf). What does collage allow for? Amalgamating figures, forms, gestures and viewpoints. Unlike painting or sculpture, it doesn't have the same history. Painting can include the legacy of the so-called Old Master 'greats'; sculpture comes with the history of artists using materials like marble on a grand scale. Collage is a newer medium which can help new things be said. Put two things together today on a page. What picture do they make?

Frida Orupabo (b. 1986) is a Norwegian-Nigerian artist who creates collages from fragmented photographs of mostly Black female figures.

Source: Binyam, Maya, 'Stealing It Back: A Conversation with Frida Orupabo', The Paris Review, 25 April 2022

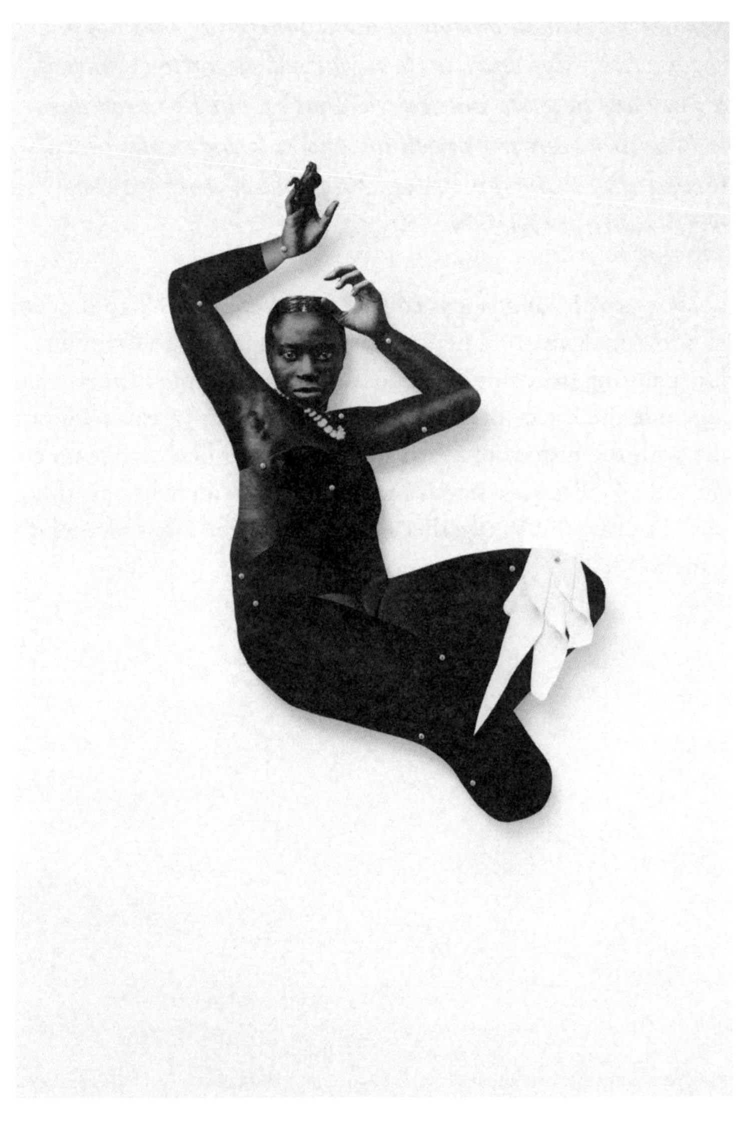

Frida Orupabo, *Untitled*, 2018

The time is now

'Reflect on what it is to be alive at any moment.' —Sarah Sze

Every day is a historical occasion. What might seem mundane or difficult now may be seen as profound in a few years. Be a conduit for the time in which you are living. Document what it is to be alive now. Reflect on it by using art as your tool. One day you might return to this forgotten account and remember something extraordinary.

Sarah Sze (b. 1969) is an American artist who explores how we make meaning from the never-ending stream of images that saturate contemporary life. In her complex interdisciplinary work, Sze destabilises the boundary between two and three dimensions, as imagery repeats across media, flowing from painting to sculpture and back again. Through this pictorial call-and-response from the physical and digital worlds, she produces intricate sculptures, paintings, drawings, prints, videos and installations that explore the precarious nature of materiality and the elliptical quality of time, memory and perception.

Source: The Great Women Artists Podcast, *2023*

Elevate the ordinary things

'That's why I like ordinary things as opposed to fine things or ostentatious things, which are already saying too much.'—Sarah Lucas

The British artist Sarah Lucas uses bananas, eggs, stockings, chairs, cigarettes and newspapers in her work, transforming them into artworks that get us to look at them differently.

What can you glean from two fried eggs on a woman's chest? How can a newspaper headline from thirty years ago speak to you about wider culture and society? What do you think of when you see a woman eating a banana? How can stuffed stockings evoke a female body?

As Lucas says, sometimes the ordinary things in life can have the best potential. It's from them that we can pull the most interesting discussions. What objects or things can you give deeper meaning to, and get us to see anew?

Sarah Lucas (b. 1962) is a British artist who uses everyday objects in her sculpture, installation and photographic works.

Source: Lucas, Sarah; Heyse-Moore, Dominique (ed.), 'Happy Gassing: Louisa Buck and Sarah Lucas in Conversation', Happy Gas, Tate Publishing, 2023

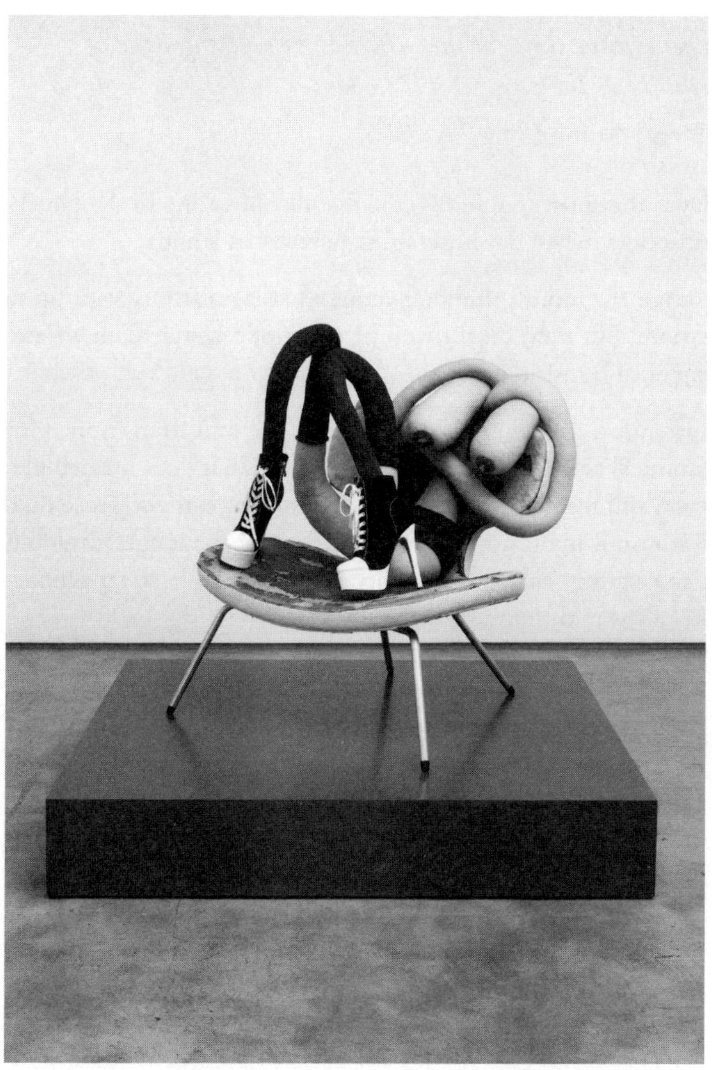

Sarah Lucas, *COOL CHICK BABY*, 2020

Spring equinox

'The crisp quiet of winter and its transition into spring is a generative time for me. There is an exciting sense of possibility as the days get a little longer and things begin to grow again.' —Naudline Pierre

Today is the spring equinox – the first day of spring in the Northern Hemisphere, when day and night are equal in length.

We began the month thinking about what it means to wake up to a new time. But now, on the tipping point of a new season, we are in a moment of transition.

Pay attention to the outside world: have the buds transitioned into blossom? What new colours have arrived? What does it smell like? Are you still feeling the quietness of winter, or can you sense that a new season is upon us? How can you look to the longer days to give you an exciting sense of possibility, as if time has been stretched as we make our way through spring?

Naudline Pierre (b. 1989) is an American artist who draws from mythology, fantasy and iconography for her vivid painterly worlds.

Source: A note to the author, January 2025

There is no limit to creativity

'You can't use up creativity. The more you use, the more you have.' —*Maya Angelou*

Look, watch, read, listen, but also draw, paint, sculpt, knit, dream, imagine . . . It's all useful and will inform everything you do – and go on to make or see. Ideas are everywhere, and endless. Creativity will never run out; it will never disappear. Trust creativity when it comes to you. Think of it like muscle building: the more you work out, the bigger you get. Inner strength is just as important/the same as outer strength.

Maya Angelou (1928–2014) was an American writer, editor, essayist, playwright, poet, educator and civil rights activist.

Source: Elliot, Jeffrey M. (ed.), Conversations with Maya Angelou, *University Press of Mississippi, 1989*

'Break' if you need to

'I always make sure to have at least six panels in progress at once. It's a hard habit to commit to when one's going well and exciting, but it's an essential rule for me. It makes sure I don't put too much pressure on any. When one inevitably isn't working and I can't figure out why, rather than forcing it I put it away and pull over a different panel.' —Aubrey Levinthal

Either it works, or it doesn't. This quote from Levinthal reminds us to relax. If you're in a groove, keep going. If it's not working, allow yourself to change. Keep multiple things going so you can make that break and change direction if you need to.

The best thing we can do sometimes is to switch it up, because doing so might just excite something we never thought we were capable of.

Aubrey Levinthal (b. 1986) is an American painter known for her intimate paintings that capture private moments that involve herself, her family or her acquaintances. With their muted or at times saturated palette, they depict the quietness of the everyday, making you notice the small moments in life and celebrate the rituals of daily activities.

Source: A note to the author, 2024

Try different mediums

'I really enjoy going from one medium to another. Some say it leads to mediocrity. It might, but I feel like if you're demanding enough of yourself, you're going to be able to create something new . . .'—Nadya Tolokonnikova

Focus isn't simply about sticking to the same medium – it's a state of mind. It requires, as Tolokonnikova says, demanding enough of yourself.

Nadya Tolokonnikova (b. 1989) is an artist, activist and founding member of Pussy Riot, the feminist art-collective and performance group, active since 2011, dedicated to fighting for freedom and confronting the dangers of the far right.

Source: The Great Women Artists Podcast, *2024*

Use all of your senses

'But the wonderful thing about writing is that it's not purely a visual medium. You can use all of your senses. So it's like you have a camera of the ear, and a camera of the skin, and all of these are instruments of the physical body that can observe, that can record, and that can be used in order to describe, and bring to life a location, or a scene or a character.' —Ruth Ozeki

How many senses do you have? From hearing to smell, taste to touch, looking to feeling . . . how can you embrace all of them? How will this open up myriad and exciting new ways of thinking, looking and experiencing?

Ruth Ozeki (b. 1956) is an American-Canadian Zen Buddhist priest, and author of the novel *A Tale for the Time Being*, as well as several other fiction and non-fiction books.

Source: The Great Women Artists Podcast, *2023*

The great web of life

'We are interconnected with a great web of life; whatever we do, it's like being a spider in a spider web. Whenever we move, many other things move around us as a result of us, of our own movement. So, there is a great responsibility that comes with just the idea of existing in the world.' —Marguerite Humeau

Everything is connected; to live artfully is to recognise that. Use this connection wisely. Create for yourself, but also understand what it will mean for others in this great web of life. What will you do today that moves other things around?

Marguerite Humeau (b. 1986) is a French artist working in London, who draws on prehistoric and futuristic worlds for her at times large-scale sculptures that investigate the mysteries of human existence. She has collaborated with scientists, anthropologists, explorers, linguists, clairvoyants and more, and uses art as a tool to explore ever-expanding ecosystems.

Source: Artist Marguerite Humeau: To Be Alive Is a Great Responsibility, *Louisiana Channel,* 2024 *(video)*

Don't be precious; make anywhere

'Colour isn't connected to specific surfaces or materials or to a particular place. A painting can land and remain anywhere: on a rubber boot, on an egg, in the crook of the arm, in the garden, on bulging folds of fabric, along a railway track, in the snow and ice, or on the beach. If painting isn't connected to place, then the imagination is not connected to place; and since imagination is immediate reality, reality as well is siteless.' —Katharina Grosse

Creativity can exist anywhere. Never be precious about where you make. Art is not limited to a canvas, nor is it limited to being shown in a gallery. When we create or stage artworks in unorthodox places, it also invites a new way of thinking about the art because of the history of the place.

In 2016, Katharina Grosse spray-painted Fort Tilden, a derelict former military building on the Rockaway peninsula in New York City, transforming the site with sprays of red, white and magenta, blurring the boundary of where an artwork begins and where it ends.

Where will you choose to make?

Katharina Grosse (b. 1961) is a German artist hailed for her wall paintings that explode with luminous colours, as well as her site-responsive paintings which she spray-paints onto rocks, walls, landscapes and architecture.

Source: McNay, Anna, 'Katharina Grosse – interview: "My eyes are my most important tools"', Studio International, *21 December 2020*

How can art enhance our daily experiences?

'Art has crept out into full-blown existence in our lives. And we dare call it art. I don't know if it is art, but it's certainly enhancing our daily experiences to come across some kind of daring thrust of colour, texture, fibre and emotional explosion of some kind, or a very intimate discovery. It may be something like a little bird's nest that fell from a tree. Or maybe a little mouse has left behind all the twigs that it gathered from the tree and made a nest for the mini mice. As you walk across in the park, you look under the bushes, and you look up at the sky, and you see leaves changing colours. So we're not talking about art. We're talking about living visual experiences.' —Sheila Hicks

Art is all around us, constantly enhancing our daily experiences. The secret is to notice it.

Sheila Hicks (b. 1934) is an American artist who uses innovative and experimental techniques for her fibre-based sculptures that range in size from small to colossal.

Source: The Great Women Artists Podcast, *2022*

We are all creative

'Everybody works in a creative way in order to survive life — some need to do this more than others. But creativity should be nurtured in all of us. Survival is part of being human and creativity is as important a tool as any other. Creativity is not in the sole possession of the artist. It is part of the human experience.' —Helen Cammock

Whatever your profession, we all need and use creativity to work out how to survive. What have you experienced? How can you channel that emotion into what you do, whether that be something you're paid to do, or something for yourself? Being creative can sometimes make us feel most alive.

Helen Cammock (b. 1970) is a British artist who works in film, photography, print, text and performance. Utilising a predominantly researched-based process, Cammock investigates the complexities of social histories and has used her art to centre marginalised voices.

Source: Phillips, Sarah, 'The experts: artists on 20 easy, mind-expanding ways to be much more creative', Guardian, 4 January 2024; reworded for the author, 2025

How can we be conscious of others, and the outside world?

'Everything that is alive thinks.' —*Etel Adnan*

How will this change the way you view and interact with the world? From an insect to a plant, the river to the sea – what is alive to you?

Etel Adnan (1925–2021) was a celebrated Lebanese-American poet, essayist and artist. She lived all around the world, including Paris and California, and could speak many languages. Her paintings consisted of simple shapes in bright colours, and what you see can change depending on how you choose to look at them.

Source: Adler, Laure, 'Beginning with Color: An Interview with Etel Adnan', The Paris Review, 4 October 2023

Fill your life with contrasts

'I start work in the morning at about ten . . . having put the washing in the washing machine, and gone to the greengrocer . . . I will read something easy to stop me thinking about the house, and then I read something difficult to make my mind be really moving – you know, like running a car in. And then after a bit if I read something difficult that's really interesting I get this itch to start writing. So what I like to do is to write from about half past twelve, one, through to about four. And then I start reading again. That would be a perfect day's work.' —A. S. Byatt

Find two pieces of writing – one easy, one hard – and see the effect they have on you.

A. S. Byatt (1936–2023) was a celebrated English novelist, critic, poet and short story writer. In 1990, she won the Booker Prize with her novel, *Possession*.

Source: Quoted in Lockwood, Patricia, 'Isn't that . . . female?', London Review of Books, *20 June 2024*

Stay eager

'Attention is vitality. It connects you with others. It makes you eager. Stay eager.' —*Susan Sontag*

Let's close the month with words of wisdom by Sontag. How can we stay eager? Write down, quickly, what you have learnt in this past month. Add five things that you want to stay eager for in the month to come.

1. ____

2. ____

3. ____

4. ____

5. ____

Susan Sontag (1933–2004) was one of the most influential American critics, essayists and authors of the twentieth century. She is best known for her works of criticism, such as *Against Interpretation* and *On Photography*, and the essay 'Notes on Camp'.

Source: Sontag, Susan, commencement address at Vassar College, 2003

APRIL

In March we reflected on looking out and observing closely; how art can exist anywhere; the excitement of sharing art and language, and passing that on.

This month, let's explore world-building – thinking collectively and working collaboratively in our communities. What magic happens when we come together and lift each other up? How does art help us understand both our common humanity and unique experiences?

What can we learn from a month like April?

'April. It teaches us everything. The coldest and nastiest days of the year can happen in April. It won't matter. It's April. The English word for the month comes from the Roman Aprilis, *the Latin* aperire: *to open, to uncover, to make accessible, or to remove whatever stops something from being accessible. It maybe also partly comes from the name of Aphrodite, Greek goddess of love, whose happy fickleness with various gods mirrors the month's own showery-sunny fickleness. Month of sacrifice and month of playfulness. Month of restoration, of fertility-festivity. Month when the earth and the buds are already open, the creatures asleep for the winter have woken and are already breeding, the birds have already built their nests, birds that this time last year didn't exist, busy bringing to life the birds that'll replace them this time next year.' —Ali Smith*

Think of April like a daisy chain, the connecting month of spring, and focus on Mary Delany's *Chrysanthemum Serotinum* (1781) – a collage of coloured papers spliced together to portray an oxeye daisy, mid-bloom and dancing against the pitch-black backdrop.

Ali Smith (b. 1962) is an acclaimed Scottish writer of fiction and non-fiction. Between 2016 and 2020, she completed a series of four stand-alone novels, grouped as the Seasonal Quartet, which track unprecedented events in living history. At the spine of each book is an artist: Pauline Boty in *Autumn*, Barbara Hepworth in *Winter*, Tacita Dean in *Spring*, and filmmaker Lorenza Mazzetti in *Summer*.

Mary Delany (1700–88) was an English artist, known for pioneering the medium of collage in producing principally botanical images, which she called her 'paper mosaicks'.

Source: Smith, Ali, Spring, *Hamish Hamilton, 2019*

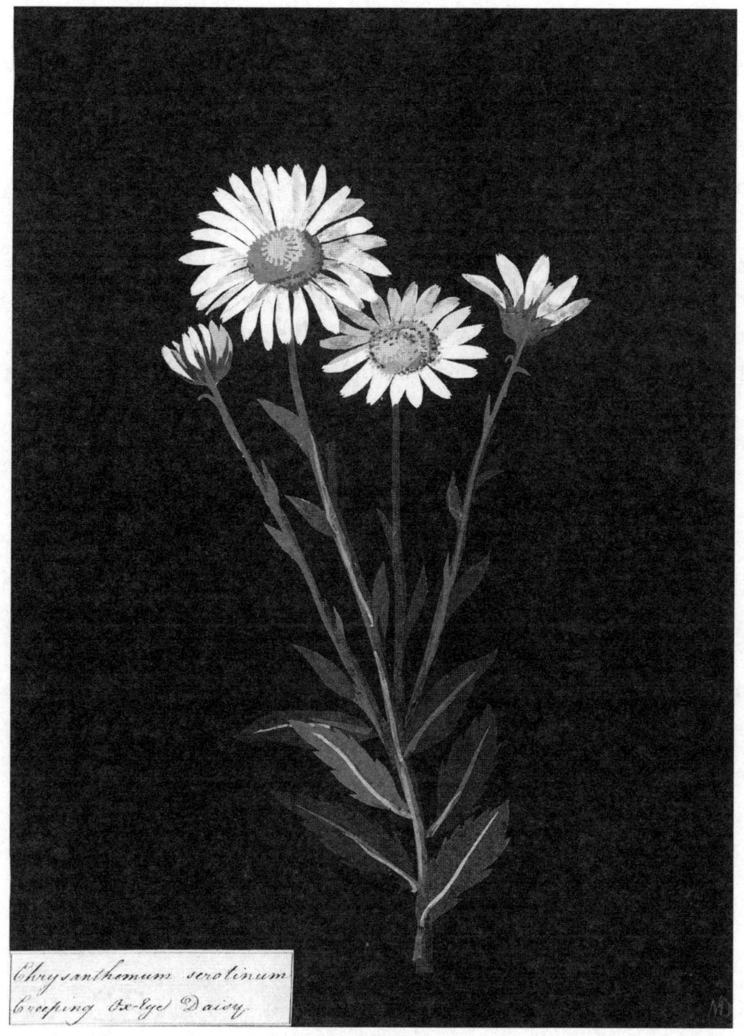

Mary Delany, *Chrysanthemum Serotinum*, 1781

Build communities

'When we went around the room to introduce ourselves, June [Wayne, a painter] encouraged me to say "Luchita Hurtado". That was a very important moment in my life, remembering my name.' —Luchita Hurtado

In the 1970s, Hurtado was part of a group of women artists in Los Angeles spearheaded by artist Joyce Kozloff. It was the time of the Women's Liberation movement and while Hurtado had always made art – and exhibited, on occasions, in the 1950s – it wasn't until she was part of this community that she felt encouraged to assert herself as an artist. Not only did she stop turning her unfinished paintings towards the wall (so they were on view for all to see), but, as she says here, she stopped using her married name when it came to her artmaking. Upon 'remembering' it, she went on to say, 'I lived again.'

Of course, we don't have to change our names and, if we do, we might wish to own that new name and be happy in it. What we can think about is the invitation Hurtado was offered by the new community around her. How can you champion friends and colleagues; offer guidance and critiques; provide space, both physically and emotionally? It could be anything from using a name that we once had, or going back to our roots to make us feel like we can 'live' again.

Luchita Hurtado (1920–2020) was a Venezuelan artist who was based in Los Angeles, USA, for much of her life. Constantly experimenting with different art forms, scales and subject matters, which created unexpected perspectives – from looking down at her body to straight up the sky – Hurtado, through cosmic motifs and geometric abstraction, investigated universality and transcendence.

Source: 'Luchita Hurtado in conversation with Hans Ulrich Obrist', in Lewin, Rebecca and Constable, Joseph (eds.), Luchita Hurtado: I Live, I Die, I Will Be Reborn, *Serpentine Galleries & Koenig Books, 2019*

Small things can make the greatest differences

'I think I really would like people to learn that they have agency. That each one of us can make a tiny, tiny bit of difference. It doesn't have to be big showy gestures, but really tiny bits of difference to the people around you, sometimes to somebody you don't know. But that is absolutely the way that change happens.' —Lubaina Himid

Change starts with small steps. Collaboration begins with one moment. What's one small thing that you can do today that will make a difference to someone else's life? Who will you instil agency in?

Lubaina Himid (b. 1954) is a British artist, born in Zanzibar. She trained as a theatre designer and works across painting, sculpture and installation. She was a pioneer of the British Black Arts movement of the 1980s.

Source: The Great Women Artists Podcast, *2020*

You never know the impact you will have

'Hope . . . is the belief that what we do matters even though how and when it may matter, who and what it may impact, are not things we can know beforehand. We may not, in fact, know them afterwards either, but they matter all the same, and history is full of people whose influence was most powerful after they were gone.' —Rebecca Solnit

You never know the impact something you do will have, whether it be now or in years to come. Think about all those who are no longer here who are still impacting us – whether it be through books, art or their spirit in our memories. Today, reflect on a moment that was given to you. Hold on to that, and the hope that person or thing might have given you. Pass it on.

Rebecca Solnit (b. 1961) is an American writer, historian and activist, and the author of twenty books on subjects that span feminism to the environment.

Source: Solnit, Rebecca, foreword to the third edition of Hope in the Dark, *Canongate, 2016*

Giving visibility

'I'm fascinated by the mystery and beauty of being, and my work is an attempt to explore it. I hope to give presence to voices that are too often left at the margins. The women in my work carry stories of movement, memory, and resilience that deserve space and light.' —María Berrío

The way we seek out stories, and the way stories have been brought to the fore, has so often been through artists' willingness to look to the margins. I believe that there are stories we would not know about without artists taking the time to capture them.

Who and what will you give visibility to, today? What can you get us to see?

María Berrío (b. 1982) is a Colombian-born artist living and working in New York City. She is celebrated for her paintings made from different types of hand-dyed textured Japanese paper. Often populated with hybridised winged or masked characters, Berrío's works reimagine mythical worlds, from Colombian folklore to tales from the artist's imagination. They can also be steeped in political realities and current events, but despite the sometimes very real narratives, her paintings are full of hope, beauty and optimism.

Source: A note to the author, 2025

Recognising strength

'There's a lot of tension simply existing as a human being, and so I like to incorporate that energy of what it means to exist.'
—Senga Nengudi

Through sculpture, Senga Nengudi visualises both the strength and fragility of our bodies. For her series, *R.S.V.P.*, 1977–2003, she stretched and attached nylon stockings to the wall, filling some areas with sand, to create bulbous and solid sacks.

These artworks show the ultimate dichotomy between hard and soft, strong and fragile, and show the incredible capacity of the body and mind to expand and contract.

Even when you are feeling fragile, notice the strength that you have within you.

Senga Nengudi (b. 1943) is an American visual artist, curator and educator. She makes work that challenges what it is like to live in a body.

Source: Senga Nengudi: 'As human beings we're fragile, yet we're so sturdy', *Henry Moore Foundation, 2023 (video)*

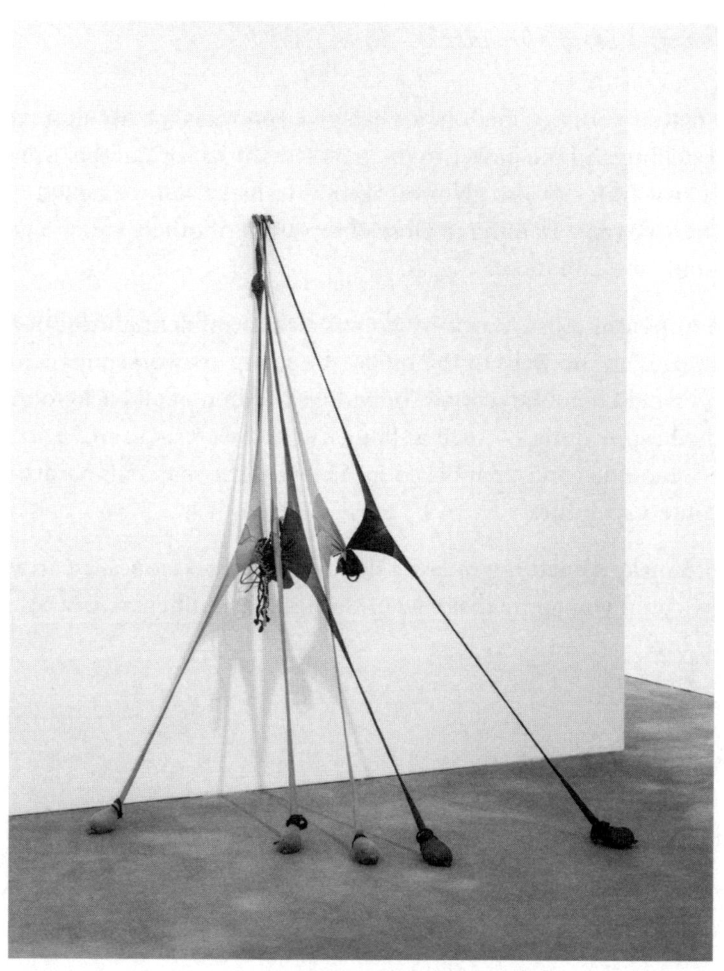

Senga Nengudi, *R.S.V.P. Reverie "Scribe"*, 2014

How can art make us more skilled?

'Art will make people better, more highly skilled in thinking and improving whatever business one goes into, or whatever occupation. It makes a person broader.' —Ruth Asawa

No matter your occupation, art can give you tools for self-expression, storytelling and the power to imagine – essential for rational thought. As a 'maker' it can also give you agency, to make something that is entirely yours: a training in close observation of others and the world around you, and more.

The American artist Asawa – who was also an influential educator – knew this all too well. In the 1960s, she set up art workshops across San Francisco public schools, providing children of all backgrounds with cheap materials – such as flour, salt and water – to make art. Once moulded and then baked in the oven, the materials hardened to become a sculpture.

Try to make something today: a doodle, a stack of stones, an artwork. How could you apply that way of thinking in a different area of your life?

Ruth Asawa (1926–2013) was an American artist recognised for her wire sculptures and public commissions, and as an influential educator and arts advocate in the San Francisco Bay Area.

Source: Nathan, Harriet, 'Oral history transcript: Ruth Asawa', Bancroft Library, 1974 and 1976

Be open to multiple points of view

'Many points of view have to be aware of each other so that there is no oppression or domination. And as time goes by it becomes more and more of a necessity to work including as many people as possible, because we have to reconnect and rebuild and reweave the notion that we have to work together. Why is that? Not only for the survival of our species, but most of all because it's joyful. Because it's fun, and it's beautiful, and it's delightful.' —Cecilia Vicuña

Reflect on your position in the world. Are you the head of a family or a team, or in a supporting role? Are you young, or old? Whatever position you have in the world, know that all of them count. No matter who we are, what our profession or status is, we always need to hear from multiple points of view. Not least, as Vicuña says, because it's fun, too!

Cecilia Vicuña (b. 1948) is a Chilean-born artist, hailed for her works that are as ephemeral as they are permanent, colossal as they are minute, fragile as they are strong, that bring together sound, weaving, language and community. Although sometimes working on a monumental scale, her work can comprise twigs, bamboo, stones and shredded textiles.

Source: Cecilia Vicuña: 'Your Rage Is Your Gold', *Tate, 2023 (video)*

Recognise our common humanity

'I really think that the underlying message is that while we are all so different and subjected to different cultural, traditional, political and religious realities, what we have in common is our humanity. We face similar dilemmas as human beings living on this planet, and share common anxieties such as fear of war, violence, abandonment, displacement and loss.' —*Shirin Neshat*

Sometimes people can feel a million miles away from us, as if they come from totally different planets. But when we think about all the things we humans enjoy, eat, listen to, read, watch and more, we are a lot more similar than we might at first gauge.

Recognise the common humanity in all of us: your perspective of someone, or the world itself, might just slightly change.

Shirin Neshat (b. 1957) is an Iranian-born artist, based in New York, known for her work in photography, film and video that delves into issues of gender, identity and politics. Her personal experiences as a Muslim woman in exile have informed much of her work, and it is through the lens of art that she explores political structures that have shaped the history of Iran. Speaking about this, she has said: 'Every Iranian artist, in one form or another, is political. Politics has defined our lives. If you're living in Iran, you're facing censorship, harassment, arrest, torture, at times execution. If you're living outside, like me, you're faced with a life of exile, the pain of longing and the separation from your loved ones and your family.'

Source: The Great Women Artists Podcast, 2020

Create space

'When we [Karon and her husband, Noah Davis] got together, we were always interested in spaces and creating spaces for other people. I would say to anyone – just go for it. Don't let anyone tell you how you're going to know if you don't try, right? Since then, I've had so many young people and young artists [come up to me and say], "I want to start a space, I want to do this." And that's the legacy of the young men and women that worked for us at this space [the Underground Museum], who helped make it happen, and [I love] seeing them out in the world now curating and performing and being their own artists and creating spaces.' —Karon Davis

In 2012, Davis and her husband, the painter Noah Davis (1983–2015), founded the Underground Museum in Los Angeles, USA, with a mission 'to ensure that no one has to travel outside the neighbourhood to see world-class art, or learn from leading thinkers, educators, chefs, and artists'. Using the money left by Noah Davis's father after he died, the couple converted four shopfronts in Arlington Heights, Los Angeles, where they invited the community to see exhibitions by the likes of Kara Walker, Lorna Simpson, Arthur Jafa and more; as well as movie nights and wellness sessions, from yoga to meditation. It was just as much a cultural centre as it was community hub. It ran, serving the community, until 2022.

What can you do to serve your community, no matter how big or small? As Davis tells us, don't let anyone tell you how you're going to know if you don't try.

Karon Davis (b. 1977) is an American artist who creates sculptures and installations of imagined and historical figures. Drawing on issues of history, race and violence in the United States, as well as her background in theatre, dance and film, Davis uses a unique plaster method, akin to Egyptian mummification practices, to sculpt entire ballets or recreations of historical events. Her life-size sculptures, covered in white plaster dust, raise questions about Western beauty standards that have been entrenched in our society since classical times.

Source: The Great Women Artists Podcast, *2023/4*

Collaborate with those of the past

'The dead surround the living.' —*John Berger*

Remember all those people who lived in this world. They're still here, among us, in what they built, made, wrote, sang, played; in what they fought for and marched for, so we can live our lives; in memory, and in spirit. Use them, speak with them, ask them questions, imagine how they might see the world today – or what they might say to you about what you're dealing with right now.

You don't have to restrict yourself to speaking to, engaging or collaborating with those alive today. For example, the writer Andrew O'Hagan uses Charles Dickens as his imaginary friend. Who would you choose? Who from the past can be your imaginary friend?

John Berger (1926–2017) was an influential British art critic, novelist, poet and painter. A writer on art and society, Berger is best known for his groundbreaking book and television series, *Ways of Seeing* (1972), and his Booker Prize-winning novel *G.* that was published in the same year.

Source: Berger, John, 'On the Economy of the Dead', Harper's Magazine, *April 2008*

We are stronger when we are unified

'From an early age, we're taught to sort and categorise our experiences. We divide the world into opposites [. . .] We assign value to everything: good or bad. Even as we mature and gain a deeper understanding, we often continue to shut our eyes to complexity and nuance.

But times change. [. . .] We've been exposed to other ways of thinking, other visions of what a world can be. [. . .] Geographically, we have learned to see, from that magnificent photo of the Earth in outer space, that we all reside on a "blue marble" going round the sun.

And yet, under pressure, we regress [. . .] We retreat into simplified categories, redividing the world into "us" and "them." [. . .]

On a personal level, we divide ourselves too — into inner and outer selves [. . .] But this strategy of self-dissection is ultimately a losing one.

This habit of division [. . .] holds us back — from being whole people, and from building a whole society. On this spinning blue marble we all share, there is no "here" or "there." As a species, our destinies are increasingly intertwined: We are one. Cooperation isn't just wise; it's essential. And recognizing that isn't just important; it's crucial.' —Martha Rosler

Rosler reminds us that we are a lot more similar to each other than we think. Seek out the sameness and recognise commonality.

Martha Rosler (b. 1943) is an American artist who works across video, sculpture, installation and photography. A leading voice within feminist histories, she is also a pioneer of collage: a medium that sees her marry two opposing images – such as capitalist advertising and documentations of war – to create a dialogue that holds up a mirror to the truth of our world.

Source: A note to the author, 2025

Be willing to not know

'One of the things I've experienced from teaching poetry is what you're really teaching people to do is think. Particularly in America, where I think thinking is sneered at, and only valued when it goes into the marketplace as something adult and respectable . . . I've had to learn to tell people to be stupid, be obvious, we can fix it later, be willing to wait, be willing to not know.' —*Eileen Myles*

No one knows anything until they think. Take time and be willing to wait for the answers. I think this is the distinction between information and knowledge.

As Myles tells us, poetry can be a great starting point to teach us how to think. Read a poem today. Sit with it.

Eileen Myles (b. 1949) is one of the most influential living poets. Born and raised in Massachusetts, and based in New York City since 1974, they have published twenty-two books, from poetry and memoir to plays and fiction, including *Not Me, Chelsea Girls, Cool for You, Skies, The Importance of Being Iceland: Travel Essays in Art* and *Inferno: A Poet's Novel.*

Source: The Great Women Artists Podcast, *2021*

Find different ways to research

'At six o'clock one morning, we went to draw at the fish market at the Rialto Bridge. Great art wasn't something far away; it was part of life.' —Jenny Saville

On her travels to different cities in her youth, the painter Jenny Saville – as well as visiting museums – used real life as research. Saville's methods – from drawing Venetian fish markets to tracing the steps of an artist or seeking out where they lived (as she did with Rembrandt) – show us that research can take many forms. You don't just have to visit the temples of art, you can look at real life: get up at dawn and notice something; hunt down the place someone from the past wrote about or drew, and try to catch the same view as them. Understanding someone's 'real life' gives you a richer, deeper sense of their work, and the world.

Jenny Saville (b. 1970) is known for her all-encompassing portraits of flesh. Theatrical and grotesque, beautiful and painful, her presentations of the body can feel almost like a landscape, pressed up against the surface of the canvas, in her masterful handling of paint that ranges from wet to dry, thick to thin. Tackling Biblical and mythological narratives, as well as her own experience as a mother, Saville has constantly configured new ways of presenting the body, and in more recent years has turned to stark, saturated colouring.

Source: Cooke, Rachel, 'Jenny Saville: "I want to be a painter of modern life, and modern bodies"', Observer, *9 June 2012*

Choose hope

'It's easy to feel overwhelmed by the huge perspective shift that our species needs to undertake, in order to survive. I have found it consoling to remember the seemingly impossible revolutions in thought that we have managed in the past.' —Es Devlin

In moments of despair, find hope.

In 2022, Devlin created a monumental installation, *Come Home Again*: a sliced-open sanctuary-like dome that mirrored the architecture of London's St Paul's Cathedral, which it stood opposite. She filled it with larger-than-life pencil-drawn cut-outs of 243 animal and plant species (such as moths, beetles, birds, wildflowers) that were all at risk of becoming extinct in London. It was also an immersive experience, featuring a soundscape of the species' names, as well as a place for diasporic choirs to sing evensong in a fusion of Zulu, Xhosa, Swahili, Bulgarian and Latin, to imprint the names of these species in her viewers' imagination further. Making this work was not only a way to amplify their beauty, and to get us to look closer at what surrounds us, but an attempt to heighten our idea of what and who we need to take better care of.

Es Devlin (b. 1971) is a world-renowned artist and stage designer working across myriad genres. She has created luminous large-scale installations at the V&A, Serpentine Galleries, Somerset House and the Imperial War Museum, and a retrospective at the Smithsonian Cooper Hewitt Design Museum. She conceives kinetic stage sculptures for musicians including Beyoncé and U2 for 100,000-seater stadia as well as small theatres with audiences of eighty.

Source: The Great Women Artists Podcast, *2019*

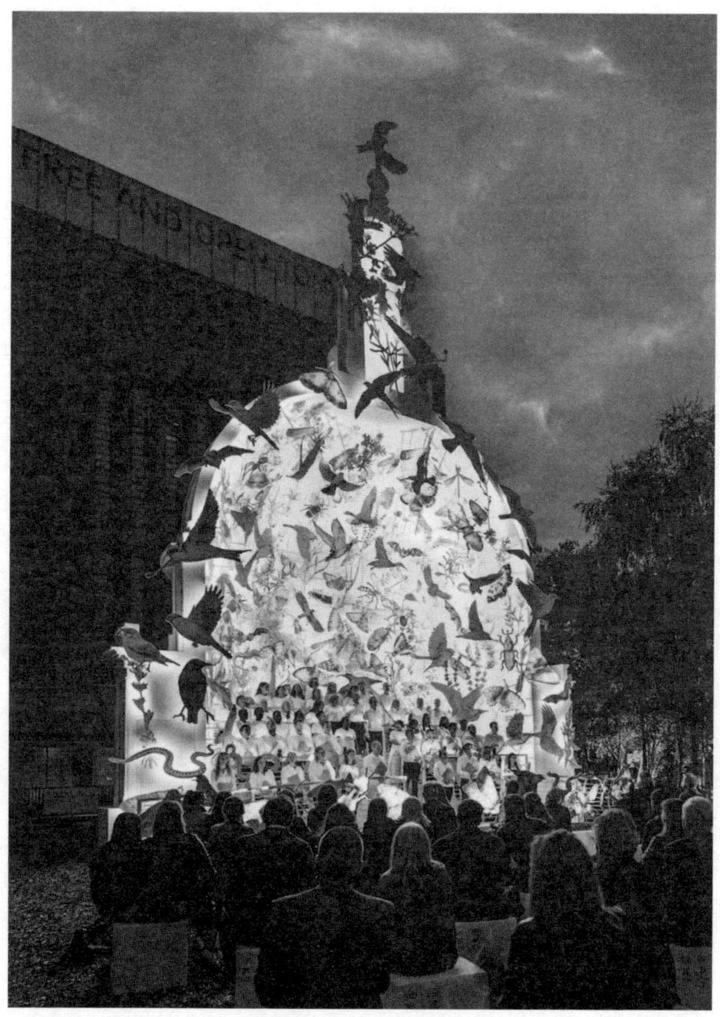

Es Devlin, *Come Home Again*, 2022

Take action!

'To dream about painting and not also to work at it doesn't ever bring about a painting. To dream about creating a new world that is not teetering on the edge of total destruction and not to work at it doesn't make a peaceful world.' —*Corita Kent*

We can dream, but nothing will happen until we take action. The relics of the world are from those who have. What will you take action with today? Start small, and go from there.

Corita Kent (1918–86) was an American, Hollywood-based former nun, artist and educator. She was hailed for her brightly coloured screenprints that address her deep concerns about poverty, racism and war. She was head of the art department at the Immaculate Heart College.

Source: Kent, Corita, with Steward, Jan, Learning by Heart, *Bantam, 1992*

We made it; we can change it

'We made this world; we can change this world.' —*Judy Chicago*

Between 1974 and 1979, Chicago and an army of volunteers constructed a colossal touring installation in the form of a dinner party (see overleaf). It awarded thirty-nine women from mythology and history a seat at the table (with the names of 999 further women marked on the porcelain *Heritage Floor* in the middle), celebrating those who dared to have vision, and work towards change.

While history has tended to overlook these women, Chicago understood that through an artwork a different 'story' could be told. Take a moment today. How would you envision missing histories?

Judy Chicago (b. 1939) is an American artist whose wide-ranging oeuvre, consisting of sculptures and installations, painting, drawing and more, is concerned with feminism and feminist histories.

Source: The Great Women Artists Podcast, *2024*

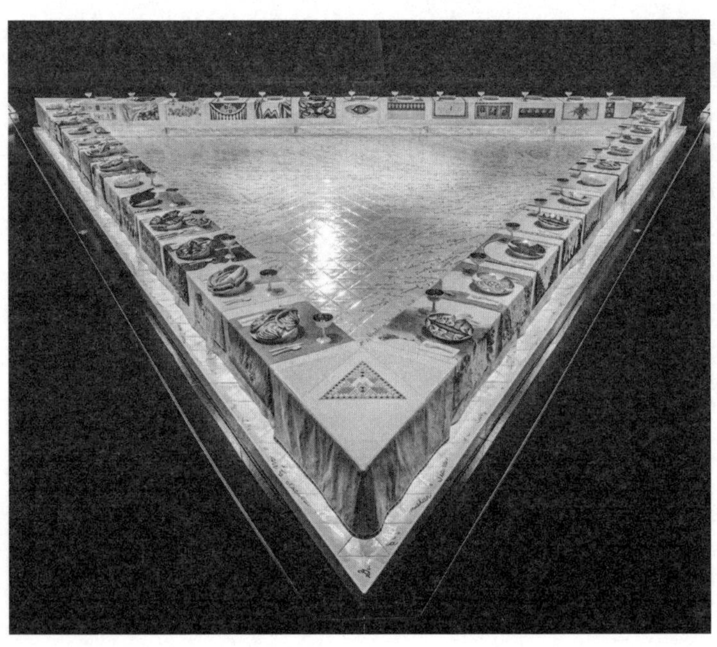

Judy Chicago, *The Dinner Party*, 1974–79

Dream

'The artist is an active dreamer . . .'—Romaine Brooks

These words ring so loudly because they can apply to anything. Keep dreaming, actively . . .

Or, you could look at this in another way: you can still be an artist while you are asleep. Creativity doesn't start from the moment we wake up – you are already doing it in your dreams.

Romaine Brooks (1874–1970) was an American painter – born in Rome and working in Paris and Capri – who was known for her commanding, ethereal and mysterious portraits of women. Often androgynously dressed, with boyish suits and sharp bob haircuts, Brooks's subjects spoke to the New Woman of the twentieth century, and were painted in her signature grey-toned palette.

Source: Brooks, Romaine, Strange Impressions, *David Zwirner Books, 2022*

Spread joy through art

'By making gay, joyous sculpture maybe I'm saying, "Look, the world is awful, but it is also great. So, let's enjoy its greatness." My work is about color, the changing of colors for dreams and emotions – red, blue, yellow, green, purple. And it's about roundness and the curves of nature. My work gives me hope, enthusiasm, structure. My work is my REAL DIARY.'
—Niki de Saint Phalle

How can you seek out the beauty in what can sometimes seem like a broken world? Can you turn to the colours that exist in nature; or look closely at the shapes and outlines of the world? How can you make with joy?

For two decades, from the late 1970s to the 1990s, the artist Niki de Saint Phalle worked tirelessly envisioning and building her mesmerising Tarot Garden, in Tuscany, Italy.

She filled it with her 'Nana' sculptures – bulbous female figures – to which she gave the form of the twenty-two Major Arcana tarot characters, from the glittering climbing structure that made up The Emperor to the sphinx-shaped Empress.

The garden was 'a magic space' for Saint Phalle, who said: 'I lost all notion of time, and the limitations of normal life were abolished. I felt comforted and transported. Here, everything was possible.'

Niki de Saint Phalle (1930–2002) was a French-American artist, working across sculpture, painting and film. She was a pioneer in performance and conceptual art in Paris in the 1960s, and went on to explore large-scale immersive environments through her joyous, bulbous and sometimes glittering 'Nana' sculptures. These include the Tarot Garden in Tuscany (1970s–1990s) and *Hon – en Katedral* (1966) at the Moderna Museet in Stockholm, where visitors entered through the giant open legs of one of her Nanas, only to unveil a twelve-seat cinema, a bar, a playground for kids, a fish pond and sandwich vending machine.

Source: de Saint Phalle, Niki, Niki Charitable Art Foundation Archives, 25 January (date unknown)

Don't police your open mind

'Anything is possible.' —Lisa Yuskavage

There's a form of policing we do to ourselves, where we shut down a lot of avenues. We don't dare admit to our dreams, our fantasies, our other worlds.

Yuskavage, however, told me that she just 'wasn't built that way'. As she continued: 'I took very seriously, as a young person, this idea that we were supposed to challenge authority, and make something to challenge people. As I went along, I started to see that a lot of people want to see the things that they already know. They're not willing to be open to being shocked or open to their cages being rattled. I rather like my cage being rattled. Isn't that sort of the point of all of this? Isn't that the idea of art, that we're supposed to be open-minded?'

What could you do to challenge systems or authority? Sometimes it starts with speech: saying something that might be uncomfortable or demanding. But the challenge can come to have a greater impact. Resist policing your open mind – and always be honest. Because the more honest you are, the greater connection you will have.

Lisa Yuskavage (b. 1962) is an American artist who began painting doll-like, pre-pubescent, semi-naked women in the early 1990s. Often emerging from a pool of saturated pinks, greens, reds or yellows, Yuskavage's figures fuse art history with the semi-pornographic images found in magazines such as *Penthouse*. She borrows painting techniques from the likes of the sixteenth-century Venetian painter Tintoretto while also looking to how some women are presented in the world today.

Source: The Great Women Artists Podcast, *2021*

Let people in

'Ultimately, I think of portraiture as a shared moment. I don't think that you can ever really capture this cliché essence of a person . . . I think that that's how I want it with the audience. But I also want to challenge their ideas and what their beliefs are. I want to try to get to a greater democracy, a greater understanding of humanity. And so, I try to incorporate that within the work by its quietness, but it also has a big voice at the same time.' —Catherine Opie

How can you use art to spread kindness? The American photographer Catherine Opie came to prominence in the early 1990s with her dignified photographs that centred those in the artist's gay leather S/M communities. It was a time, due to the AIDS crisis, when society judged or 'othered' them. Opie used photography as a means to give people space and to show that their story belonged in the museum, too. Referring to sixteenth-century Old Master paintings, with their sumptuously textured backgrounds, she told me: 'I wanted to honour them [her community] in the way that Holbein did around the royal family.'

How can you make from a place of kindness, and use art to spread beauty and give visibility? Art can be a very powerful tool in showing that people belong in places which had previously shut them out. The bigger the range of stories you tell, the richer the pool becomes.

Catherine Opie (b. 1961) is an American photographer of people, landscapes, the urban environment and American society. First picking up a camera aged nine, it was in the 1990s that she began to gain recognition for her studio portraits of gay and transgender communities who appear painterly and defiant, powerful and regal. Travelling across the world, in particular different areas of North America, Opie has documented masculinity through high school footballers; politics and culture through her images of the 2008 presidential election; the landscape through images of sparse urban environments; and memorial through images of items once owned by Elizabeth Taylor.

Source: The Great Women Artists Podcast, *2022*

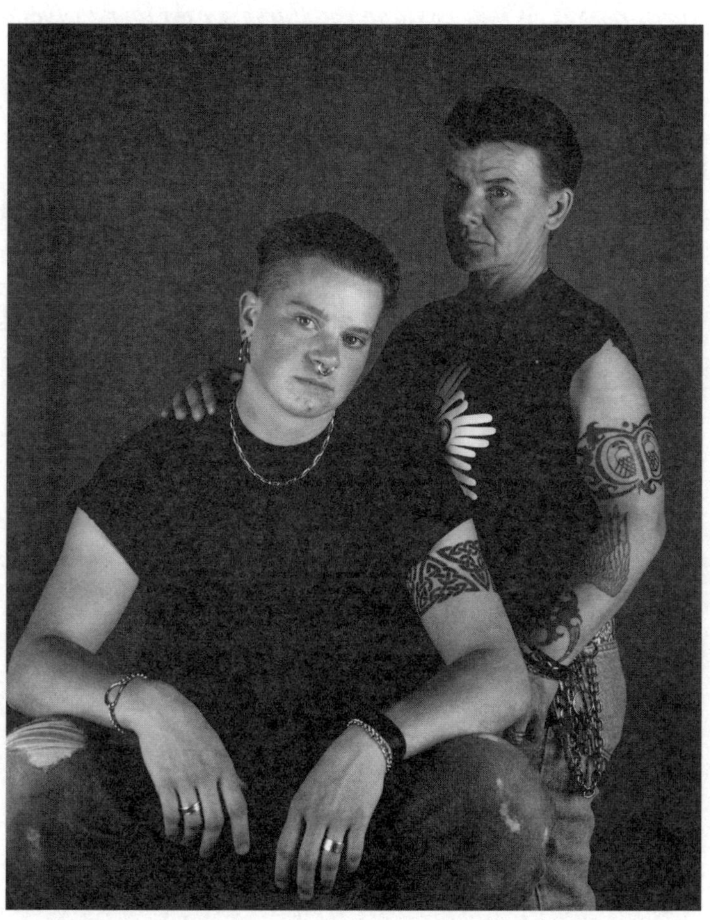

Catherine Opie, *Matt and Jo*, 1993

Think about the Earth

'To look at the Earth from space is a bit like a child looking into a mirror and realising for the first time that the person in the mirror is herself. What we do to the Earth we do to ourselves and what we do to life on Earth, human and otherwise, we do to ourselves.' —Samantha Harvey

Today is Earth Day, a day of honouring the planet, first held on 22 April 1970. It's a reminder that in order to sustain the life of our species, we must protect and not injure the very place on which we walk. As Harvey says, think of our planet as a metaphor for our own bodies. If it stops breathing, we stop breathing; if it breaks, we break. Take care of it like we would ourselves: it's a living entity. What can you do to feed the Earth today?

Samantha Harvey (b. 1975) is an English novelist, and the author of five books. In 2024, she won the Booker Prize for her novel, *Orbital*, a story told over a twenty-four-hour period about six astronauts and cosmonauts who, orbiting the Earth, watch sixteen sunrises and sunsets across myriad weathers and seasons.

Source: Samantha Harvey, Booker Prize acceptance speech, 2024

Sing in harmony

'I look at works by various artists and their language and what they're trying to say and I think we are a chorus of women . . . who are all singing this one thing, but we all have our solo act. We all have our lines that we can sing. And I like that, I think it makes a great harmony.' —*Deborah Roberts*

This is a great reminder when you find yourself looking to the side, and to what other people are doing rather than what you are doing.

Remember, as Roberts says, we are all solo acts. But, together, we can also sing in harmony. Is it not what we are all doing living our life? We all need teams – whether it's our friends, our family, our community, our government – that support us to sing. One way to live an artful life is to find others to sing with. The more you do it, the more it will enhance them. The more they do it, the better your voice will sound.

Deborah Roberts (b. 1962) is an African American artist who uses collage to explore race, identity and gender. Exploring the lived experience of young Black children, she combines a range of different facial features – from James Baldwin to Michelle Obama – with a variety of skin tones, hairstyles and patterned and striped outfits. As she has said: 'With collage, I can create a more expansive and inclusive view of the Black cultural experience.'

Source: Panel discussion for From Near and Far *(exhibition at Stephen Friedman Gallery): Katy Hessel in conversation with Kenturah Davis, Genevieve Gaignard, Deborah Roberts and Amy Sherald, 22 July 2022*

Hold out for those who give you time

*'The desire to love and be loved makes all things beautiful! . . .
What I think is, that to meet anyone really sincere to one's ideas is
very rare. I had the good fortune to do so in Paris and they have
remained my friends in spite of the six years' war . . .'*
—Marlow Moss

We don't all have the same ideas or like the same things. So when
you find people whose ideas are interesting, or who are interested in
yours – that is when the excitement happens. Hold on to those people.

When it comes to speaking about our work, or even discussing books
or art with other people, they don't necessarily have to be a good
friend, partner, sibling or parent. People can serve different purposes.
Bonds over interests can be some of the most fulfilling relationships
we can have, and sometimes that *is* the bond. Think about the people
you know. Who would you most like to go to an art gallery with?
Who is that person you like to attend talks with? With whom do you
like to discuss ideas?

Marlow Moss (1889–1958) was a British painter and sculptor, based mainly in Cornwall, who
worked in the style of Constructivism. Moss pioneered the 'double-line' (two thin black lines
running in parallel with each other), often with block primary colours, and developed a
Constructivist style by moving into mechanical steel sculptures.

*Source: Handwritten letter from Moss to Paule Vézelay, dated 14 April 1955, held in the Tate
Gallery Archives*

Look to icons to understand our strength

'You learn a lot about people by what they do with other people, even if it is an icon, right? I think that we look to icons, because we're trying to understand our own greatness, our own strength.' —*Rose B. Simpson*

The world is full of icons – in the form of religion, celebrities, historic figures, miracle-makers, and more. What icons do you look to, and why do you look to them? What is it about that figure that gives you strength, or helps you understand your own strength?

The icon I like to look to is Frida Kahlo, the Mexican painter who was famed for her self-portraits in various guises. Despite the many physical and emotional challenges she faced in her life, she had an extraordinary ability to see the joy amidst hardship; to reinvent; to learn; to be unafraid to say how she saw the world. It's this that gives me strength.

Rose B. Simpson (b. 1983) is a mixed media artist who lives and works in Santa Clara Pueblo, New Mexico, and is from a long lineage of women working in ceramics in her tribe.

Source: The Great Women Artists Podcast, *2024*

Make something shine from something thrown away

'When you look at trash, it's something that everybody throws out. It's something that doesn't hold any value any more to a person who considers it trash or garbage at that particular time [. . .] So the only way to bring the value of us – the "trash" – is by showing how important we are, how vocal we can be, how professional we can be, how talented we are.' —Leilah Babirye

Babirye's works are made up of recycled, previously thrown-away trash, a metaphor for how she and her LGBTQI+ community have been treated in her native Uganda, where it is illegal to be queer. To configure them, she resurrects and transforms something that was unwanted into something beautiful.

What can you make shine from something that has been thrown away? How can you transform something unwanted into something beautiful?

Leilah Babirye (b. 1985) is a Uganda-born, US-based artist working across painting, sculpture, assemblage on paper, ceramics and wood. She uses experimental techniques such as carving, burnishing, weaving and welding, and addresses narratives surrounding identity, sexuality and human rights.

Source: The Great Women Artists Podcast, *2021*

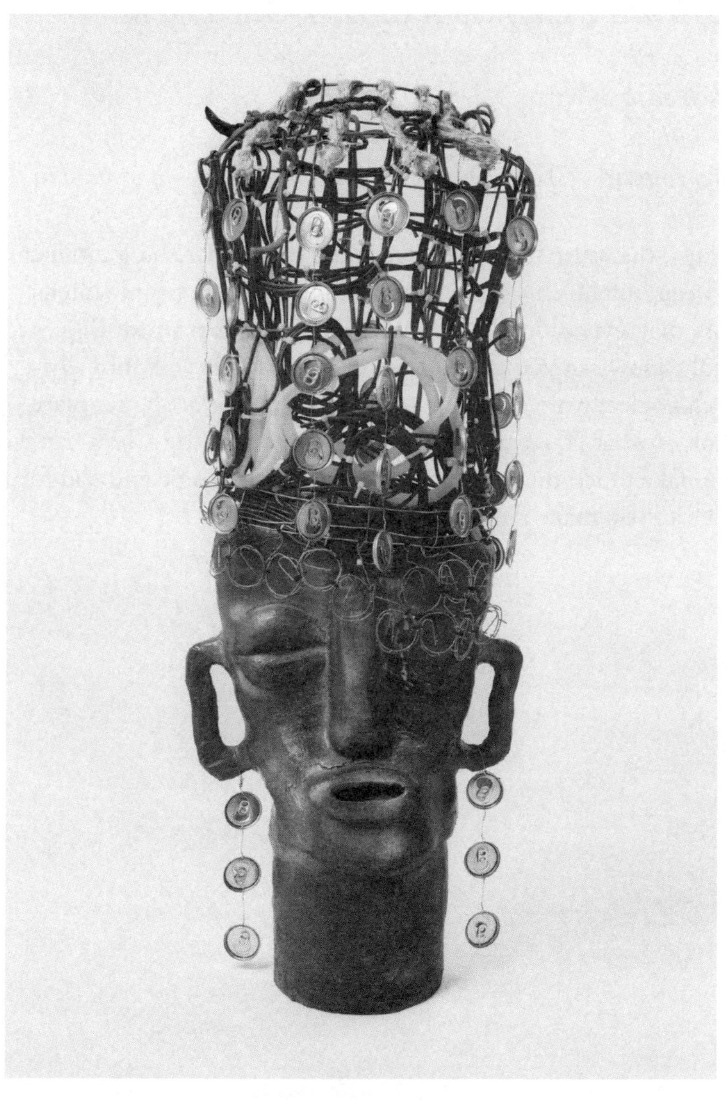

Leilah Babirye, *Senga Muzanganda (Auntie Muzanganda)*, 2020

Listen to Yoko!

'TOUCH POEM FOR A GROUP OF PEOPLE

Touch each other

1963, winter' —Yoko Ono

In 1963, the artist Yoko Ono was aware of the increasing distance between humans. Decades later, in a world where people interact more than ever online, rather than in real life, her words ring loudly. How can you touch someone – physically, emotionally, psychologically or artistically – to make the world a better place? Think of what you're doing as giving someone a hug – how can what you make touch them in ways that feel warm, magic and comforting; how can you make them feel held?

Yoko Ono (b. 1933) is a Japanese-born artist, musician and activist, hailed for her participatory performances and conceptual artworks.

Source: Ono, Yoko, Grapefruit, *Sphere Books, 1970*

The fundamentals of love

'Love is the extremely difficult realisation that something other than oneself is real.' —*Iris Murdoch*

As we approach the end of April, and think about world-building – is love not at the very core of all of this: of bringing people together, building communities, caring for others, making work that will make others feel seen? While love can be defined through stories, artworks, gestures and more, Murdoch captures its fundamentals through words. If we love, we acknowledge that something other than ourself is real. Love is the instrument that gets us to look outside of ourselves.

Iris Murdoch (1919–99) was an Irish-born British novelist, philosopher and poet, and author of twenty-six novels, seven of which were nominated for the Booker Prize.

Source: Murdoch, Iris, Existentialists and Mystics: Writings on Philosophy and Literature, *ed. by Peter Conradi, Chatto & Windus, 1997*

Write a letter

'To A Young Woman Artist . . . I hope you make your art accessible to more people, to all women and to everybody; I hope you think about that now and aren't waiting till you make it, because that's likely to be too late. I hope you remember that being a feminist carries with it a real responsibility to be a human. I hope and I hope and I hope . . . love, Lucy Lippard.' —Lucy Lippard

Today, I invite you to write a letter – to someone you know; someone you don't know; or, like Lippard, a group of people not yet at the same stage as you in your life. Use your wisdom; pass it on; or ask questions to those older than you. Who would you write to?

I love to write letters to female artists no longer here, asking them questions about their life, how they persevered in hard times, what the treatment of women was like in their lifetime, and telling them what life is like now for me. In an unrequited and unanswered letter to the great sixteenth-century painter, Sofonisba Anguissola, I once wrote:

> *Why art? Why portraiture? What were the 1500s like, specifically as a woman? What opportunities did you have? Was it difficult? You were so successful and the work you left behind makes it look like you were confident . . . Where did that come from – that drive – and how did you put yourself out there?*

Just like Berger's comment about the dead still walking among us, we can still write letters, whether we receive a reply or not.

Lucy Lippard (b. 1937) is a trailblazing American activist, writer, critic and champion of feminist art. She is the author of numerous books and articles on contemporary art, and the curator of over fifty exhibitions, including the groundbreaking 'Eccentric Abstraction', featuring the work of Louise Bourgeois and Eva Hesse, that engaged in the language of feminism prior to the Women's Liberation movement of the 1970s.

Source: Letter, 1974, in Usher, Shaun, Letters of Note: Art, *Canongate Books, 2020*

1,000 Eggs

'I like doing things with other people. And I like it to be part of my life and part of my social life. It's been mixed up, really . . . I sometimes ask myself what's more important to me: art or people? And it would be people, I expect . . . You want things to happen, don't you?' —*Sarah Lucas*

Since 2017, Sarah Lucas – in Berlin, Mexico City, New York and London – has staged a performance called *1000 Eggs: For Women*. It has seen her assemble women – or those who identify and dress as women – to lob 1,000 eggs at white gallery walls.

Why the egg? What does it symbolise? A seed, vessel, femininity, fertility? Nutrition, health, sustenance? For centuries, it has been used in art, as a subject as well as a medium (egg tempera has been used by artists since ancient times).

What would throwing an egg at a wall, along with women all around the world, mean to you? How can we paint a collective portrait, while having fun with other people?

(Note: she uses pullet eggs – those usually rejected by supermarkets because they are considered too small.)

Sarah Lucas (b. 1962) is a British artist who uses everyday objects in her sculpture, installation and photographic works.

Source: Lucas, Sarah; Heyse-Moore, Dominique (ed.), Happy Gas, *Tate Publishing, 2023*

MAY

How to Find the New

In May – the zenith of spring, a gateway to the summer – let's look at how and where we can find inspiration. Artists can help us get out of creative ruts and give us simple resources that help us reframe our way of looking.

As the American painter Georgia O'Keeffe tells us on 2 May, when we take time, we see something so much larger, broader and wide-ranging than we could have ever first imagined. Let's deep-dive into a month of looking and refocus our attention to a world that is brimming with inspiration, without us even realising it.

Starting points

'I think the starting point is just being curious.'—Kapwani Kiwanga

What is the potential that one tiny object, like a bead, can hold? Can this be a starting point for a discussion that can speak to globalisation, look at the history of trade, and tell a story of a place?

In 2024, Kiwanga represented Canada at the Venice Biennale. She filled her pavilion with over 7 million tiny glass Murano beads in different tones and shades in an installation called *Trinket*. Each smaller than a lentil, some of these beads had existed for hundreds of years.

Hung together, the beads created serene draped tableaux, and told multiple stories – about trade (the beads were once used as currency); globalisation (as they had been sourced all over the world); community (the beads were strung together by a wide range of people); and even their setting (the island of Murano in Venice – a city steeped in artisanal culture for hundreds of years – produces this beautiful glass).

Today, take a moment to think of something small that you own that contains a whole array of stories. How can it be a starting point for something much bigger?

Kapwani Kiwanga (b. 1978) is a French and Canadian artist whose work is deeply rooted in history, archives and questions of power.

Source: Silver, Hannah, 'Kapwani Kiwanga considers value and commerce for the Canada Pavilion at the Venice Biennale 2024', Wallpaper, 16 April 2024*

What do you see?

'In a way – nobody sees a flower – really – it is so small – we haven't time – and to see takes time like to have a friend takes time.' —Georgia O'Keeffe

What do we see when we really take the time to look?

Georgia O'Keeffe spent her long career painting the same New Mexican landscape and elements of nature – such as skulls or flowers – in sequences. By really looking, and studying that one thing over again, she showed us the minute details that exist within nature, while also reminding us that we should look to the smaller aspects of life, and give our attention and time to the things that we might miss.

If you were to look, really look, at the same something or someone every day, what would you notice? Choose someone or something, and find out.

Georgia O'Keeffe (1887–1986) was one of the most significant American artists of the twentieth century and a pioneer of modernism. Her career spanned seven decades and encompassed luminous paintings of New York City skyscrapers, magnified depictions of flowers and the expansive landscapes of New Mexico.

Source: O'Keeffe, Georgia, 'About Myself' in Georgia O'Keeffe: Exhibition of Oils and Pastels, *An American Place (Gallery), 1939*

Take in the world, piece by piece

'Sometimes you can take the whole of the world in, and sometimes you need a small piece to take in. I think that is really what a work of art is: it is a small piece that you can ingest, that gives you an idea of the richness of the whole.' —Corita Kent

Today I want to tell you about a practical way of looking, as masterminded by the former nun, educator and screenprinter, Corita Kent.

Her teaching methods were about looking closely at the world. When she was head of the art department at the Immaculate Heart College, Sister Mary Corita encouraged her students to use a 'viewfinder'. They used a piece of paper or cardboard with a square hole cut out, which they would hold up to see the smaller picture amid the bigger picture outside the frame.

The viewfinder can be made by any one of us as a tool for looking. Make one by getting a piece of paper and cutting a square in the middle, then look through the square. What will you see?

Corita Kent (1918–86) was an American, Hollywood-based former nun, artist and educator. She was hailed for her brightly coloured screenprints that address her deep concerns about poverty, racism and war. She was head of the art department at the Immaculate Heart College.

Source: Corita Kent in We Have No Art, *film by Baylis Glascock, 1967*

Long looking vs short looking

'I began to think about how long will anyone actually look at these works, as they're going from A to B? What if I make sculptures that are actually about being walked past than being stood in front of and gazed at for many minutes? What about making work that is intentionally and purposefully about being glimpsed, or just caught?' —*Phyllida Barlow*

We need the glimpsing moments in our life just as much as we need the more long-lasting ones. While we can stop, focus and pause on something, it's also important to simply glance at something, or look at it almost subconsciously. Not everything is about that long look, nor is everything long-lasting.

It's like the people we meet just once, or come into our lives just briefly, but who have a profound effect on us; the single events we go to that shape us for the rest of our lives; or the glimpse of blossom on a tree that puts beauty into our eyes for a moment on our daily commute.

As Barlow continued: 'Maybe not all art is about that long look, maybe there is art that's like being on a train journey, where you see things and they absolutely capture you. But you've only had a split second to absorb it . . .'

What are those fleeting, precious moments in your life?

Phyllida Barlow (1944–2023) was a celebrated British artist, mostly known for her work in sculpture that could be simultaneously colossal and intimate, precarious and triumphant, made from cement, cardboard, fabric and chicken wire. An influential educator at the Slade School of Art, London, for four decades until 2009, Barlow represented Britain at the Venice Biennale in 2017.

Source: The Great Women Artists Podcast, *2021*

How can we be both strong and fragile?

'I've been a giant in my strength and my work has been strong and my whole character has it inside. But somewhere I'm a terribly frightened person.' —Eva Hesse

How can something be so strong, but so fragile? While Hesse's structures might appear flimsy and skin-like, they are also hard and solid. Her works get me to think about ephemerality, and our nature as humans: as both strong and weak, solid and fragile. For example, look at *No title*, 1970. While it appears stringy, and is delicate, it's also very tough. It wouldn't have survived more than fifty years had it not been strong.

We need fragility and vulnerability as well as strength. It's these tensions that make us human, and forever interesting.

Eva Hesse (1936–70) was a German-born, American sculptor who lived and worked mostly in New York City in the 1960s and early 70s. Despite her brief, only decade-long career, Hesse was a profound experimenter. Always searching for a new material or form, she fused incompatible substances found lying about on her studio floor for her process-based work.

Source: Nemser, Cindy, Art Talk: Conversations with 15 Women Artists, *HarperCollins, 1995*

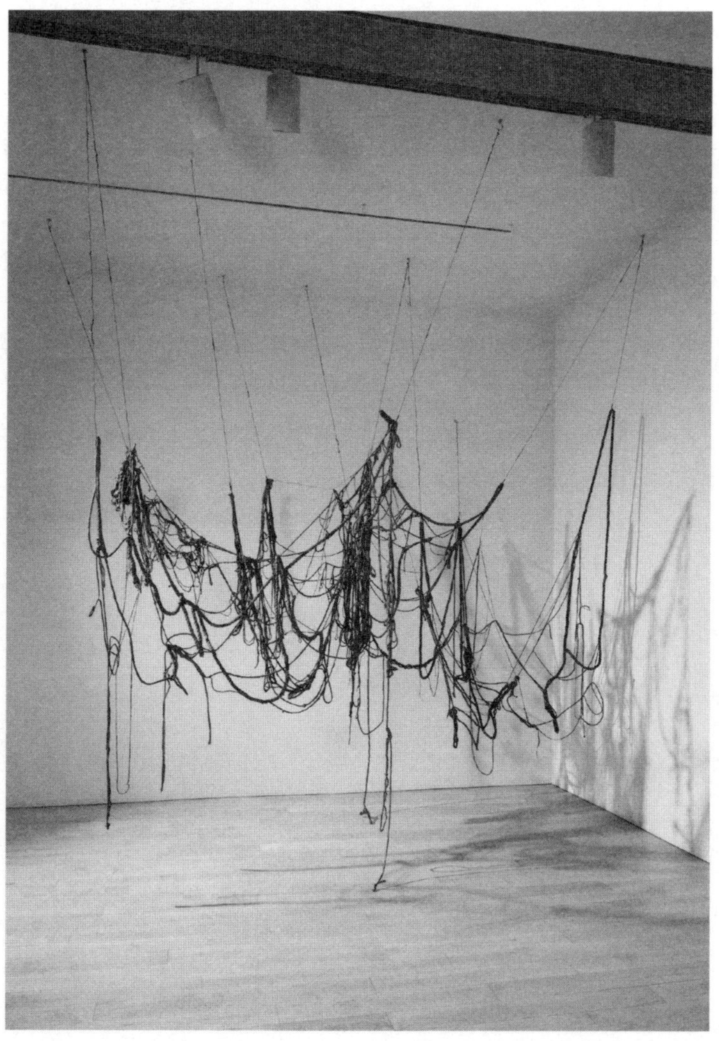

Eva Hesse, *No title*, 1969–70

Look anew

'I think we must try to look in through the smog in ourselves and ask who or what is this, and what within this we could evolve, live, grow.' —*Leonora Carrington*

Our bodies are miraculous. Think about all the things they are capable of, what they can grow both physically, mentally – and artistically, too.

Remind yourself of all the miraculous ways you've grown and evolved before.

Leonora Carrington (1917–2011) was a British-born artist and writer who lived in France and Spain before settling in Mexico during the Second World War. She painted fantastical beings and creatures within scenes that were enigmatic, otherworldly, yet strangely familiar.

Source: Carrington, Leonora, 'What Is a Woman?', 1970, reproduced in Rosemont, Penelope (ed.), Surrealist Women: An International Anthology, Athlone Press, 1998

Deal with the blank space

'It's like taking medicine. Sometimes we have to take political medicine, and it doesn't always taste good. I think the great thing about my work is that I am the honey in front of the medicine. So the first taste of it, you might say, "Oh, this is beautiful" – until you start unpacking some of these meanings, what I'm trying to say, and how the work affects you, how the work challenges you.

That's one reason why my work has no background, because you've seen it in a white space. And the only thing you can do is concentrate on that one image. So I want people to understand it. I'm trying to say "look at my humanity", mainly.' —Deborah Roberts

Roberts reminds us of the power of concentration in order to better see ourselves, and our world.

Look at her images (see overleaf). While they might seem like joyful images of children, notice how they are in fact made up of a range of components – such as James Baldwin's eye.

What is the significance of this? Would this have been less noticeable had there been a background? What happens when we really concentrate on a portrait of humanity and let the background fall away?

Deborah Roberts (b. 1962) is an African American artist who uses collage to explore race, identity and gender. Exploring the lived experience of young Black children, she combines a range of different facial features – from James Baldwin to Michelle Obama – with a variety of skin tones, hairstyles and patterned and striped outfits. As she has said: 'With collage, I can create a more expansive and inclusive view of the Black cultural experience.'

Source: The Great Women Artists Podcast, *2020*

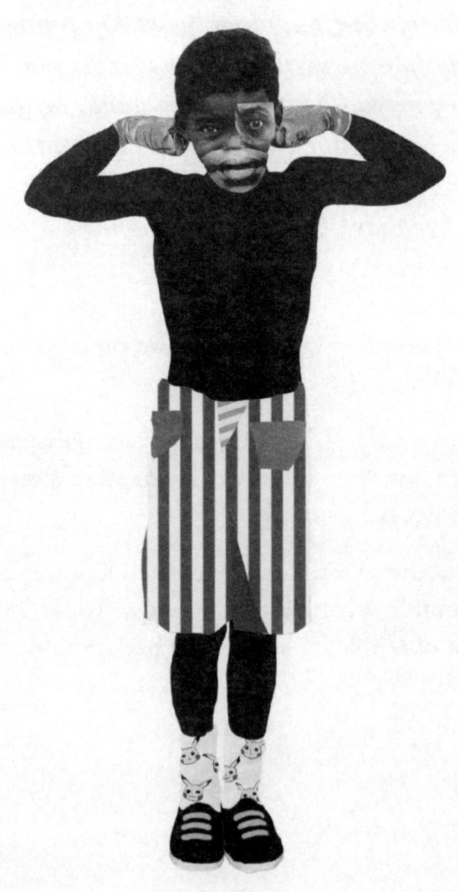

Deborah Roberts, *Man[ly]*, 2019

Look within you

'I do remember when it occurred to me the first time, when I got the idea of painting the way I feel at a given moment. It was in my studio in Klagenfurt. I was sitting in a chair and felt it pressing against me. I still have the drawings where I depicted the sitting sensation. The hardest thing is to really concentrate on the sensation while drawing. Not drawing the buttocks because you know what they look like, but drawing the buttocks sensation.' —*Maria Lassnig*

What does it look like to capture yourself from within? The Austrian-born artist Maria Lassnig created what she called 'body awareness' or 'body sensation' painting. This means that she would paint exactly how she physically felt, picturing her bodily sensations through paint. If there was a part of her body that she didn't feel anything in, she would omit it from the canvas. But if there was a part that she felt a particularly strong sensation in, she would paint it larger, or in a more heightened colour.

If you were to draw how you were feeling from within, what would your body look like? What colours would you use, and what features would you distort?

Listen to your body and think about how it makes you feel. Then capture it.

Maria Lassnig (1919–2014) was an Austrian artist known for her analytical self-portraits, drenched in an often acidic-like palette, based on her theory of 'body awareness'.

Source: Obrist, Hans Ulrich, Pakesch, Peter and Poschauko, Hans Werner (eds.), Maria Lassnig: Letters to Hans Ulrich Obrist: Living with Art Stops One Wilting!, *Walther König, 2020*

Make a list

'If I am at a loss I make a list.

Looking though my notebooks, I find lists of the Greek names for the winds, of the different journals filled by a long-departed Parisian cousin, the colours of the pigments used in Siena, all the pseudonyms used by Coleridge . . . I find the same word repeated, listed until it becomes incantatory. I find a list of possible titles for works. I think of the people whose work I love and name them, one after another.

I think of Cy Twombly: his paintings are a mass of marks, erasures and words. Phrases come and go. Sometimes you read a fragmentary part of a poem, or an allusion to a classical text, only for it to be crossed out. There are puns and odd misspellings: erudition giving way to doodling at the back of the class. And this is what I love – the slippage between an intended epic expression and a failure to finish. In his work he has both the shopping list and the great list of ships sent to attack Troy.

Lists work. They give you space to start again.'
—Edmund de Waal

Lists tend to be made up of single words, and yet they often spark ideas. From colour pigment types to lists of those you admire – write them down, as de Waal says, and see what comes. How will words and names resonate in ways you might never expect? What conversation will they spark in your mind?

Edmund de Waal (b. 1964) is a British artist who writes. Much of his work is about the contingency of memory: bringing particular histories of loss and exile into renewed life. Both his artistic and written practice have broken new ground through their critical engagement with the history and potential of ceramics, as well as with architecture, music, dance and poetry. De Waal is also renowned for his bestselling family memoir, *The Hare with Amber Eyes* (2010), in addition to *The White Road* (2015), *Letters to Camondo* (2021) and *An Archive* (2025).

Source: A note to the author, 2025

How does context determine perception?

'[The canon] changes even with some of these male artists who are now seen as gods – their fates weren't sealed from the very beginning. Our contexts determine perception.' —Siri Hustvedt

We think of 'canons' as fixed – as revered names always belonging to history, but in reality, they are constantly evolving entities. What was in favour or beloved in the nineteenth century was different to that in the twentieth, and now twenty-first.

For example, the Renaissance painter Sandro Botticelli, famed for *The Birth of Venus*, was largely forgotten for 300 years after his death in 1510. Similarly, the seventeenth-century Dutch painter Johannes Vermeer was 'rediscovered' in the nineteenth century.

As Hustvedt says, our context determines whether we consider something to be great or not, and even what is meant by great changes over time too. Who gets to decide what is great? Is it you? How would you change what we see? It takes us to do the work, to bring people and their work to the fore. This is how the context – and therefore perception – will change.

Siri Hustvedt (b. 1955) is an American novelist, essayist and author of eighteen books. From memoir to poetry, non-fiction to fiction, Hustvedt's groundbreaking writing has touched on the topics of psychoanalysis, philosophy, neuroscience, literature and art.

Source: The Great Women Artists Podcast, *2023*

Disrupt the 'single' perspective

'In school, we are taught perspective drawing by sketching a triangular road that tapers into a vanishing point with a horizon line running through it . . . What if there were many vanishing points, many overlapping histories and intersecting narratives . . . shifting perspectives, or altered horizon lines?' —*Ayesha Singh*

What is perspective? Often, we are taught that it is a particular viewpoint, as Singh told me, as in 'what school and society teach us, or what the idea of tradition is'.

What if that singular perspective was a metaphor for a dominant and prescribed way of thinking? What if that perspective was opened up to many vanishing points? What if we flipped the lines, and saw history anew? There is no limit to how many narratives of history we can create for ourselves, and share with others.

In 2025, Singh created an artwork that covered the entire facade of a building, disrupting a 'single' perspective by creating multiple vanishing points. The vanishing points led to images of structures built or commissioned by women, from the eleventh to the twentieth centuries, who were instrumental in shaping architecture in India but whose voices are often cut out from the so-called 'canon'. Singh showed how history can be rewritten through art.

Ayesha Singh (b. 1990) is an Indian artist whose work disrupts the idea of dominant perspectives in myriad ways. Through her research and interventions in architecture, she exposes the gaps in our cultural histories, including those that have for too long kept women out.

Source: Artist statement, 2025/conversation with the author, 2025

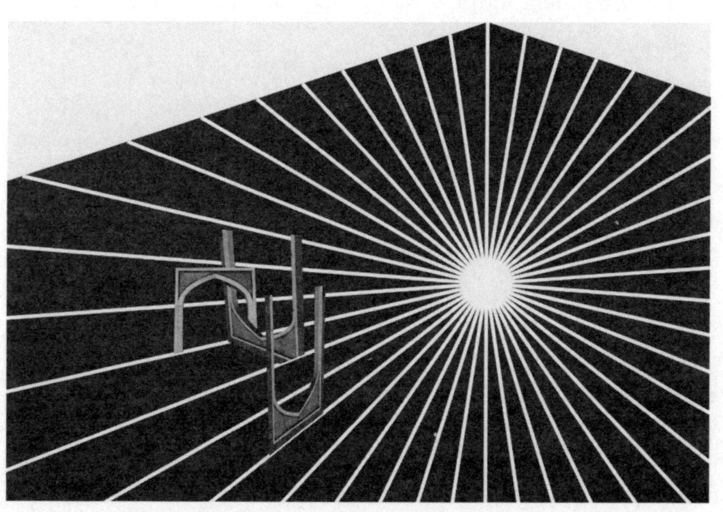

Ayesha Singh, *Skewed Histories and Site Lines*, 2025

Believe in the future

'The future is now. It is not in fifty years' time, it's now and I think we have the means, the skill, the knowledge to build great stuff.' —Zaha Hadid

Zaha Hadid was one of the most influential architects of the twentieth and twenty-first centuries. While her job was quite literally to design buildings for modern living, we can also use the idea of being an 'architect' in a metaphorical way. What future will you design?

Zaha Hadid (1950–2016) was an Iraqi-born, British architect and artist, known for her futuristic, bold style that employs yonic forms melded with sharp edges. Notable buildings include the London Aquatics Centre and the Serpentine North Gallery, London.

Source: Al Aan TV interview with Zaha Hadid in Beirut, December 2014

Go to children's books

'Children's books are, too, the great floodlit gateway to ideas.' —Katherine Rundell

Katherine Rundell is a writer for both children and adults (her specialism is the work of the sixteenth-century English poet, John Donne). As Rundell writes in her book, *Why You Should Read Children's Books Even Though You Are So Old and Wise*, 'Children's fiction does something else too: it offers to help us refind things we may not even know we have lost.'

Choose to read a children's book – for yourself – this year. What might you discover about the great themes of life, from beauty and joy, to struggle and pain?

Katherine Rundell (b. 1987) is an award-winning writer of children's fiction and adult non-fiction, including the *Impossible Creatures* series, and *Super-Infinite: The Transformations of John Donne*.

Source: Rundell, Katherine, 'Why children's books', London Review of Books, 6 February 2025

Blur the lines

'I would like to blur the firm borders that we human beings, cocksure as we are, are inclined to erect around everything that is accessible to us. [. . .] I want to show that small can be large, and large small, it is just the standpoint from which we judge that changes, and every concept loses its validity, and all our human gestures lose their validity. I also want to show that there are millions and millions of other justifiable points of view beside yours and mine. Today I would portray the world from an ant's-eye point of view, and tomorrow, as the moon sees it, perhaps, and then as many other creatures may see it. I am a human being, but on the strength of my imagination – tied as it is – I can be a bridge.' —Hannah Höch

In 1918, the German-born artist Hannah Höch joined forces with the Berlin Dada group. Made up of painters and performers, and growing out of the horrors of the First World War, Dada was a form of art that refused to define itself as anything at all.

Höch chose photomontage as her medium. This lends itself to attaching images of body parts together to make a picture that would never otherwise exist. Splicing photographs from magazines and journals, Höch could capture the disjointed reality and political chaos of the era.

Today, put at least two images together and see what conversation they make.

Hannah Höch (1889–1978) was a German artist who worked mostly in photomontage, adopting a distinct feminist and queer stance in her art. Using images and text from journals, newspapers and magazines, she engaged with contemporary social and political issues and gave a voice to those so often dismissed.

Source: Foreword to the catalogue for Höch's first solo exhibition at the Kunstzaal De Bron, The Hague, 1929

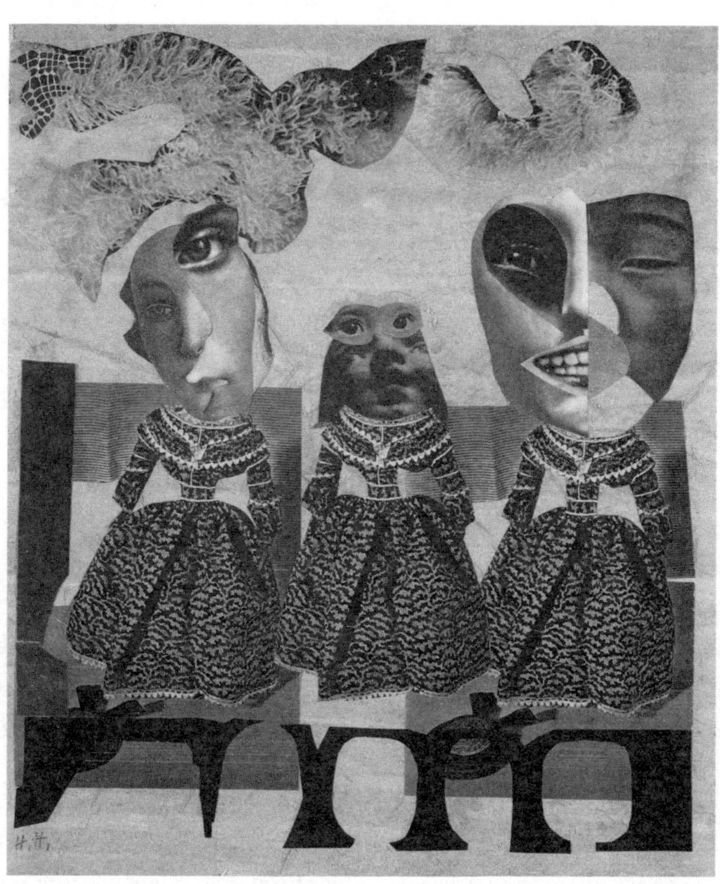

Hannah Hoch, *Modenschau*, 1925–35

Let go

'Some years ago, I made a garden, out of a field, in Dorset. I divided my time between London and Dorset and when I was in London I was in my studio and when I was in Dorset I was in my garden. I began to see painting and gardening as equal acts of creativity. In some ways I could lose myself more completely outside, living in and organising this three-dimensional space. Its ever-changing nature, its colour, its sheer exuberance.

I now live in London full time, my children and husband have all, happily, left home, the garden no longer calls, and the fact my attention is now focused solely on painting has opened up a world I almost didn't realise was there. Something feels complete. I have learnt to concentrate absolutely because I now have the time to sit and stare and let my mind wander. This is a priceless luxury, particularly for a woman.

But then the spring comes around again with its buds and shoots and, as Philip Larkin says, "their greenness is a kind of grief". So I walk in the park before starting work, still managing to absorb some of spring's miraculous energy. And London at this time is as beautiful as any city. And I get on with my work knowing I am the only person who can do what I do and that the heart-breaking greenness will get on with its life without me.'
—Anne Rothenstein

Like Rothenstein's walks in the park, what small things can you do to remind you of another time, as a way of unlocking and seeking out inspiration? Was there a meal you used to cook for someone, or a song they played you? What gives you that miraculous energy?

Anne Rothenstein (b. 1949) is a British artist who works in painting and collage. She captures vivid, imaginary worlds of faraway landscapes, or figures enraptured in solitary moments.

Source: A note to the author, 2025

Work at different 'desks'

'I work at three different desks, with a different project open on each, let's say, so one is academic, one writerly, and one art. I go at these erratically, sometimes to all three desks within an hour. They cross-pollinate one another.' —Anne Carson

While you don't need to have three different physical desks, you can go to different places to get different things out of them – like a local library for one thing and a café for another, or you can walk a particular route when you want to figure out a specific idea.

Anne Carson (b. 1950) is a Canadian poet, essayist, professor of Classics and celebrated translator of the ancient Greek poet Sappho, as well as the writers Euripides, Simonides, Sophocles and more.

Source: Aitken, Will, 'Anne Carson, The Art of Poetry No. 88,' The Paris Review, *Issue 171, Fall 2004*

Embrace your contradictions

'Because humanity is filled with contradictions, we are all made up of numerous paradoxes that form our personalities and that influence various aspects of our lives, whether these are cultural, political, personal, environmental and so on. These contradictions also make us intriguing and interesting most of the time. Nothing we do is ever black or white, it's this grey area I'm interested in.' —Sanam Khatibi

We live in a world where, increasingly, we have to be either/or. Yet we are all made up of the paradoxes that form our personalities, and it's that 'grey area', as Khatibi calls it, that we can try to embrace. What contradictions live within you?

Sanam Khatibi (b. 1979) is a Belgian artist (with Iranian heritage), working with paint, embroidery, tapestry and sculpture. The crux of her paintings is often a seemingly luscious, verdant landscape, but upon a closer inspection, unsettling images – in contradiction to the landscape's beauty – begin to arise. She gets me to ask: is all as it seems?

Source: A conversation with the author, 2024

Anonymity is generosity

'There's a reason I'm anonymous in my work: I like to be absolutely out of view and out of earshot. I don't sign my work because I think that would diminish its effectiveness. It would be the work of just one person. I would like it to be more useful than that — to be of utility to as many people as possible. I think if it were attributed to me, it would be easier to toss. I want people to concentrate on the content of the work and not "who done it?".' —Jenny Holzer

Jenny Holzer's work utilises words and phrases in an array of different mediums – from electronic signs to public billboards (see overleaf). While her work can be identifiable, by her not 'signing' it with her name, it can also be purposefully confused with advertisement and the media. I like how this gets us to think deeper about what these signs are saying in the first place.

Jenny Holzer (b. 1950) is an American artist known for her text-based and politically ambiguous work. In the 1970s, Holzer began by making her *Truisms* (essays and sentences shown out of context) on storefronts or billboards in Times Square, which can provoke a spectrum of responses, depending on how the viewer reads them. Examples include *Abuse of Power Comes as No Surprise* or *Protect Me from What I Want*.

Source: Holzer, Jenny, '"For 7 World Trade" and "Redaction Paintings"', Art21, undated interview

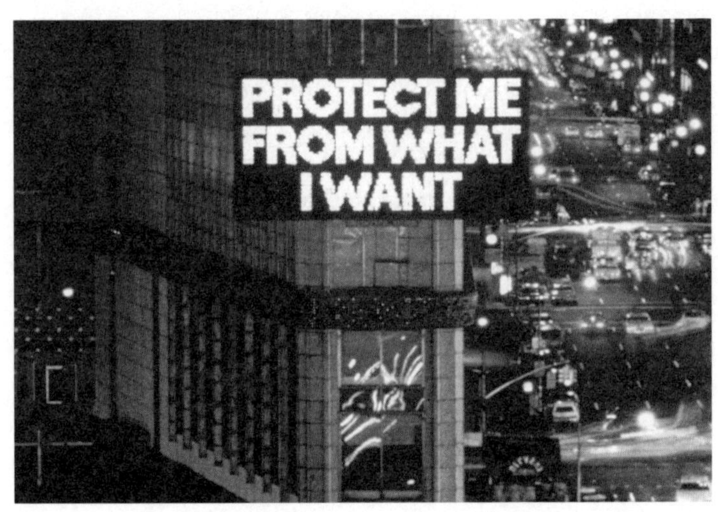

Jenny Holzer, from *Survival* (1983–85), 1985

Transcend symbols

'I thought of them [my paintings] as transcending the mundane circle . . .'—*Howardena Pindell*

Much of Pindell's work employs the motif of the circle (see overleaf).

For Pindell, the 'circle' is not just a shape: it has historical connotations, too. She has recalled memories of growing up during segregation, and having root beer with her father. At the bottom of their glasses was a red dot, signalling that this glass was for Black people – and that glassware couldn't be shared with whites.

Seeking to 'undo' the derogatory nature tied up with the circle, Pindell transforms it into something beautiful and multi-layered.

What does the circle mean to you? What do you associate it with?

How could you take something derogatory in the world, and transcend it into something hopeful?

Howardena Pindell (b. 1943) is an American artist, who, since the 1970s, has been working across a spectrum of mixed media, including painting, video and more.

Source: The Great Women Artists Podcast, *2021*

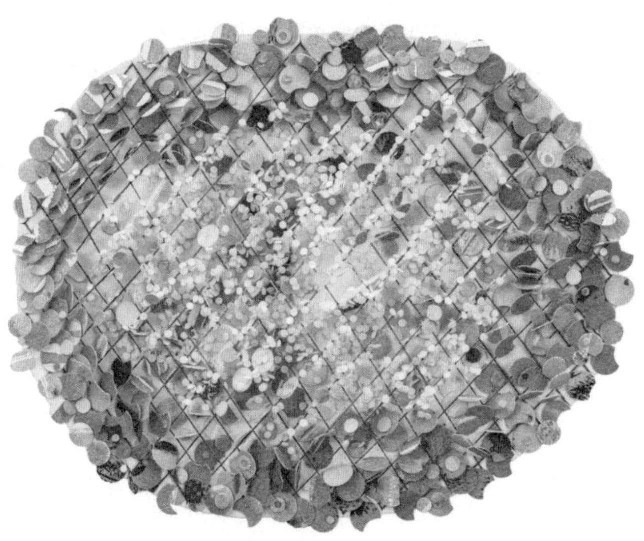

Howardena Pindell, *Untitled #49*, 2010

Flip the script

'The two sentences differ by only a single character.' —*Ghada Amer*

There's a famous ancient Arabic proverb: 'A woman's voice is shameful.' But by changing a single character in the Arabic script, you can create a new saying which translates: 'A woman's voice is a revolution.' It was a phrase common during the Arab Spring in 2011, and it was used by Ghada Amer for the title of an exhibition in 2022.

What famous lines, slogans or sentences do you feel could have a shake-up/do you find uncomfortable/do not comply with your views? How can you look to these phrases or sentences, sometimes entrenched in history, as inspiration, and transform their meaning? How can you flip the script from something negative into something positive?

Ghada Amer (b. 1963) is an Egyptian-born artist who works with embroidery to create canvases celebrating female sexuality.

Source: Vogel, Wendy, 'Ghada Amer: Fighting for equal rights one stitch at a time', Art Basel website, 2022

Keep what you have

'You don't have to give up your culture. You just carry the stories that you brought with you and exist next to other people, and it actually makes for a richer world.' —*Njideka Akunyili Crosby*

Akunyili Crosby was born in Nigeria, and went to the US to study aged sixteen, where she still lives today. In some of her work, she fuses modernist American architecture with patterns and fabrics from Nigeria.

Whether via the identities of our youth, or the countries and cultures we were born into but no longer live in, we will always be made up of stories of all sorts – they never leave us. Take a moment to reflect on the story of where you have come from.

Njideka Akunyili Crosby (b. 1983) is known for her multi-layered paintings of family gatherings, conversations between loved ones, or weddings that reflect a life lived between two countries: Nigeria and the USA.

Source: 'In Conversation: Njideka Akunyili Crosby with Jason Rosenfeld', The Brooklyn Rail, July/August 2020

Switch up your ways of working

'I started working on the floor, and for me, that was very liberating. You walk on your canvases and it becomes a mess, and so do your feet. You become involved, you're really in it – not just standing there looking at it, but really standing in the work. You can walk across it, you can work upside down, you can pour the paint directly onto the canvas and it won't trickle off.' —Rose Wylie

When you are stuck, or want a change in working, why not flip the book upside down; change your position; start from the end; liberate your routine; write by hand instead of typing; or use the other end of a paintbrush. Switch up your way of working.

Rose Wylie (b. 1934) is a British painter based in Kent. Her recognisable painting style is filled with text and image, referencing film, sports stars, mythology and everyday life.

Source: Robertson, Emma, 'Rose Wylie: "If it works, it works"', The Talks, 26 January 2022

Hustle

'I had written to the ambassador of Pakistan to the US, saying that it would do Pakistan well if they supported young artists. It would be a great thing for their image. And eventually she wrote back, and I ended up travelling to the US, to Washington, DC, courtesy of the Pakistani government, to showcase my paintings at the embassy.

I was up for a few days a week, possibly, but nothing sold. And I think I was imagining I was going to sell the work and put myself through school.

But what was so interesting is that I took all that work and called up a lot of art schools on the East Coast and physically took myself and my work to these different schools, and that's how I ended up getting accepted at the Rhode Island School of Design's graduate programme.

Artists unfortunately have to hustle all the time.'
—Shahzia Sikander

It's very rare that the things we want fall into our laps. Whether it be inspiration or opportunity, we usually have to seek it out.

While flying across the planet might be possible for some, remember, 'hustling' – as Sikander refers to it as – can happen in myriad ways. It doesn't have to be great, grand gestures. Take a moment to work out what you're looking for, and then try to think of one thing you could do to help make it happen, whether it's writing a letter, attending an event in the hope of making connections, reaching out on social media, or staging an exhibition or a play – this could even be in your own living room. Be alert and look around you: maybe you're already equipped with the tools to take that extra step right now.

Shahzia Sikander (b. 1969) is a Lahore-born, New York-based artist who is widely celebrated for her work that subverts tradition and reclaims narratives – such as of Central and South-Asian manuscript painting – and for launching the form known today as Neo-Miniature.

Source: The Great Women Artists Podcast, *2024*

Stay focused

'Keep your eye on your inner world and keep away from ads and idiots and movie stars, except when you need amusement.' —*Dorothea Tanning*

What do you want to do? How are you going to get there? The only way is to use time wisely. Listen to Tanning. Take stock of where and how you waste your time – and write down what you could be doing instead.

Dorothea Tanning (1910–2012) was an American artist who lived in Paris for much of her later life, hailed for her Surrealist-inspired paintings and soft sculptures. She was also a writer and poet, and famously said, 'Don't ask me to explain my paintings.'

Source: Glassie, John, 'Oldest living surrealist tells all', Salon, 11 February 2002

Make the work

'People associate artists with being very whimsical in their application, but they are the opposite, because otherwise nothing happens. I learnt my work ethic from sitting for my father and watching him . . .' —*Bella Freud*

It's easy to imagine that artists have a particularly louche life. But as the fashion designer Bella Freud, whose father was the painter Lucian Freud, reminds us, artists wouldn't be artists if they didn't have the work to show for it. Sometimes they are the most disciplined of all.

Bella Freud (b. 1961) is a British fashion designer, known for her sharp-cut suits inspired by nineteenth-century poets and 1970s rock stars.

Source: Freud, Bella, Fashion Neurosis with Nick Cave, *2024/5 (podcast)*

Listen to music

'I listen to Maria Callas a lot when I work. The human body at full capacity operating at the top of her range. That's what I aspire to . . .'—*Liza Lou*

What music gives you that lift so you can fly on your own accord? Put it on.

Liza Lou (b. 1969) is an American artist known for her paintings and installation work that often employ the medium of the bead.

Source: Lou, Liza, 'Everything More Ideal', artist statement, Lehmann Maupin, 2024

Relish the act of making

'For me, the act of doing, creating, painting holds the highest and only priority, without ever having the expectation that a piece of work is "finished" . . . When it is "finished", it becomes, like, dead!' —Eva Beresin

Today, when so much of what we see is online, consumed at a rapid pace – and often on a surface level – it can be easy to forget how something was made, the time spent on it, and that the journey of making is often the point.

Ultimately, the joy and meaning in making art is in the process: of figuring something out, trying to comprehend a thought. While this can be both euphoric and painful, the act of 'doing' is not dissimilar to the act of 'living'.

So give yourself a different perspective on your process. See if you can relish its joys and hardships, love and pain. You might even think about showing the process itself.

Eva Beresin (b. 1955) is a Hungarian painter based in Vienna, known for her graphic and washy, fantastical scenes of animalistic figures that seem to both explore the banality and humorous aspects of life, as well tragedy and existentialism.

Source: A note to the author, 2024

Relinquish routine

'There's nothing routine about making art: you're facing your demons and teachers at every turn; climbing mountains; sleepwalking through a maze with a million doors; all the while holding on to your sanctuary and the curious child in you who believes that you are going to meet the all-seeing, all-knowing, all-hearing shaman sent by your ancestors to guide you.' —Bharti Kher

Kher reminds us that it is OK to confront the unknown. When we make or create, we are bringing our entire lives with us. But we still pull through, make mistakes, climb that mountain, because what and who we will meet along the way will always be worth it.

What demons are you facing; which teachers? What mazes do you walk through? How can you use those, at times, painful experiences as inspiration? Art can be a way to confront what we fear and hide most. It's easy to build up all kinds of emotions in our heads, but when we face them by drawing or writing them down, not only do they give us a sense of release, but by making them external – and something you can contemplate from a distance – they don't feel so difficult to understand.

Bharti Kher (b. 1969) is an Indian-based artist known for her wide-ranging art practice, from bindi-based abstract paintings that border maps, or appear like cells, to hybridised sculptures of goddess women.

Source: A note to the author, 2025

Leave the room

'When you start working, everybody is in your studio – the past, your friends, your enemies, the art world, and above all, your own ideas . . . But as you continue painting, they start leaving, one by one, and you are left completely alone. Then, if you're lucky, even you leave . . .'—Philip Guston recalling what the composer John Cage told him

The best moments in life, I think, are when we lose our sense of ourselves entirely. I don't mean this in the literal way – but more when we are so engrossed in something that we forget to be self-conscious. How can you get to that point, and lose yourself – as if you are leaving a room? Could it be as simple as walking down the street and admiring the spring flowers that May has to offer, taking time to meditate, engaging in a piece of art, reading a great piece of fiction, going out dancing or making something with your hands? To achieve transcendence requires you to get outside of yourself. How will you leave yourself behind today? Where will you go to?

Philip Guston (1913–80) was a Canadian artist who made paintings that captured the tumultuous and fractured world.

John Cage (1912–92) was an American composer, music theorist and artist.

Source: Guston, Philip, quoted in wall text at Tate Modern, 2023

Be alert

'I am a sort of spy.' —*Vivian Maier*

Vivian Maier was a street photographer who spent her day job as a nanny. Despite taking pictures incessantly – and amassing more than 100,000 negatives – she never published or exhibited in her lifetime.

Maier's photographs reveal a woman who had empathy for her subjects – from children to the elderly – though they were often unaware of her presence.

She famously worked with a Rolleiflex camera (see overleaf), which didn't need to be brought up to one's eye and enabled her to catch her subjects off-guard.

It was only after her death that her work was printed for the very first time – and more is still being unveiled today. Her photographs show us the uncanniness of the everyday, and off-guard, private moments.

Are all artists spies? On each other, our inner worlds, and the outer ones, too? How can you be a spy – on yourself, or the world at large?

Vivian Maier (1926–2009) was an American photographer who, using the streets as her stage, captured the uncanny moments of daily life.

Source: Bannos, Pamela, Vivian Maier: A Photographer's Life and Afterlife, *The University of Chicago Press, 2017*

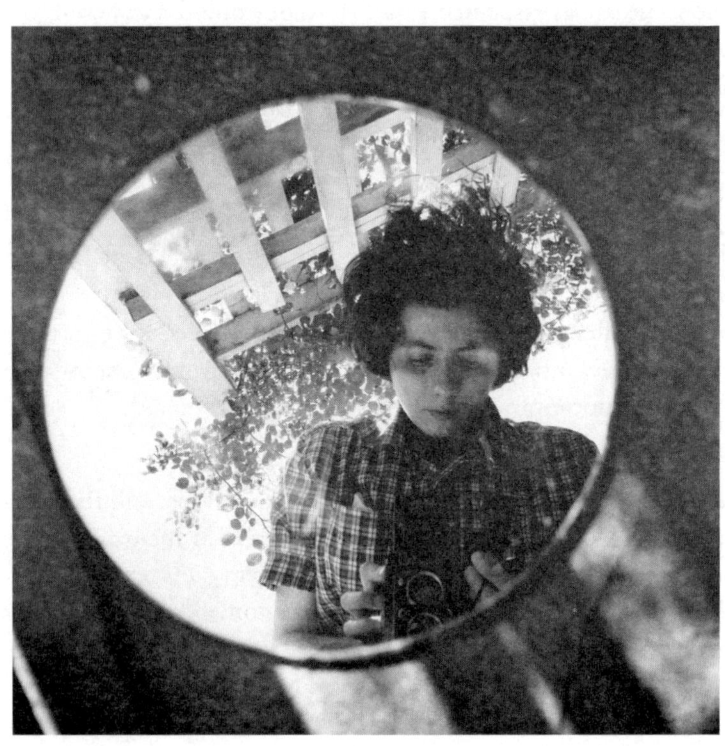

Vivian Maier, *Self Portrait*, 1953

Go out out!

'When in doubt, go out.' —*Jeffrey Hinton*

I saw this quote at an exhibition at the Tate Modern in London about Leigh Bowery (1961–94), an Australian-born performance artist and hugely influential cultural creative pioneer who was part of London's club scene in the 1980s. He was best known for using make-up as painting (to confront and mix up the norm) and designing his clothes as sculpture (blurring all boundaries between his life and his art).

Hinton was a DJ at 'Taboo' every Thursday in the mid-1980s, a nightclub run by – and revolving around – Bowery, as well as being a multimedia artist and Bowery's close friend and collaborator. Together, they used nightclubs – and 'going out' – as a way of teasing new looks and performances, and to see how others reacted.

As we learnt from Marina Abramović in January, the studio can be a 'trap'. If we only stay indoors – both literally and psychologically – then nothing will ever happen. Get dressed up and go outside. Whether it be the streets, the nightclub or the supermarket – practise what you're working on. Provoke a response. Be alert to catch ideas. Let's close the month of May with a reminder – you never know when the inspiration will hit. In the spirit of Hinton and Bowery, have fun while you're at it.

Jeffrey Hinton (b. 1959) is a British visual artist, producer and DJ.

Source: Bowery, Leigh, quoted in wall text at Tate Modern, curated by Fiontán Moran, 2025

JUNE

Despite the destruction that has been inflicted throughout history, artists have continued to make, sculpt, dance, envision, speak, sing, play and lift others up, collectively making something beautiful, hopeful and full of wonder in the process. Sometimes art can be the only thing we have to hold on to.

I think of Brazilian artist, Anna Maria Maiolino (b. 1942) who, living under a strict military dictatorship in Brazil for two decades from the mid-1960s, made work using her body (as 'performance'), or smaller, ephemeral forms – such as eggs – so as to avoid censorship and leave no trace. She also worked in this way for practical reasons, due to the scarce art materials available to her at the time.

In 1981, she performed *Entrevidas* ('Between Lives') (overleaf), where she scattered chicken eggs and literally 'walked on eggshells'. By using the egg – a symbol of life not yet born or ideas still embryonic – she shows us her belief in the possibility of the future, and hope for the next generations.

Maiolino's art was a form of resistance. Let's take this energy into June.

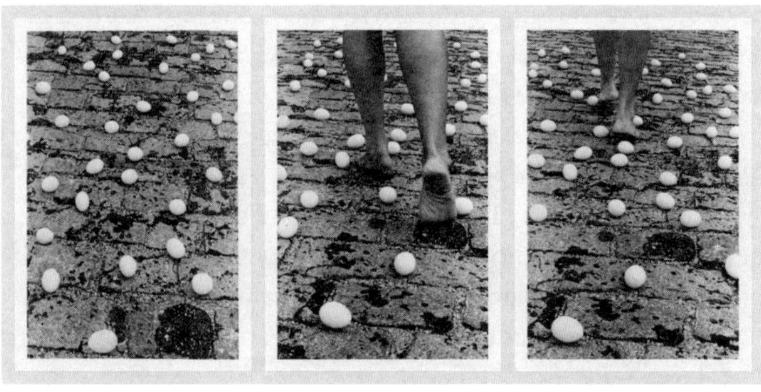

Anna Maria Maiolino, *Entrevidas (Between Lives)*, from *Fotopoemação
(Photopoemaction)* series, 1981

Resistance begins in art

'Resistance and change often begin in art.' —*Ursula K. Le Guin*

There are so many ways to resist and provoke change, from organising demonstrations to protesting in any way you can. Art is also a very effective tool, in all its myriad forms. Ursula K. Le Guin was best known for writing science fiction books, and understood the power of fantasy as a vessel to spark discussions about good and evil. As she said in 2004:

> *Fantasy is a literature particularly useful for embodying and examining the real difference between good and evil. In an America where our reality may seem degraded to posturing patriotism and self-righteous brutality, imaginative literature continues to question what heroism is, to examine the roots of power and to offer moral alternatives.*

Le Guin prompts me to ask: how different is the evil that exists in fantasy books, versus the evil we see in the world?

There are many ways to teach people about resistance: start in art.

Ursula K. Le Guin (1929–2018) was an American author, best known for her science fiction books. In her lifetime, she wrote twenty-three novels, twelve volumes of short stories, eleven volumes of poetry, thirteen children's books, five essay collections, and four works of translation.

Source, quote 1: Acceptance speech for The National Book Foundation Medal, 19 November 2014; quote 2: 'Some Assumptions about Fantasy', a speech by Ursula K. Le Guin, presented at the Children's Literature Breakfast, BookExpo America, Chicago, 4 June 2004

You can't argue with the facts

'There had to be an in-your-face, disruptive, better way to convince people that the art world was a patriarchy.' —Guerrilla Girls

The Guerrilla Girls, the activist artist collective, use statistics in their art as a weapon for telling the truth. As a result, their bold, loud, text-and-image artworks, made in the style of advertisements – which they print out as posters, and stick on the side of buildings near museums to call out gender disparities inside those very buildings – have made some of the greatest contributions to combating gender imbalances in the art world.

Examples include: *Do Women Have to be Naked to Get into the Met. Museum?* from 1989, which goes on to say: 'Less than 5% of the artists in the Modern Art sections are women, but 85% of the nudes are female.'

What I like is that they approach their anger with a sense of fun. How can you find a positive emotion or impetus inside something that enrages you? How could doing so help you fight? And show the facts. After all, they never lie.

Guerrilla Girls (1985–present) is a feminist activist artist collective who protest to fight sexism, racism and corruption in art, politics and culture. They work anonymously, shielding their identity by wearing gorilla masks.

Source: The Great Women Artists Podcast, *2020*

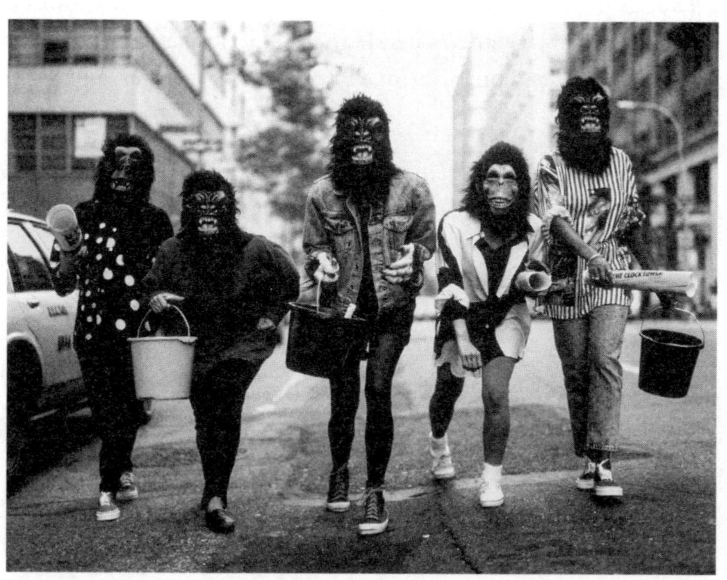

Guerrilla Girls, George Lange, 1991

Art is the only language

'Art is about the only language which nations can speak together and they don't quarrel. And yet in times of stress and war, the tiny grant which the State provides to maintain the visual arts is the first to go.' —*Barbara Hepworth*

Why is it that our governments do not prioritise art? Why do they put first violence, war, arms, destruction? Not only is art essential for offering us hope, a way out, a route from despair, but *making* it is key for working through all sorts of issues.

Barbara Hepworth (1903–75) was a giant of British sculpture. Born in Wakefield, Yorkshire, she carried with her the rhythms of the Northern hills. From 1939, she was based in St Ives, a fishing village in Cornwall famed for its rocky beaches, and the weathered lines and ocean swirls of her surroundings made their way into her highly textured sculptures. Working in an interior and exterior environment, Hepworth interacted with the natural forms of the landscape, as well as analysing the many forms that the human body can take.

Source: Bowness, Sophie (ed.), Barbara Hepworth: Writings and Conversations, *Tate Publishing, 2015*

Art is a universal language

'We could not speak German. Germans were hated. We had to learn French and English. We were always travelling somewhere else, speaking something else. But I had a Romanian governess who taught me how to draw. I did not have to draw in German or French or English. I could just draw.' —Rebecca Horn

Art can be a universal language that people, no matter where they are from or what they have experienced, can use to connect to each other.

The German-born artist Rebecca Horn grew up during postwar Germany – a time of tension, shame and poverty. But the act of drawing gave her freedom – a language untied to any culture, a method of communication, and a tool from which to make something beautiful and hopeful.

We can find ourselves overwhelmed by the historical events we live through. No matter how your government works, no matter what your country stands for, look to art as a place of solace and positivity.

Take a moment today and look at Horn's *White Body Fan*, 1972 (overleaf): a sculpture she wore to extend the limits of the body.

Rebecca Horn (1944–2024) was a German multimedia artist, known for her performances, films, sculptures, kinetic installations and drawings.

Source: Winterson, Jeanette, 'The bionic woman' (interview with Rebecca Horn), Guardian, *23 May 2005*

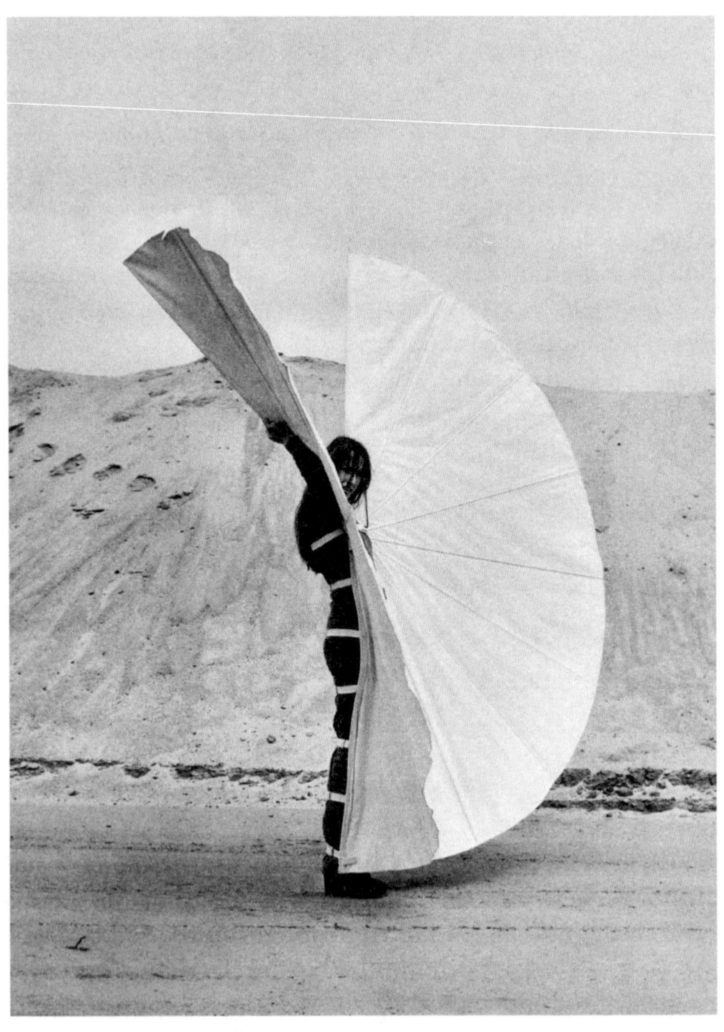

Rebecca Horn, *White Body Fan*, 1972

Art is a way to fight pain

'I fight pain, anxiety and fear every day, and the only method I have found that relieves my illness is to keep creating art.' —Yayoi Kusama

'Art as resistance' can speak on a global and political level, but it can also console us from within, on a smaller, everyday scale.

The Japanese artist Yayoi Kusama began experiencing visions as a child. To work through this, she turned to art, despite her mother taking away her drawing materials. (As an alternative, she might have found materials at school, and used seed sacks as canvases.) Nine decades later, she is still creating dazzling and dotty sculptures, pumpkins, and mirrored infinity rooms that offer an insight into how she sees the world, and lives it, day by day.

Yayoi Kusama (b. 1929) is a Japanese painter, sculptor, installation and performance artist, filmmaker, and more. For seven decades, she has worked with the motif of the dot, repeating it to the point of infinity whether it be in her immersive mirror rooms or covering entire paintings or sculptures.

Source: Kusama, Yayoi; McCarthy, Ralph (trans.), Infinity Net: The Autobiography of Yayoi Kusama, *Tate Publishing, 2011*

Art is a way to change systems

'Well, how do you write a female character that interests me? It's not a general thing. She's got to have some sort of interior life; what is she there to do? I often ask myself this. In many films, I think, what are the women in this film here to do? Apart from service everyone else's desires, and be sexy, and be desired too. You know nothing about them. And apparently just being desired is to know a lot about them.' —Deborah Levy

So much of the histories of art or film have reduced women to two-dimensional characters. What is the impact of this? How can we raise our consciousness to resist this troubling 'default' that has stuck for so many years, and to recognise the depth and interiority of all people?

I often think about the French artist Suzanne Valadon (1865–1938), prominent in 1920s Paris, who painted her rich interior life in a self-portrait, *The Blue Room*, 1923.

Look at this image. Valadon was an artist-model-turned-artist who was never formally trained but rather learnt from those who drew her. She had her first solo exhibition aged forty-six, and was a financially independent woman living in Paris at a time when women were still very much second-class citizens. Here, she paints herself in her own space, taking on the reclining Venus pose that had objectified women for centuries. To me she exudes freedom, upending the tradition of painting nude women in this pose.

Deborah Levy (b. 1959) is a South African-born, British writer, and the author of several critically acclaimed novels and non-fiction works, including her 'living autobiographies' on writing, gender politics and philosophy: *Things I Don't Want to Know*, *The Cost of Living* and *Real Estate*. She has been shortlisted twice for the Goldsmiths Prize and the Booker Prize.

Source: The Great Women Artists Podcast, *2021*

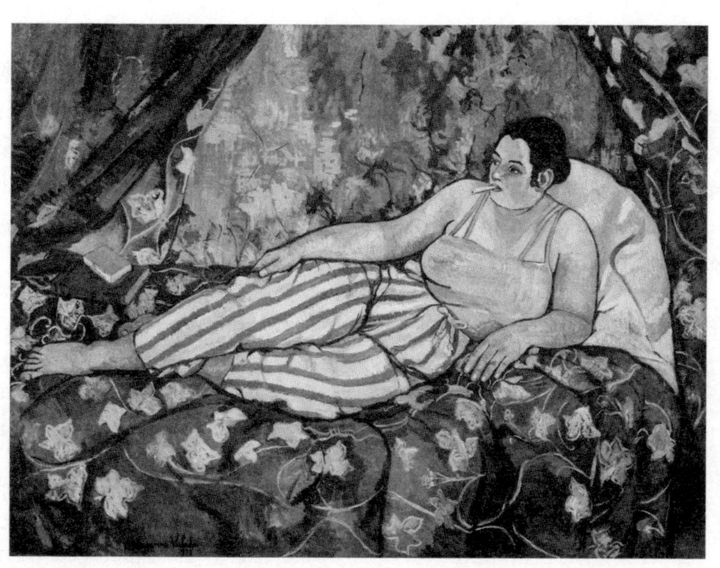

Suzanne Valadon, *The Blue Room*, 1923

Art is a way to show who we are

'Figurative paintings are deeply rooted in our human lineage and will continue to play a vital role in telling our stories for as long as we exist' —Mickalene Thomas

How do we remember people? We immortalise them by telling their story – through painting, photography, sculpture, film – and by keeping their memory alive for the next generation.

Mickalene Thomas is an American painter acclaimed for her striking, rhinestone-encrusted large-scale paintings of Black women confidently claiming space. Drawing from Black American culture and western art history, she reimagines iconic poses and compositions – such as the reclining goddess Venus – and transforms figures once objectified, marginalised or overlooked because of their gender and/or race into representations of power, beauty, joy and love.

Thomas has spoken extensively about the transformative role of portraiture: 'Portraits allow us to see ourselves reflected in images – they serve as mirrors of our identity and intimate extensions of our being. Through them, the artist weaves a narrative shaped by their own personal story.'

Mickalene Thomas (b. 1971) is an African American artist known for her exuberant paintings and collages that celebrate Black women, from a specifically queer lens.

Source: The Great Women Artists Podcast, *2023; a note to the author, 2025*

Beauty as resistance

'If you want to dignify a human life then you have to come back to beauty . . .' —Doris Salcedo

It can feel uncomfortable to think about beauty in times of trouble. But beauty and wonder should always be cherished to remind us that we are bigger than evil, violence, betrayal and hurt.

The Colombian artist Doris Salcedo is hailed for her artworks that commemorate those who have lost their life to violence. She will often use everyday objects, such as chairs, candles or fabrics.

Her artworks regularly pay homage to victims of Colombia's fifty-two years of civil war, although can be open to interpretation.

In 2007, Salcedo and other participating artists placed almost 24,000 candles in Bogotá's main square, Plaza de Bolívar, surrounded by official state buildings such as the Palace of Justice and the National Capitol.

Creating a space for thought and contemplation – in a temporary memorial titled *Acción de Duelo* (overleaf) – she invited spectators to mourn. But despite the respectful silence that occurred throughout the evening, the message spoke louder than words, with the lives of the victims remembered through light, beauty and community.

Doris Salcedo (b. 1958) is a Colombian artist who works with public – at times participatory – installation, and found objects, such as chairs, roses, tables. While her work draws on her experiences of Colombia's violent political history, it can also speak to wider and timeless global issues.

Source: Salcedo, Doris, 'Memory as the essence of work', recorded interview, San Francisco Museum of Modern Art, 2004

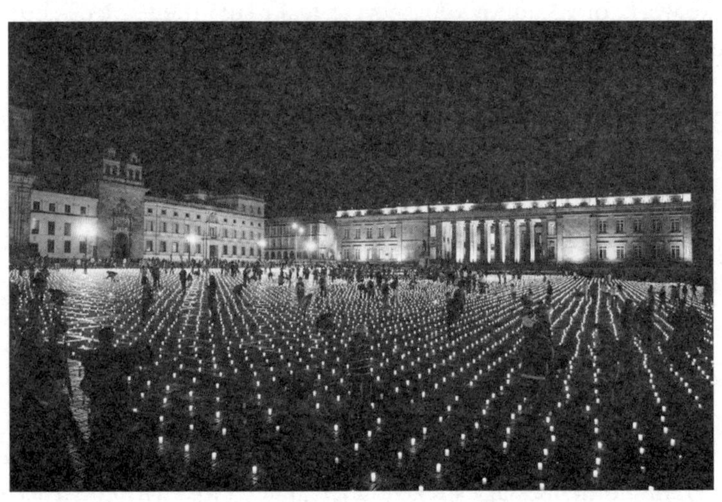

Doris Salcedo, *Act of Mourning, Plaza de Bolívar, Bogotá, 2007*

Keep making

'So if we're going through a stage of mega conservatism, it's women who are going to be at a massive disadvantage in every way possible. That's part of what I make my work about. And if it's unpalatable, then I'm sorry, but I'm not going to stop making work.' —Tracey Emin

Who in your community is the most disadvantaged? How can you make work, or go out of your way, to make sure their voice is heard? If everyone was afraid of being 'unpalatable' then no change would occur. Keep making, fighting, shouting, protesting, campaigning. Raise your voice, and bring others up with you. Make yourself and others feel uncomfortable – if you're not, ask yourself whether you're hiding from and avoiding the truth.

Tracey Emin (b. 1963) is one of the most influential British artists, looking to her life for primary material, and creating work across painting, sculpture, installation, drawing and more.

Source: The Great Women Artists Podcast, *2022*

Turn dismissal into energy

'I've had slight dismissal from male artists I know, which makes me get galvanised and get myself together even more. In fact, it's a trigger for you to go on . . . so the people doing it should perhaps reconsider doing it because it has the reverse effect of where they are trying to position me . . .' —Rose Wylie

Rose Wylie is now one of the most acclaimed British painters. But she didn't always get this attention. Having gone to art school in the 1950s, Wylie put her practice to the side until she was in her forties and even then it wasn't until the 2010s, when she was in her eighties, that her work began to be lauded. All that time she was making art in her Kent-based studio, conjuring her iconic painting style.

We may not ever experience success of the kind that Wylie found later in life, but we can take inspiration from the way she took that dismissal from others and turned it into something energising for her.

Rose Wylie (b. 1934) is a British painter based in Kent. Her recognisable painting style is filled with text and image, referencing film, sports stars, mythology and everyday life.

Source: Rose Wylie in conversation with Frances Morris, Royal Academy of Arts, 2019

Resist labels

'We're supposed to fit into a certain box but a lot of us work in different forms and ways and we're constantly feeling like we have to explain why this or why that, and I just like this idea of the box having all these doors and we're just coming in and out as we need to' —*Genevieve Gaignard*

Have you ever felt like you are being put into a box?

It is impossible for us to ever fit in one – our lives our too multitudinous. Often, when we get told to fit into a box, it's because we might be considered something 'other' than the default, so it's easier to place us as such. But in reality, it's impossible to fence us off, to say we're 'other'. We can find connections if we look. There is strength in that.

Genevieve Gaignard (b. 1981) is an American multidisciplinary artist who explores race, class and gender.

Source: Panel discussion for From Near and Far *(exhibition at Stephen Friedman Gallery): Katy Hessel in conversation with Kenturah Davis, Genevieve Gaignard, Deborah Roberts and Amy Sherald, 22 July 2022*

Find the light

Interviewer: 'Ms Hatoum, do you see darkness in your art?'
Mona Hatoum: 'I think your personal experience shapes the
way you view the world around you. With fifteen years of civil
war in Lebanon and conflict in the Middle East ever since I
can remember, there is nothing very uplifting about it and this
inevitably filters through my work. So, yes, there is darkness but
there is lightness as well. There are often two sides to each piece,
not just one meaning. Duality and contradictions exist in most of
the work: darkness and light, heaviness and humour, beauty
and danger . . .'

Palestinian in heritage, Hatoum often addresses conflict and exile in her work.

We see this in her work, *Current Disturbance*, 1996, an installation full of contradictions. On the one hand it could feel like a cage, a place of imprisonment. But on the other, the fluctuating lights and sounds are mesmerising.

Without hope, there is no life. You have to always be able to see the light among the darkness.

Mona Hatoum (b. 1952) is a British-Palestinian artist, born and raised in Lebanon, who often makes politically charged works across installation, sculpture, video, photography and works on paper.

Source: Robertson, Emma, 'Mona Hatoum: "It's about shattering the familiar"', The Talks, 19 October 2016

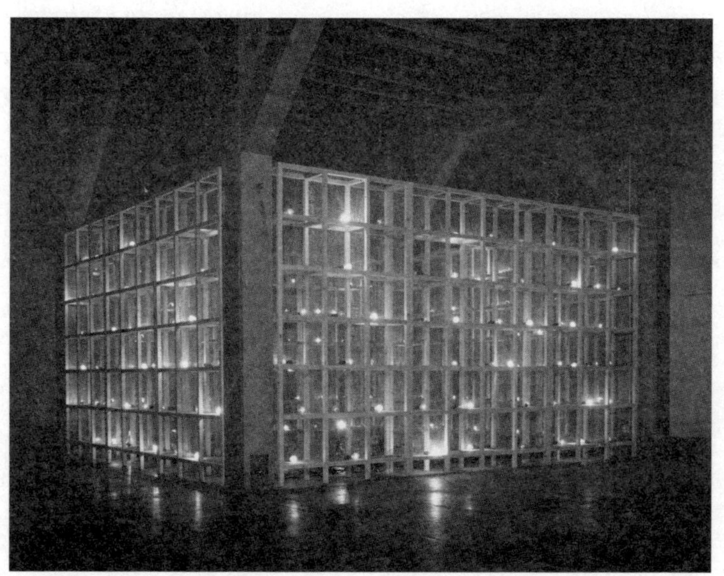

Mona Hatoum, *Current Disturbance*, 1996

Resist knowing

'Most of the things that I draw, I don't know what they are by name. People say, "Nellie, what is that?" I say I don't know, it is what it is. That is all I know. But I know one thing, I draw what is in my mind. I draw things you haven't seen born into this world, but these things may someday be born but I'll be on through.' —Nellie Mae Rowe

When we create, we have – in lots of ways – no idea where we are going, or what the outcome of what we are making will be. In part, this is because it might be viewed or read by people who will exist long after we have existed, and spark in them an idea beyond your imagination.

Rowe's words are a reminder that it's not only OK to not know, but we should actively embrace not knowing.

Nellie Mae Rowe (1900–82) was a self-taught African American artist who grew up on her family's sharecropping farm in Fayette County, Georgia. Inspired by her parents' handcrafting skills, she began making art as a child, using whatever materials she could find. Married at sixteen, she spent many years working in domestic service before returning to art after being widowed at forty-eight. In the decades that followed, she joyfully transformed her home and yard – what she called her 'Playhouse' – into a vibrant, ever-evolving world of drawings, collages, handmade dolls, chewing-gum sculptures and found-object installations. Today, her work is held in museums and private collections around the world.

Source: 'About Nellie Mae Rowe: In Her Own Words', interview by Judith Alexander, 1982, The Judith Alexander Foundation

Be human

'I read a lot of books, like Simone de Beauvoir, and they had a great influence on me. I've always been a sucker, always doing what I'm told. I became aware of things that I hadn't been aware of before – like independence. It was exciting to think that women could do what men could do. It felt just. I don't use the ideas directly but I try and get justice for women . . . at least in the pictures. Revenge, too.' —Paula Rego

You don't always need to do what you are told on the grounds of your gender or background. Books and art can be a means to seek out ways to rebel and rattle against the constraints.

The Portuguese-British artist Paula Rego liked to use well-known stories and fairytales as the foundation for her pictures, reworking characters – such as Snow White or the Virgin Mary – from a female perspective. By doing so, she gets me to think about the gender expectations that are so deeply ingrained in our culture, and how it takes us to flip the script so as to break the cycle.

How can you look to artists to give you permission to bend the rules, and rework well-known stories from a different perspective? Which writers or artists help give you your voice? Take a moment and write down their names.

Paula Rego (1935–2022) was a British artist, who was born in Portugal. For over seven decades, she made paintings, pastels, drawings and sculptures that dealt with secrets, desires, fears; family dynamics and art history; and, using stories as a framework, upended fairytales, myths, or passages from the Bible. Through her highly political work, Rego fought for reproductive rights and the rights for women, and stood against fascism in Portugal and Salazar's colonial wars.

Source: Gosling, Emily, '"I'm All Too Human": Paula Rego in Her Own Words', AnOther Magazine, *28 February 2018*

Choose the less well known

'Historical images – I believe – carry a weight of authority and familiarity, which I like to disrupt. When I reinterpret these images, it can be [as] a bridge connecting the past with the present day, looking at struggles, triumphs and questions. They help us to see the echoes of history in the now. It's about holding a mirror to our shared histories and asking how we can use them to foster, I guess, a more reflective, inclusive and equitable contemporary narrative world.' —Barbara Walker

Since 2018, the British artist Barbara Walker has been working on a series called *Vanishing Point*, which obscures the dominant white subjects (through blind embossing) in the Old Master paintings, and instead highlights the Black subjects (by drawing them in graphite), who have historically been pushed to the sidelines by the main narrative of Western art history.

Walker's words and art remind us to resist looking only at what has been termed the 'main event'. What are we not seeing? What could we find? Next time you decide to go and look at a work of art, rather than choosing the most talked-about show or artwork, what could you choose to go and see instead?

Barbara Walker (b. 1964) is a British artist who creates works on paper, paintings on canvas and large-scale charcoal wall drawings. They are filled with empathy, depth and emotion, and address the state of Black communities, their experiences and histories.

Source: The Great Women Artists Podcast, *2024*

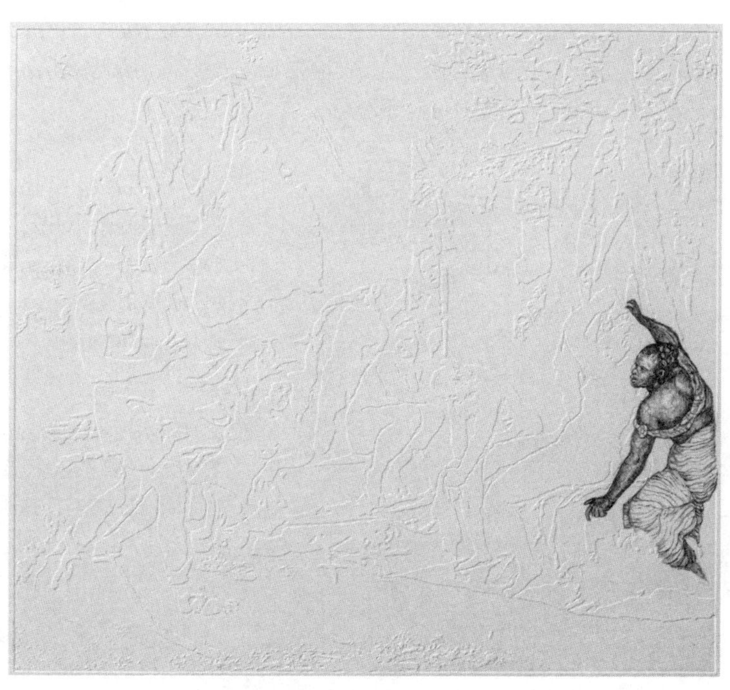

Barbara Walker, *Vanishing Point 7 (Titian)*, 2018

Resist convention

'There are no "shoulds" . . .'—Jadé Fadojutimi

Just because society tells us we 'should' do something doesn't mean we have to abide by it. What convention do you want to resist in your own life?

Jadé Fadojutimi (b. 1993) is a British artist known for her abstracted canvases, infused with vivid colour and myriad textures. Standing in front of one of her paintings is like witnessing a theatrical performance unfold in front of your eyes. She is influenced by Japanese anime and the props and items that she collects in her studio, and, when painting, blasts musical soundtracks that add to the all-encompassing worlds she seeks to create.

Source: The Great Women Artists Podcast, *2020*

Find a way to revolt

'I always imagined I would have a life very different from the one that was imagined for me, but I understood from a very early time that I would have to revolt in order to make that life. Now I am convinced that in any creativity there exists this element of revolt.' —*Leonor Fini*

Following on from yesterday, what life do you want to live? Take a moment and write down how it will feel to live that life.

Leonor Fini (1907–96) was an Argentinian-born painter, designer, illustrator and author, based in Europe for most of her life. She was known for her realist-style 'Surrealist' pictures of inventive worlds filled with sphinx-like figures. She had many lovers, and lived with seventeen cats.

Source: Winter, Nina, Interview with the Muse: Remarkable Women Speak on Creativity and Power, *Moon Books, 1978*

Turn to something else

'All the paintings had been painted as far as I was concerned and I became a photographer.' —Lee Miller

The American-born Lee Miller began her career as a model before becoming a photographer. She worked with the Surrealists in Paris, setting up a commercial studio both there and in New York, followed by a brief time living in Egypt, until eventually she settled in England, where she was to become an official war photographer for British *Vogue*.

Always interested in what hadn't been done, she constantly sought out new ways of looking and handling her medium: the camera. What has not been 'done' in your world? How could you begin to do it?

Lee Miller (1907–77) was an American-British photographer. Using both her Surrealist eye (adept at seeing the strange in the familiar) and the photographic techniques that she helped develop (like solarisation: exposing light in the darkroom to create a silvery effect), Miller captured friends, objects, fashion items, Paris in the 1920s and the expansive Egyptian desert. Most notably, she caught the horrors and reality of – as well as women's vital contribution to – the Second World War. Following the war, she became a celebrated chef with her recipes published in *Vogue*.

Source: Amaya, Mario, 'My Man Ray: An Interview with Lee Miller Penrose', Art in America, May–June 1975

Recycle

'I personally feel moved when I see the scraps of material, knowing whom they came from, what I remember and associate with them, and whom they belonged to.' —*Małgorzata Mirga-Tas*

Małgorzata Mirga-Tas compiles scraps of fabrics, from clothing to curtains, that she recycles into her artworks. Not only does she resurrect these materials, she uses them to create positive, women-led community scenes that purposefully defy stereotypes about Romani people.

I love how, in the work overleaf, it's as though the women are physically sewing together the scene in front of us, reminding me of the artist's power to visualise truth and counter stereotypes.

What can you recycle into something beautiful, powerful?

Małgorzata Mirga-Tas (b. 1978) is a Polish-Romani artist, activist and educator.

Source: Unravel: The Power and Politics of Textiles in Art, *Barbican, 2024*

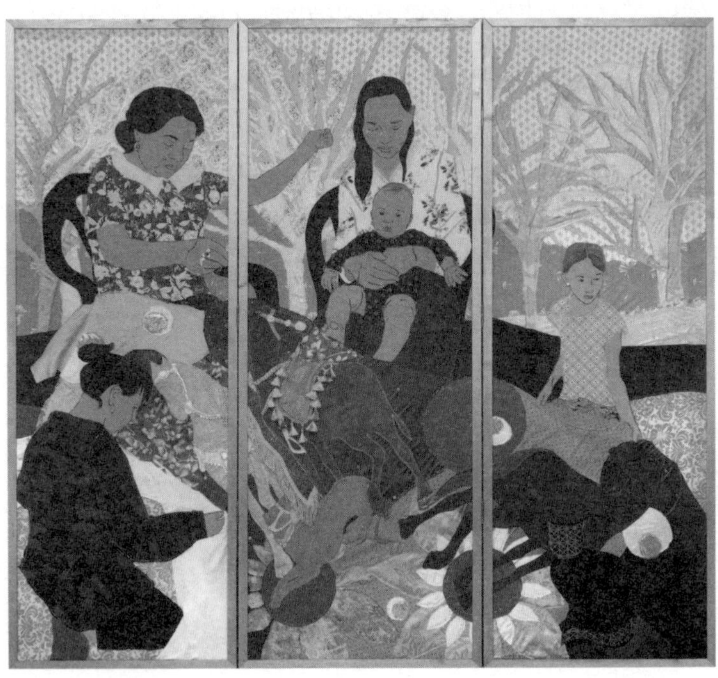

Małgorzata Mirga-Tas, *Untitled (After Gentile da Fabriano)*, 2023

March to the beat of your own drum

'I realise now I'm neurodivergent and so I didn't see the world in quite the same way as everybody else. I was always teased for being weird and I kind of marched to the beat of my own drum. And I thought it was natural, I thought everybody did that, until I realised that I was being laughed at, and then I kind of suppressed it. The thing that I suppressed and tried to excise from myself is actually the thing that drove me and turned me into a writer and made me persevere. It's the thing that I embrace now, but it took me a long time to learn to do that.' —Malorie Blackman

What is unique to you? How do you see the world in ways that no one else does? How can you embrace what might be considered something 'other' and turn it into a superpower? Finding the magic within you is the key. Always march to the beat of your own drum.

Malorie Blackman (b. 1962) is a celebrated British writer, most famous for her young adult novels, such as the *Noughts and Crosses* series.

Source: Malorie Blackman in conversation with Bernardine Evaristo, British Library, 23 February 2024

Look up, look out

'I am giving back to people through art what they already have in them.' —Nancy Holt

Today marks the summer solstice, when the sun will appear at its highest elevation.

Lying in the Great Basin Desert, Utah, are four giant concrete tubes installed by Nancy Holt between 1973 and 1976, called *Sun Tunnels*. They are tall enough to walk through, and face each other in an X formation.

During the day, you can see through them the expansiveness of the arid landscape and sky. If the sun is out, light dapples through holes in the pipes arranged in the constellations Capricorn, Columba, Draco and Perseus. Pass through them and it's as if you're walking on stars.

Twice a year, on the summer and winter solstices, the sun will align exactly with the openings of the tunnels, and light pours through.

Accentuating the natural world that constantly surrounds us, as Holt says, she's just giving back what we already have.

Nancy Holt (1938–2014) was an American artist who worked with the land through her innovative site-specific installations, pushing the boundaries in terms of where art could be found and viewed.

Source: Holt/Smithson Foundation, holtsmithsonfoundation.org

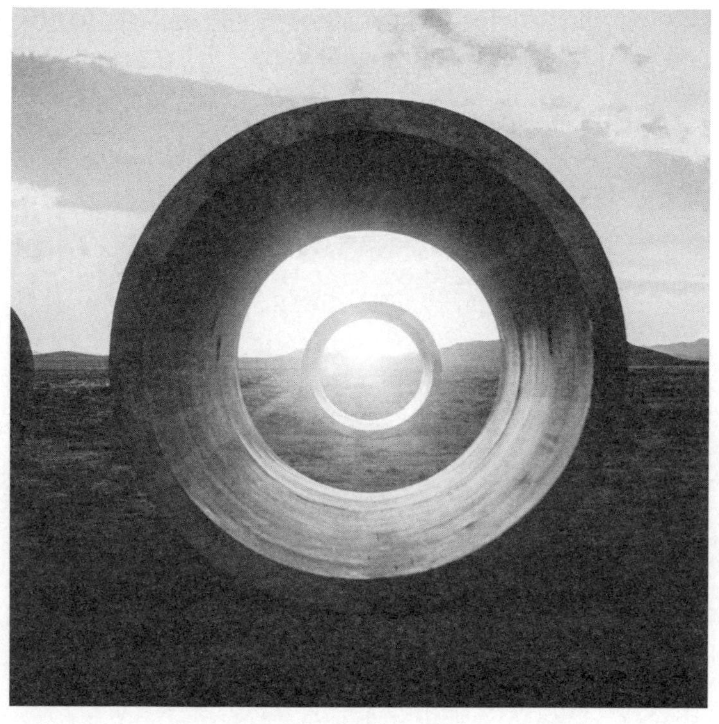

Nancy Holt, *Sun Tunnels* (1973–76). Great Basin Desert, Utah. Concrete, steel, earth. Overall dimensions: 2.8 x 20.8 x 16.2 m. Photograph: Nancy Holt. Collection Dia Art Foundation with support from Holt/Smithson Foundation © Holt/Smithson Foundation and Dia Art Foundation / Licensed by DACS, London

Close off unwanted comparisons

'There are many things written on my studio wall. Some are lines for inspiration, some just phone numbers I don't want to forget . . . one is "Play the music just for you" . . .' —*Catherine Goodman*

When the British artist Catherine Goodman attended a classical music concert in Delhi with her friend, the writer Vikram Seth, he observed, listening to the tabla player, 'It sounds as though he's just playing for himself.'

How can we close off unwanted comparisons? Not just in our work, but in all aspects of our life? Play the music just for you.

Catherine Goodman (b. 1961) is a British artist hailed for her intensely expressive and atmospheric paintings that explore both figuration and abstraction through her unique employment of oil paint and oil stick. She has been a pioneering educator as the co-founder of the Royal Drawing School, London.

Source: A note to the author, 2025

Sometimes you have to wait

'Sometimes you have to wait for culture to catch up with you. Remember, they just don't get it, but one day they will.' —Linder

If you have belief in what you are doing, making, creating, culture will likely catch up. Resist doing what everybody else does simply because it's what everyone else is doing: if you do what is true to you, it will always be radical. Perhaps we need to remind ourselves of this every day.

The legendary British artist **Linder** (b. 1954) is hailed for her scalpel work and radical feminist photomontages. Part of the Punk scene of the 1970s, in 2025 at aged seventy, she had her first major London museum exhibition, at the Hayward Gallery, to great acclaim.

Source: Dinsdale, Emily, 'Linder: "Global conflict alone is so much more shocking than porn"', Dazed, *12 February 2025*

The artist's perspective

'Artists are people who are very good at imagining a thing and finding the way in which that can be built and exist for others.' —Tania Bruguera

Why do governments or corporations so rarely go to artists for ideas? Why isn't there an artist on the board of every company? Artists are visual trailblazers – they can help envision a new reality in whatever field you're in. Use them; ask them questions; seek them out.

Tania Bruguera (b. 1968) is a Cuban activist and artist known for her politically driven work that spans installation, performance, sculpture, film, writing, large-scale interventions that involve the public and more. She is interested in raising questions around authoritarian control, borders and migration. In 2008, she sent in two policemen on horseback at the Tate Modern to highlight Cuba's strict authorities for her work *Tatlin's Whisper #5*; in 2009, for *Tatlin's Whisper #6* at the Havana Biennial, she created a space for free speech, which is normally denied in Cuba.

Source: Sollins, Susan, 'Defining an Artist' (interview with Tania Bruguera), Art21, *March 2014*

Don't censor yourself

'I don't think that you can make great art if you're censoring yourself or you're afraid of a response or a reaction.' —*Sheila Heti*

How can you create more moments when you're less self-conscious? Where do you find yourself free? And how do you bring those moments to your work, to more of your daily life? Is it in movement, in song, with your family or friends, in reading? Seek out those times, and see if you can take the sensation with you.

'That kind of courage or lack of caring is one of the most important things in the moment of creation,' Heti continued. 'Obviously, you don't have that every single moment that you're making something. But if you can – for a writer anyways, with editing – take away the stuff that you wrote while you were more self-conscious, and leave the stuff that you wrote when you were less self-conscious . . . I think you always want to catch the moments where you didn't think about the thing being seen.'

Sheila Heti (b. 1976) is the author of eleven books, including novels and novellas, short stories and children's books. Recent books include *Alphabetical Diaries* (2024), which ordered a decade's worth of diaries in alphabetical order, and *Pure Colour* (2022), a novel that explores grief, art and time.

Source: The Great Women Artists Podcast, *2024*

Embrace the now

'A really good picture looks as if it's happened at once. It's an immediate image. For my own work, when a picture looks labored and overworked, and you can read in it – well, she did this and then she did that, and then she did that – there is something in it that has not got to do with beautiful art to me.

And I usually throw those out, though I think very often it takes ten of those over-labored efforts to produce one really beautiful wrist motion that is synchronized with your head and heart, and you have it, and therefore it looks as if it were born in a minute.' —Helen Frankenthaler

One way to overcome self-consciousness is through preparation and repetition: think of scales for pianists, or the repetition of a series of yoga poses. How do you achieve that great piece of work that looks effortless and 'synchronized with your head and heart' as if 'born in a minute'? It might take ten tries to get there, at least, but the tries and the final piece are always worth it. The more you know, the more you do, the more you prepare – the better that single thing will be.

Helen Frankenthaler (1928–2011) was an American painter and printmaker commonly associated with the postwar artists in downtown New York City. Working alongside the Abstract Expressionists, she pioneered a type of painting called the 'soak stain' technique.

Source: Rose, Barbara, Frankenthaler, Harry N. Abrams, 1975 (second edition)

Go back to your beginnings

'Much of what I experienced as a child takes place again much later on the stage.' —Pina Bausch

Whether by drawing on the historical, personal or societal events that we witnessed in our youth, or by referencing a pivotal moment that shaped who we are, we can use art as a tool, a means of going back to our beginnings and working them out. Making art can be a process of self-discovery and even healing, a way to make sense of events in our lives.

Pina Bausch (1940–2009) was a highly influential German-born dancer and choreographer. Fusing dance with speech, music, sets and props, she led the dance company Tanztheater ('dance theatre').

Source: Bausch, Pina, Kyoto Prize speech, 2007, via the Inamori Foundation

Have an open mind

'If you have space in your mind that is open, you can let things in, and you have a natural fluid understanding of it. But if you put up a resistance to things, you'll never understand anything . . .'—*Tracey Emin*

Do you feel like something is missing in your life, something that you want but haven't quite figured out how it can be accommodated? Could it, therefore, not have happened yet because you haven't made room for it? Today, think about how you could open up a space in your life for a new reality. From letting someone into your life to learning a new skill – how can you work on opening your mind, in both the literal and psychological sense?

Tracey Emin (b. 1963) is one of the most influential British artists, looking to her life for primary material, and creating work across painting, sculpture, installation, drawing and more.

Source: Tracey Emin in conversation with Jennifer Higgie, Fane Productions, 2024

Stick with it

'I took photos. I photographed. If a writer wants to write, they've got to write. If someone wants to paint, they've got to paint, right? It's in the doing of it, the repetition of it. Then the conversation is between your work and you. It's not about anybody else. It's just you and your work . . . I decided if my work was good or not.' —Ming Smith

How do we know if we are good at anything? We don't know until, firstly, we try it. Secondly, stick with it. See where it gets you – *then* decide for yourself whether you're good at it or not.

Ming Smith (b. 1947) is an American artist who has worked in photography since the 1960s. She uses a slow shutter speed to impart a dreamlike, hazy quality to her images, and to capture the feeling of her subjects. The first Black woman photographer to have work in the collection of the Museum of Modern Art in New York, Smith has ventured from Harlem to Ethiopia for her art, recording a changing society in her distinctly ethereal lens.

Source: 'A Portrait of the Artist, Ming Smith in conversation with Janet Hill Talbert', in Smith, Ming, Ming Smith: An Aperture Monograph, Aperture, 2020

Never lose your spirit!

'I never lost my spirit. I always spent my time painting because they kept me going with Demerol, and this animated me and it made me feel happy. I painted my plaster corsets and paintings, I joked around, I wrote, they brought me movies. I passed [the year] in the hospital as if it was a fiesta. I cannot complain.' —Frida Kahlo

Let's close the month of thinking about resistance and learn from Kahlo.

How can you resist losing your spirit and make the most of what you have around you – transforming something typically full of pain into an object of beauty, to let the light in? Kahlo wore a back brace during her life – but look at how she made it into a beautiful artwork.

Frida Kahlo (1907–54) was a Mexican artist remembered for her self-portraits imbued with vibrant colours that address every emotion. Although spending much of her life in physical and emotional agony – as a child she had polio; in her teens she was involved in a bus crash that left her body shattered; as an adult she was in a tumultuous relationship with the artist Diego Rivera – Kahlo, through art, transformed pain into beauty, from painting tears like white crystals, to depicting a fluted column that thrusts through her body as a stand-in for a spine, keeping her head held high, queen-like, and alive.

Source: Quoted in Herrera, Hayden, Frida: A Biography of Frida Kahlo, *Perennial, 1983*

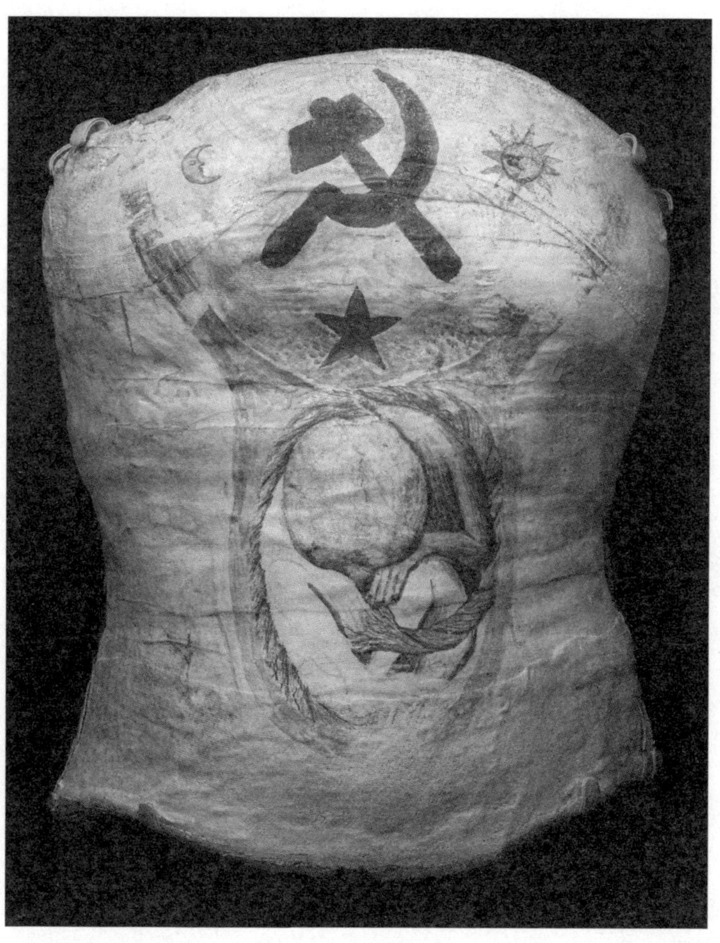

Frida Kahlo, *Hammer and Sickle (and unborn baby)*, c. 1950

JULY

Freedom

In her essay titled 'The Island' (1961), artist and Moomin creator Tove Jansson envisioned freedom as an island: 'privacy at last – distance, intimacy, a self-contained universe without bridges and fences'. Perhaps you will go to an actual island, or create one for yourself at home – an island of time, a secret place to lie in the sun. This month makes me think about stealing time, losing the routines that control us for so much of the year.

As we go into summer, I encourage you to hold in your mind thoughts of what makes you happy, building summer routines to maximise that sense that normal life might have retreated for a while.

Find freedom

'The minute I sat in front of a canvas, I was happy. Because it was a world, and I could do as I liked in it.' —Alice Neel

Of course, making something creative *is* freedom: once you're there, there are no hierarchies, no structures, no rules except those you choose for yourself. Build the characters, set the scene, choose the year, select the colours; decide where to start, and how fast – or slowly – you go.

But today, think about how you can apply Neel's words to your life outside of making art. Neel's happy place is in front of her canvas; take a moment and visualise your own. Is it a chair where you like to sit, a garden you like to tend, a gallery, a community centre you're a part of? Or is it a person, someone whose presence makes you lighter?

For me, it's a library, specifically the London Library. I go there most days. Books line every inch of the walls and there's a hall of fame with portraits of many of my favourite writers who were also members in their time, reminding me that this was clearly a place of freedom for them, too.

Alice Neel (1900–84) described herself as a 'collector of souls'. She was a painter of people, and always worked in her home-based studio in Spanish Harlem, and later the Upper West Side.

Source: Hills, Patricia, Alice Neel, *Harry N. Abrams, 1983 (reprint 1995)*

Embrace nature

'An artist should stay for long periods of time at waterfalls. An artist should stay for long periods of time looking at fast-running rivers. An artist should stay for long periods of time looking at the horizon where the ocean and sky meet. An artist should stay for long periods of time looking at stars in the night sky.' —Marina Abramović

Do you remember what Nan Goldin told us on 6 January? She told us to put down our phones as we had 'a lot to experience in the real world'.

While great things can come out of digital technologies – global connectivity; community building; movement-making – it's key to be aware of the more nefarious aspects encoded in their design.

In a month where we are thinking about freedom, embrace the world outside: meet the earth, feel the ground below your feet, gaze at the mystical expanse that is the sky – it's free! – and do as Marina Abramović tells us.

Marina Abramović (b. 1946), was born in Yugoslavia (now Serbia) and is considered as a pioneer and 'warrior' of performance art. Since the beginning of her career in the 1970s, Abramović has stretched the limits of the body. Early works include *Rhythm 0* (1974), which saw her declare herself as the object, and instruct the audience to use props on her as they wished. She has continued to break boundaries for the last five decades and counting.

Source: Abramović, Marina; Warsh, Larry (ed.), Abramović-isms, *Princeton University Press, 2024*

Let things happen

'I don't have any rules. I don't have any sketches. If I have one sketch, I'll turn up with ten physical works, because every time I try to get to the sketch, it directs me differently, it wants to be something else. It's like children in the womb, you don't know who they're going to be, who they're going to resemble.' —Leilah Babirye

All we can do is have an open mind. We can't impose rules onto creativity, because we have to see how it is going to turn out. We might have an idea of what something looks like, but in the end it will always be different to how you first interpreted it. The joy is in the discovery – in letting things happen. It's a reminder to put pen to paper, or charcoal on the page. The best thing is to do it. Get the first draft down, see how it ends up. Every decision will inform another one, and you can take it from there.

Leilah Babirye (b. 1985) is a Uganda-born, US-based artist working across painting, sculpture, assemblage on paper, ceramics and wood. She uses experimental techniques such as carving, burnishing, weaving and welding, and addresses narratives surrounding identity, sexuality and human rights.

Source: The Great Women Artists Podcast, *2021*

Learn to flourish

'I am flourishing in a new garb. Intensely exciting. Everybody likes it . . . I hope you will like it because I intend to wear that sort of thing always.' — Gluck

Gluck was part of a generation of queer artists, based between London and Cornwall, who didn't conform to dressing in ways dictated by traditional gender roles in society.

Gluck favoured the sharp suit, often with a silk tie, and a cropped hairdo – as captured in a painting by a friend and fellow artist, Romaine Brooks, *Peter (A Young English Girl)* (1923–24; overleaf).

Artists can be your guiding light in helping you to feel a sense of freedom in how you look, dress or express yourself in different guises – and how in doing so you can flourish as you are. Artists give us permission to be free.

Gluck (1895–1978) was an artist famed for their paintings of crisp flower bouquets (set in their three-tiered 'Gluck frame'), and self-portraits and portraits of those they loved.

Source: A letter to Gluck's brother, 1918, via the Smithsonian American Art Museum

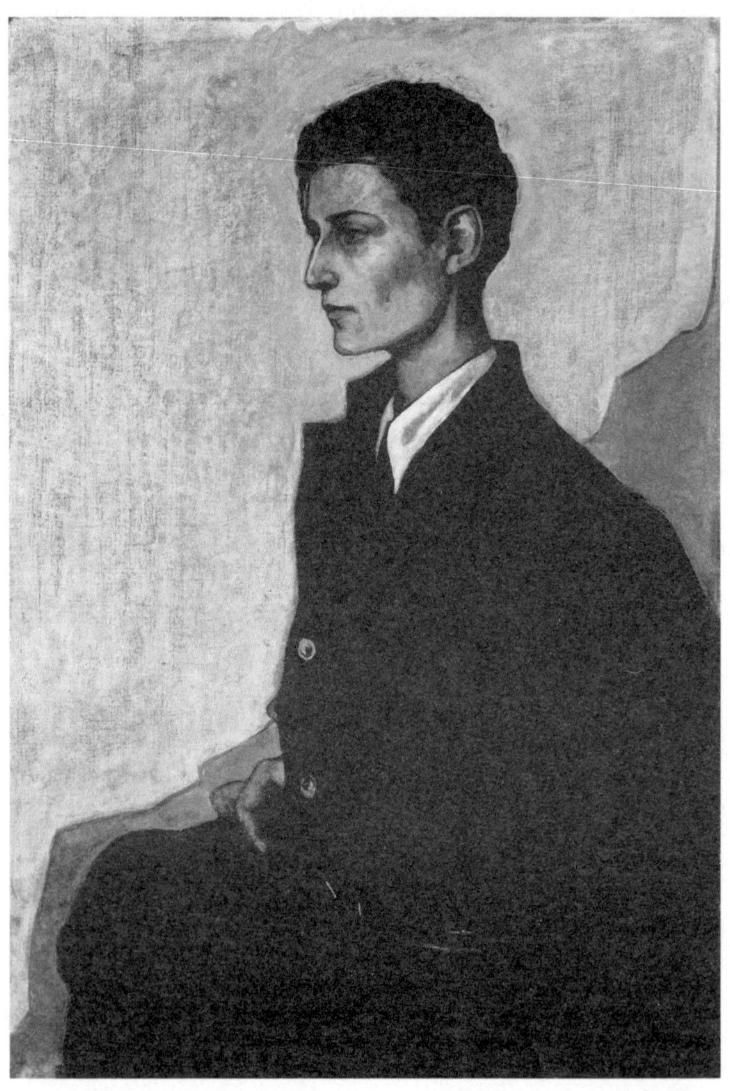

Romaine Brooks, *Peter (A Young English Girl)*, 1923–24

Wear a mask

'As a child I began to fall under the spell of masks and costumes, and once this bewitchment dug in there was no turning back. And why would I dream of such a thing? To dress up, to put on costumes is the magic that lets me merge into other dimensions, species, worlds. [. . .] Playing at being another person or even one's imagined self is all about self-invention, melting into another being, transforming and multiplying identities to the limit of one's capacity to do so. Let me convey one or multiple representations of myself. Let me bring on my own fantasies. Where is that costume? This goes beyond narcissism, which is simply cherishing one's own self. Wearing disguises is a sort of multiple narcissism because there are many versions of yourself involved – so you go into a trance of multiple identities, which engenders a state of crowded isolation from the outside world (reality?). Is this a negation of reality? Who cares?' —Leonor Fini

Across history, artists have used 'masks' as part of their art, as well as to help them forge a new identity – from the Guerrilla Girls who wear gorilla masks to remain anonymous, to the British artist Gillian Wearing who has photographed herself in lifelike masks to take on different guises (her younger self, Andy Warhol), to Fini who famously wore lion-like headdresses when she painted, perhaps to merge with different worlds, species and dimensions.

If you were to put on a mask, who or what would you become?

Leonor Fini (1907–96) was an Argentinian-born painter, designer, illustrator and author, based in Europe for most of her life. She was known for her realist-style 'Surrealist' pictures of inventive worlds filled with sphinx-like figures. She had many lovers, and lived with seventeen cats.

Source: Overstreet, Richard, 'Leonor Fini in Her Own Words' (translation, no date), via Leonor Fini: Catalogue Raisonné of the Oil Paintings, *Scheidegger & Spiess, 2021*

Create when the feeling comes

*'If I want to know if I'm honest in my work at the studio . . .
I try to listen to my motivation to paint. Do I or don't I feel like
painting today?*

Let me explain:

*Sometimes when I don't feel the urge to go to the studio,
I ask myself: how urgent for me is what I paint now? The lack
of motivation can simply result from the fact that I didn't
pick a subject I really care about deeply . . . There is no real
purpose . . . which is something I need to feel drawn to in order
to work.' —Nathanäelle Herbelin*

Herbelin's words speak universally. Even when we're in love with something, or someone, it's not always smooth sailing. It's even harder when our heart isn't in it. Our lack of motivation can be so difficult, confusing and scary – sometimes we don't recognise ourselves in these instances. How do we get back to a place of meaning?

In January, we heard from Kiki Smith, who told us to 'catch' ideas, to be attuned and present to them. And we mustn't beat ourselves up when those creative bursts or instincts don't come. Sometimes it really is about taking a break.

Today, I encourage you to do something that occupies a different part of your brain from usual. Go on a walk; climb a tree; play a game; make something with your hands – from cooking a meal to arranging a bunch of flowers. Watch a talk online; engage with someone who is a totally different age to you and ask them about their life.

Nathanäelle Herbelin (b. 1989) is a French-Israeli painter based in Paris, whose figurative works explore the raw intimacy of her subjects and scenes from daily life, with an acute awareness of how the personal and collective intertwine.

Source: A note to the author, 2025

What makes you feel alive?

'It makes me feel alive, thinking about colour.' —Rachel Jones

Yesterday we focused on getting outside of yourself as a way to access new energy. Today, take a moment to reflect on those times you've felt most alive. What, and who, gives you that energy? How can you tap into that?

For the British artist Rachel Jones, it's colour. She has a very sensual relationship to colour: she moves when she thinks of colour; or it might suggest a certain taste. Witnessing one of her paintings, composed of swathes – or even mountains – of bright reds, magentas, blues and oranges that dance and bounce off the canvas, it's as though she is taking the energy of colour and feeding it back to us. Not only does colour make her feel alive, but being in front of her work makes me feel alive.

Much of her work takes the 'mouth' as its core motif – like we are witness to all of its tastes and senses.

Practise the same thing: how does yellow make you feel; what does it taste of? How can red represent different aspects of your life? What about the many shades of blue? (The artist Felix Gonzalez-Torres once said, 'If a beautiful memory could have a colour, that would be light blue.')

Look around you, or within you. What colours do you see? What do they remind you of?

Rachel Jones (b. 1991) is an artist working across painting, installation, sound and performance. Her practice is rooted in an ongoing exploration of identity and selfhood, particularly in relation to Black culture and community. Her work is held in major public collections including the Tate, Hammer Museum, ICA Miami and Stedelijk Museum among others. In 2024, she designed the BRIT Awards trophy, joining a lineage of artists including Zaha Hadid and Tracey Emin.

Source: Rachel Jones in conversation with Erin Jenoa Gilbert for the Yale Center for British Art, July 2022; Felix Gonzalez-Torres interviewed by Tim Rollins, A.R.T. Press, 1993

Building confidence

*'Drawing is a great way of loosening up and getting acquainted
with your idea.*
Get large-scale papers and draw with pencils or charcoals.
Try watercolours with long-haired brushes.
See how your body reacts to fluid, uncontrollable materials.
Make a lot. Throw away a lot.
The more you make the more confident you become.
Great paintings are made of confidence and energy.
Be fearless.' —Sofia Mitsola

To build confidence is a slow process; it can take months, years,
decades. The best thing you can do, as Mitsola says, is keep at it. No
one ever got anywhere immediately – think of your heroes, or the
'greats' in history, and the amount of time they invested to perfect
their craft.

Throwing away doesn't just mean physically cutting things up, either.
It can mean editing, layering, cropping or concealing. It is only by
getting to know your method, your medium and your subject matter
better that your confidence will build. And once you've established
those building blocks, you will feel a great sense of freedom.

Sofia Mitsola (b. 1992) is a Greek-born painter, based in London, who, through painting,
investigates the many aspects of the female form in her signature larger-than-life characters,
with features that blend motifs from Greek mythology and Japanese animation.

Source: A note to the author, 2025

Look to the unfashionable

'One of the things that draws me to it [the Rococo] is how unfashionable it is. How it's a bit kitsch and over the top, and that's a fun place to be in the studio . . .' —*Flora Yukhnovich*

Don't just follow what everyone else is doing – look to the 'unfashionable'. Go with what draws your eye; come to something with your set of ideas, not anyone else's. Only then will you be able to look at something for what it is, and from there, form your own ideas.

Take the British painter Flora Yukhnovich, who was studying for her Masters in London when she came across the eighteenth-century French painter Jean-Honoré Fragonard, in particular, his painting *The Swing* (1767). While few of her peers were looking to this French style – which was considered 'unfashionable' for its frivolous garden scenes and florid features – Yukhnovich saw something in it.

Using it as a reference for her large-scale paintings, she brought modernity to the style, and by doing so brought the ideas of eighteenth-century French culture into dialogue with ideas of today. Just because something is considered unfashionable doesn't mean you can't use it.

Flora Yukhnovich (b. 1990) is celebrated for her large-scale paintings that bridge figuration and abstraction. Steeped in the Rococo, they also draw on R'n'B music videos and postwar American-style Abstract Expressionism; classical mythology and Walt Disney movies.

Source: The Great Women Artists Podcast, *2020*

What is beautiful?

'I was just thinking about how interesting it is that art in its time can be looked at so differently from art in twenty years and fifty years to a hundred years. And how things that look ugly at first can come to look beautiful.' —Sheila Heti

What we might think of as ugly now – perhaps ourselves, perhaps a work of art – might surprise us in years to come. It can be difficult to know if something is beautiful in the moment. It is often only when we look back on it in retrospect, or sit with it a while, that beauty comes through – sometimes from the most unexpected places.

Heti teaches us that we shouldn't be so quick to say something is ugly, especially ourselves! I remember learning this from the photographer Mary McCartney, who said that you might think you look one way in a photograph now, but you'll realise how beautiful you actually are in five years' time – a reminder to not dismiss your image so quickly.

Sheila Heti (b. 1976) is the author of eleven books, including novels and novellas, short stories and children's books. Recent books include *Alphabetical Diaries* (2024), which ordered a decade's worth of diaries in alphabetical order, and *Pure Colour* (2022), a novel that explores grief, art and time.

Source: The Great Women Artists Podcast, *2024*

Create your own language

'My goal is never to copy. Create a new style, clear luminous colours and feel the elegance of the models.' —*Tamara de Lempicka*

Tamara de Lempicka offers us the power of invention – in creating a new style, look, world, woman.

Born in 1898, in Warsaw, Poland, de Lempicka – famed for her stylised portraits that captured the spirit of the new age (see overleaf) – lived in a time when women in Europe were beginning to gain more rights and freedoms than ever. Through painting she envisioned the modern woman.

What is new about your life? What could you capture of it that could only be happening now?

Tamara de Lempicka (1898–1980) lived in Russia, France and the USA, and died in Mexico. In 1920s Paris, she found herself at the centre of the avant-garde society. She constructed some of the most radical and liberal images of women, reworking traditional subjects and capturing a fast-paced industrialised world.

Source: De Lempicka-Foxhall, Kizette, Passion by Design: The Art and Times of Tamara de Lempicka, *Abbeville Press, 1987*

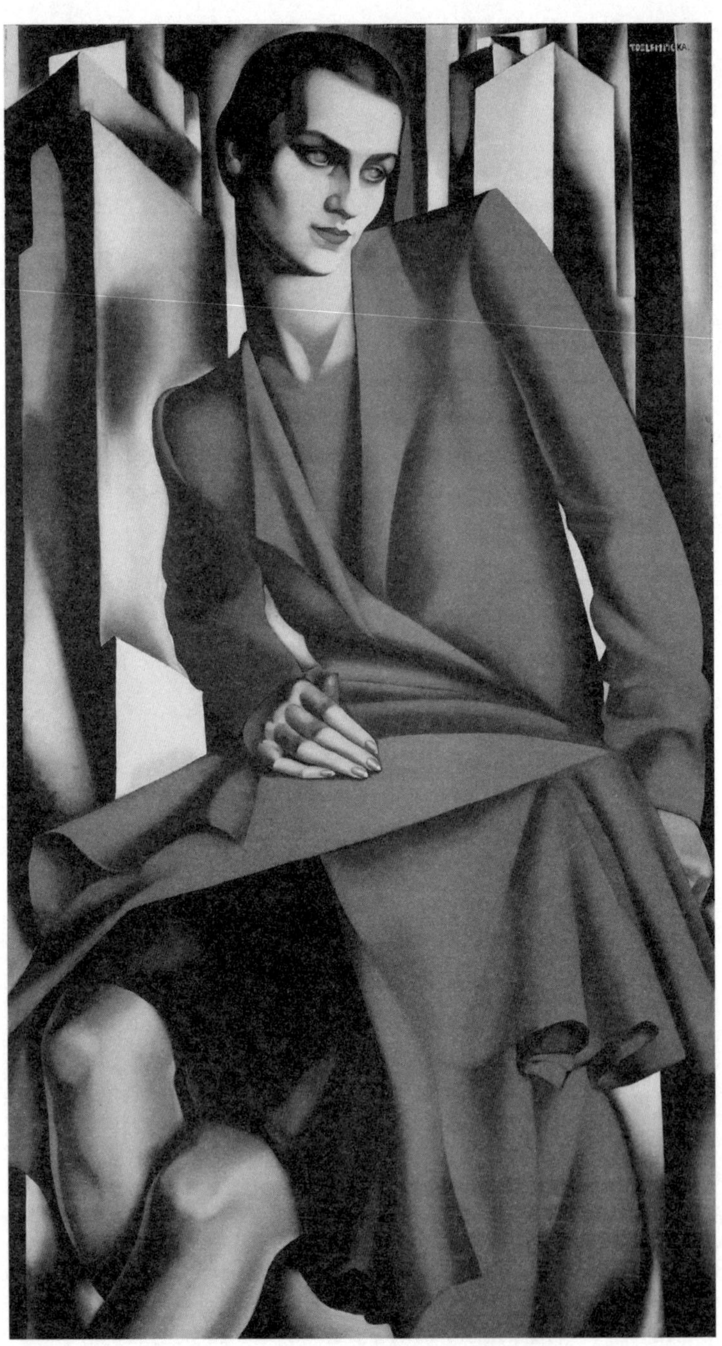

Tamara de Lempicka, *Portrait de Mrs. Bush*, 1929

Get outside of yourself

'Most of the time we fail to see the big wide real world at all because we are blinded by obsession, anxiety, envy, resentment, fear. We make a small personal world in which we remain enclosed. Great art is liberating, it enables us to see and take pleasure in what is not ourselves . . .'—Iris Murdoch

Go to great pieces of art. It's impossible to remain 'enclosed' in our own worlds when there is so much to see, read, do, taste, listen to.

There are infinite ways in which the imaginary can enrich the living . . .

Iris Murdoch (1919–99) was an Irish-born British novelist, philosopher and poet, and author of twenty-six novels, seven of which were nominated for the Booker Prize.

Source: 'Literature and Philosophy: A Conversation with Bryan Magee' in Murdoch, Iris and Conradi, Peter (ed.), Existentialists and Mystics: Writings on Philosophy and Literature, *Chatto & Windus, 1997*

Think out your own process

'For me, using an adaptation of the Method [acting technique] has proved invaluable. Others get there in other ways. Ultimately each artist creates their own process. But the Method taught me how to see in the dark, then to recognise the components of all kinds of other people in there.' —Eimear McBride

When the Irish novelist Eimear McBride began writing fiction at twenty-three she was served by her urgent impulse to create, but she struggled to expand beyond, as she wrote, 'those first fragmentary bursts'. So, she decided to utilise her previous experience of being at drama school – a three-year Stanislavski-style 'Method acting' course – which had given her an intense training that sees actors constantly embodying and inhabiting the experience of their characters. She has written, 'I wanted to see the world through others' eyes. More, I wanted to experience their experience of life.'

What methods can you draw from that have an entirely different set of rules and ideas from the ones you're already using?

Eimear McBride (b. 1976) is a celebrated Irish novelist, known for *A Girl Is a Half-formed Thing* (2013), which won the inaugural Goldsmiths Prize and the Baileys Women's Prize for Fiction, *The Lesser Bohemians, Strange Hotel* and *The City Changes Its Face.*

Source: McBride, Eimear, 'Studying method acting taught me how to write', Guardian, 8 February 2025

'Go to work'

'There's that famous Picasso quote that resonates with me — "inspiration has to find you working". I find great meaning in daily rigorous practice. I enjoy early mornings and am propelled by the conviction that I'm "going to work". Because it is work. Painting is a discipline. To me, a type of deep research. Of course, moments of inspiration can and do appear anywhere, but it requires a strong and established working pattern to inform my practice.' —Louise Giovanelli

What does 'going to work' look like? Is it a physical space, a psychological or emotional one? I find it interesting to imagine how you can give freedom to your day by imposing a rigorous structure.

Louise Giovanelli (b. 1993) is a British painter known for her luminous canvases of curtains, film or music-video stills, metallic shirts, classical sculptures and architectural details. Giovanelli's paintings fuse art history – harking back to the techniques employed by Renaissance painters – with the modern, pop culture-filled world, referencing music videos and cultural figures. Her delicately painted works are explorations into the dazzling and enchanting transient nature of light, solidifying something that is fundamentally ephemeral.

Source: A note to the author, 2025

Give freedom to others

'I struggle with time, I lose track of time, somehow clock time has not been drummed into me, both a failing and perhaps an act of resistance. My partner, also an artist, and I have rationalised time into a strict weekly routine that allows us moments to transcend it. We give each other long stretches a week without any household or child-rearing responsibilities, an expanse of time to work late, eat irregular meals at irregular times, to write, stare out the window, feel unbound by structure. This has become very important for my creative process.' —*Clementine Keith-Roach*

How can we enable other people's creative processes, and how can other people's routines enable ours – especially in a creative partnership? Cooperation is key, whatever field we are in. Transcendence doesn't happen in a vacuum – we need others to help us flourish. Cooperation and freedom go hand in hand.

Clementine Keith-Roach (b. 1984) is a British artist. She is an art historian by training and a former set designer, whose practice is imbued with these different approaches. Merging antique vessels with plaster casts of body parts – hands, feet, breasts – she draws on both Surrealism and the ancient world. While her sculptures might appear archaeological, their surfaces aged and weathered, they are in fact illusionistically painted, blurring the boundaries between vessel and body, terracotta and skin.

Source: A note to the author, 2025

Embrace and value your inner world

'[My paintings] feel more like reality than the world I step into every day. That's why I can't stop making. The place we live in, where everyone defines themselves or feels the need to define something, doesn't resonate with how I am as a person. So I guess really, what you see in my work is how I see the world.' —*Jadé Fadojutimi*

Fadojutimi creates abstracted landscapes filled with colours that crash and collide, and brushstrokes that dance or flutter like birds. While there are suggestions of textiles, animals, plant-like forms and recurring patterns, there is no perspective, no fixed image, no one thing that we are looking at. I resist the word 'viewing' when I talk about her work, because it's more of an all-encompassing experience.

When the world gets too much, you can always go to your imagination. It's not an optional extra: it's a tool, a muscle, a place that we can step into every day. Because isn't that what artists do, anyway? They go to that magical place deep in their heads and show us what they find there. Art wouldn't exist if it wasn't for people spending time in their inner worlds.

Jadé Fadojutimi (b. 1993) is a British artist known for her abstracted canvases, infused with vivid colour and myriad textures. Standing in front of one of her paintings is like witnessing a theatrical performance unfold in front of your eyes. She is influenced by Japanese anime and the props and items that she collects in her studio, and, when painting, blasts musical soundtracks that add to the all-encompassing worlds she seeks to create.

Source: The Great Women Artists Podcast, *2020*

The artist as an architect of the body

'I'm dealing with my body, and breaking my experiences of my own body into geometric forms – and trying to use the rectangle of the canvas as a landscape in which to situate these experiences that I have. In a lot of ways, I feel like I come to my work as an architect or trying to create a blueprint of an experience.' —Loie Hollowell

The image of the mother and motherhood has been imprinted in art history, and popularised in an idealised form, for millennia. When we see copious images like this, it can affect how we feel about our own bodies. Art can challenge these age-old stereotypes and expectations, altering how we understand the body that we inhabit. Hollowell sets it free by creating, as she puts it, a blueprint of experience, especially for the pregnant or post-pregnant body.

If you were to draw your body, or use words to describe it, what would it look like?

Loie Hollowell (b. 1983) is an American artist who creates tightly rendered sculptural paintings that evoke bodily landscapes. Verging on the threshold between figuration and abstraction, Hollowell's paintings – employing geometric shapes, varied textures and a strong, pulsating colour palette – allude to the human form, in particular women's bodies. They reimagine the way we don't just see, but experience the transformational abilities of women's bodies in painting.

Source: The Great Women Artists Podcast, *2020*

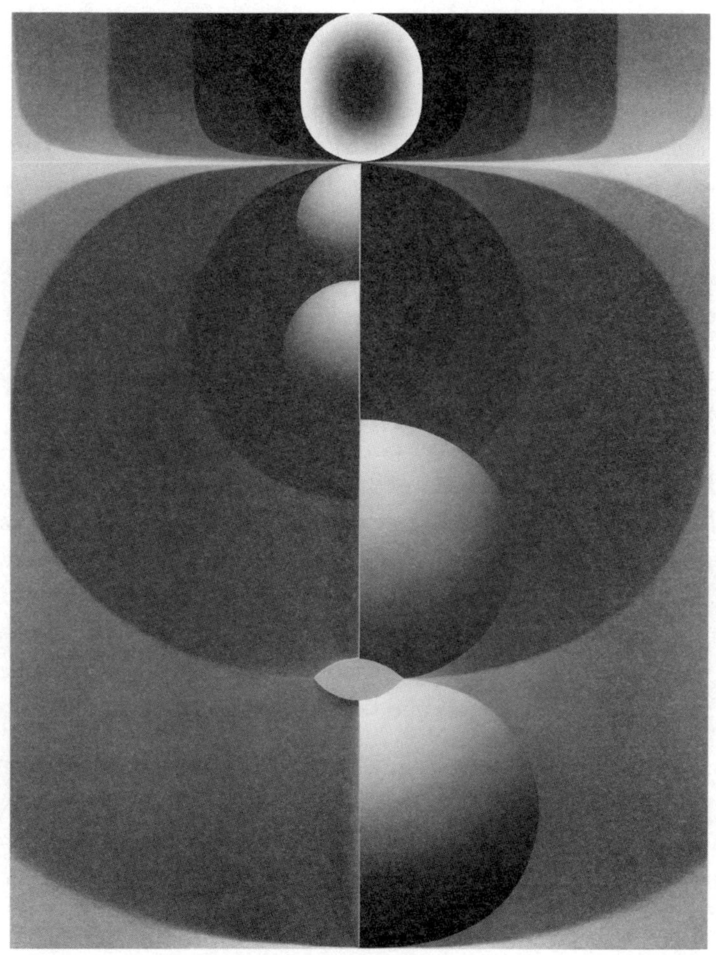

Loie Hollowell, *Standing in Blue*, 2018

'Absolute freedom'

'It's this need for ultimate freedom. Absolute freedom, that's the term I'm using at the moment, of absolute freedom.'
—Kudzanai-Violet Hwami

Categories, structures, binaries, classifications, borders: they make up so much of our world but keep us apart; narrowing the story rather than telling it from multiple perspectives; looking to restrict us, to rein us in.

Hwami's exuberant and vivid paintings of herself and her extended family offer something outside the rigid structures of our world.

Drawing on family photographs, memory, dreams and more, Hwami achieves this by using the language of collage: an art form which by its very nature can merge narratives and states of being, create unexpected links, and tie together histories and cultures. 'Collage is the language of today. I don't know if there's any other method that can properly tell the times of today,' as she told me. We are continuously overwhelmed with disjointed images and connections in the modern world, whether it's the tabs we see on a screen, the plethora of images we look at on our phones, or the people, buildings, pavements, grass and sky that we see outside.

Today, I encourage you to make a collage of your world, breaking down the edges of what is often clearly defined. What references will you draw on? What will you show? Who will you bring into it? How can you splice together contrasting entities that, ultimately, present a portrait of freedom?

Kudzanai-Violet Hwami (b. 1993) is a Zimbabwe-born, UK-based artist. In 2019, she was included in the 58th Venice Biennale, as part of the Zimbabwe Pavilion, and in the Biennale's main exhibition, 'The Milk of Dreams', in 2022. Her paintings, which collapse geography, time and space, have been presented all over the world.

Source: The Great Women Artists Podcast, *2021*

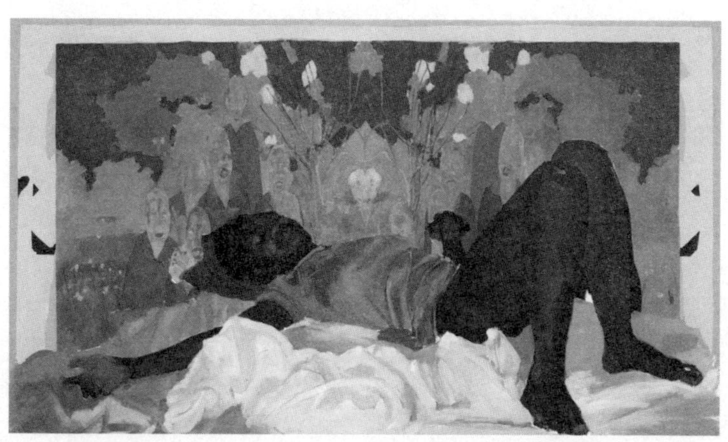

Kudzanai-Violet Hwami, *You are killing my spirit*, 2021

Say no

'You have to be willing to be able to say, "No, that doesn't work for me".' —Lorna Simpson

This is a hard, and occasionally contradictory, one. But you have to take time for yourself and not jump at every opportunity. Think carefully. Give yourself permission to say no. By doing so you can say yes to yourself.

How could you remind yourself to say no? Perhaps it's as simple as a NO Post-it note or sticker near your desk.

Lorna Simpson (b. 1960) is an American artist who gained widespread recognition in the 1990s for her pioneering approach to conceptual photography. Mainly working in photography, video and collage, her artworks raise vital questions about gender, race, memory and history.'

Source: Beete, Paulette, 'Lorna Simpson on Perspective, the Complexity of Layering, and Doing What She Wants', Colossal *magazine, 5 June 2023*

Get into trouble

'I used to have people come in all the time and say you're gonna get into a lot of trouble if you do this. But it's not like I had a choice in the matter, I had to do it. I think most of the artists I know feel that way – they just have to make what they make.' —Marilyn Minter

No one did anything revolutionary without breaking the rules. They are made to be broken. Chances are they were 'broken rules' in the first place. Who gets to make them anyway?

Minter, who makes graphic, photorealist paintings, challenges the idea of beauty as dictated by the media and pop culture.

The 'trouble' she is referring to is the way she has presented women throughout her oeuvre: sexually explicit, without shame – or maybe just 'free'. But the critics weren't happy. Minter took no notice and continued with her art.

Marilyn Minter (b. 1948) has been a legend on the New York art scene for over fifty years, as a pioneer of graphic, photorealist paintings. Cropping her images, and zooming in on highly charged moments, Minter's brightly saturated paintings of a tongue or high heel are highly ambiguous. They ask contradictory questions, such as is it beautiful, is it abject, is it pretty or is it dirty?

Source: The Great Women Artists Podcast, *2023*

Make a 'fuck you' painting

'I guess the ultimate thing that I'd like my paintings to teach people is, on a lot of different levels, to be your own person, be free, and you know, make the "fuck you" painting. Everybody out there – make a "fuck you" painting!' —Lisa Yuskavage

Make a 'fuck you' painting!

Lisa Yuskavage (b. 1962) is an American artist who began painting doll-like, pre-pubescent, semi-naked women in the early 1990s. Often emerging from a pool of saturated pinks, greens, reds or yellows, Yuskavage's figures fuse art history with the semi-pornographic images found in magazines such as *Penthouse*. She borrows painting techniques from the likes of the sixteenth-century Venetian painter Tintoretto while also looking to how some women are presented in the world today.

Source: The Great Women Artists Podcast, *2021*

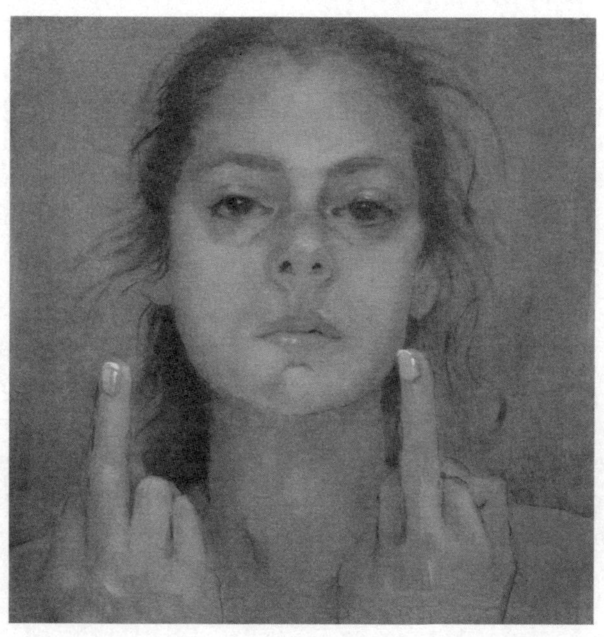

Lisa Yuskavage, *The Fuck You Painting*, 2020

Meditate

'The thing to do is to learn to accept the truth as it comes into your mind. Give up logic, deductions, and application and reference.' —Agnes Martin

Agnes Martin was a Canadian artist as well as a student of the Taoist and Buddhist teachings about awareness and perception. She was known for her delicately applied canvases, which she coated in restrained, repeated forms with startling control. Translating human emotions into abstract paintings in works titled *Friendship* or *Loving Love*, she said, 'I believe in living above the line. Above the line is happiness and love, you know. Below the line is all sadness and destruction and unhappiness. And I don't go down below the line for anything.'

Although raised in a strict Calvinist family, Martin embraced the Zen Buddhist belief that all humans could achieve enlightenment. Martin saw art as a vessel with which to access the sublime, and witnessing her paintings is an act of meditation in itself. But meditation as a practice can help people access freedom. See if you can bring it into your life, whether through a form of movement, such as yoga, or through reading spiritual works.

Agnes Martin (1912–2004) was a Canadian-born artist, who lived mostly in Taos, New Mexico. She was known for her six-foot square canvases made with subtle pencil marks, or serene bands of diluted colour.

Source: Martin, Agnes, faculty lecture, Skowhegan School of Painting & Sculpture, 3 July 1987 (audio recording)

Use the story you want

'We interpret the world through stories . . . everybody makes in their own way sense of things, but if you have stories it helps.' —Paula Rego

When Paula Rego was alive, she would talk about interpreting the world through stories. Since she was a child, Rego loved reading fantastical tales, having been introduced to Disney and Dante by her father. But once she began to depict the story – and work through it – the original narrative changed and became about her own experiences.

Sometimes it takes a strong reference for us to springboard into something else. Rework traditions in your own ways – you never know what you might find out, or the freedoms it might give, either to you or to someone consuming what you've made.

Take Snow White and the Seven Dwarfs, which is at times a complex and disturbing story, yet we are led to believe it is a fantasy story – a fairytale.

In her pastel work, *Snow White and her Stepmother* (overleaf), Rego used the characters to address the complexity of her own relationship with her mother. Here, she captures the shame Rego felt as a young girl going through puberty with a conservative, Catholic mother, who was also a product of the oppressive society in 1930s/40s Portugal.

Rego uses the Snow White image as a gateway for her own experience. Stories are out there: show them to us anew.

Paula Rego (1935–2022) was a British artist, who was born in Portugal. For over seven decades, she made paintings, pastels, drawings and sculptures that dealt with secrets, desires, fears; family dynamics and art history; and, using stories as a framework, upended fairytales, myths, or passages from the Bible. Through her highly political work, Rego fought for reproductive rights and the rights for women, and stood against fascism in Portugal and Salazar's colonial wars.

Source: Secrets and Stories, *directed by Nick Willing, 2017 (documentary)*

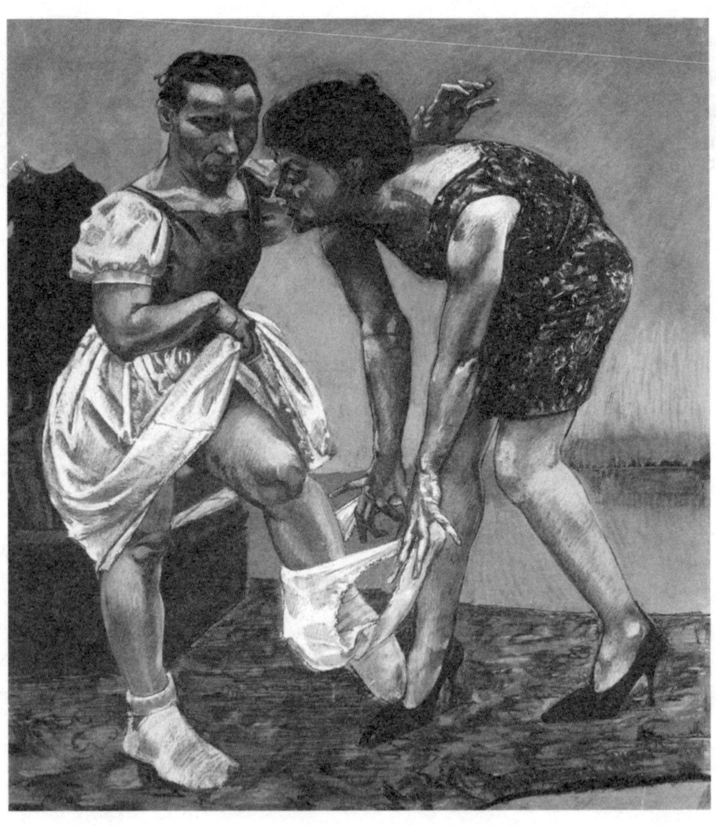

Paula Rego, *Snow White and Her Stepmother*, 1995

Dive into the ocean

'At times, to connect with a sense of totality, the sea becomes essential. A dive into the ocean, that merging with something greater, can be profoundly inspiring. It's a moment of expansion that's part of my routine and, in some way, always finds its way into the art. And I believe this holds true not just for artistic practice, but for anyone – it's a kind of nourishment for the soul.' —Adriana Varejão

Be at one with nature; dive into water for that sense of expansion, and for the ultimate route to freedom. Nourish your soul!

Adriana Varejão (b. 1960) is a Brazilian artist. Best known for her semi-architectural sculptures, and paintings that extend far beyond the frame, Varejão has tackled themes of Brazilian cultural hybridity, challenged ideas of monuments and, in her art, exposes postcolonial truths through historical research.

Source: A note to the author, 2025

What is freedom?

'I think this question of freedom is not something that is an isolated, individual thing. We can only be free through our own social ability to create a space to be free; it's dependent on all of us.' —Sonia Boyce

Freedom can only be achieved together. As Boyce continues:

> *Freedom does not exist in a vacuum. It requires systems to change, to collectively and consciously empower . . . It's not dependent on one or another, or singularly; freedom is something that we all have to have in order for freedom to possibly exist. I'm not the first person to say this. But I do think it is really true that we create the systems by which we live, not one person, or another person, or someone who's empowered – we collectively make those decisions, or even if we're not consciously feeling that we are, we do.*

Sonia Boyce (b. 1962) has a constantly evolving artistic practice spanning drawing, printmaking, photography, installation, video and sound; focusing on collaboration, often with an emphasis on improvisation, by working with other artists. Instrumental in the British Black Arts movement of the 1980s, Boyce remains one of Britain's foremost artists, having represented the UK at the Venice Biennale in 2022.

Source: The Great Women Artists Podcast, 2023

Use anything

'If you ask me, why do I work with all this material? It's not because I want to create something interesting. Oh, no, I don't think that way. It is because all these things are interesting of their own accord, you see. I have to do nothing except be with them, consider what they want, what is possible.' —Cecilia Vicuña

Twigs, wood, wool, string, found objects, plant fibres, rope and cardboard . . . While these materials might start out small and fragile, they have the power and possibility to create the most extraordinary entities – including everything that can be made from them in the world (clothes, houses, gardens, containers), but also, as depicted in Vicuña's work: language.

Vicuña is known for her installations that take the form of 'quipus', which means knots in Quecha: a system of encoding information from the Andes that conveys as much information as the alphabet. It was used for 5,000 years, before being wiped out during colonisation.

By presenting us with what she calls 'precios' (precarious) objects, Vicuña gets us to see their potentials. As she tells me: 'You are educated by the materials you see.'

How can you see the possibilities in materials?

Cecilia Vicuña (b. 1948) is a Chilean-born artist, hailed for her works that are as ephemeral as they are permanent, colossal as they are minute, fragile as they are strong, that bring together sound, weaving, language and community. Although sometimes working on a monumental scale, her work can comprise twigs, bamboo, stones and shredded textiles.

Source: The Great Women Artists Podcast, *2024*

What does your island look like?

'It is astonishing the number of people who go around dreaming of an island. Sometimes they're deliberate people who search for their island and secure it, and sometimes the island dream is a passive symbol of what lies one step out of reach. The island, privacy at last – distance, intimacy, a self-contained universe without bridges and fences.' —Tove Jansson

What does your island look like? Is it a place at all? Will it be just you, or will you have people there beside you? What does freedom look like to you?

Tove Jansson (1914–2001) was a Swedish-speaking Finnish writer, artist, painter, cartoonist, novelist, illustrator and children's book author, best known for creating the wondrous world of the Moomins: the tales of Moominmamma, Moominpappa and Moomintroll, and their adventures in Moominvalley.

Source: 'The Island', 1961, found in Jansson, Tove; Teal, Thomas (trans.), Notes from an Island, *Sort of Books, 2024*

Return to nature

'When we turn our gaze toward the plant kingdom, it gives us information about the composition of our own being.'
—Hilma af Klint

Af Klint is famed for her diagrammatic paintings of the spiritual world. For decades, she worked mostly in secret, guided by spirits, for her large-scale paintings that she filled with symbols, ranging from doves to circles, spirals and orbs.

In 1917, af Klint began to turn away from the cosmic and towards nature, closely analysing jewel-like plant forms – tulips, lily of the valley, water avens and buttercups – as if to seek out the interconnectedness of wider ecosystems.

How can we look to the nature that already exists around us, to understand our place in the world? In the same way that we get to know our fellow humans, how can we take time with natural elements, and make discoveries about who we are?

Hilma af Klint (1862–1944) was a Swedish-born artist who, in her early artistic career, made expressive paintings of landscapes. However, in the 1890s, after becoming interested in Spiritualism, she began to meet in secret with a group of four friends (they called themselves The Five). Together, they held seances to connect to spirits who were thought to guide their hand across the canvas. In 1906, af Klint ventured on her own, creating hundreds of small- and large-scale paintings – some over three metres tall – that aimed to show humanity the matters of the spiritual realm.

Source: As quoted in 'Hilma af Klint: What Stands Behind the Flowers', Museum of Modern Art exhibition catalogue, 2025, p.11 (first quote); p.121 (second quote)

Emancipate yourself

'I shall obtain it [being an artist] only by persevering and by making no secret of my intention of emancipating myself.'
—Berthe Morisot

Born into upper-middle-class nineteenth-century Parisian society, Morisot lived in a very different world to the one we do now. Although she went on to become a very successful artist – and the only woman to exhibit at the first Impressionist exhibition in 1874 – art wasn't a route that could have ever been planned out for her. Not abiding by societal rules, or the opinions of a former tutor who said it would be 'catastrophic' if she pursued art full-time, Morisot had no choice but to break out from the confines of womanhood, and the expectations of her gender. She had to assert the fact that she was, and would be, an artist, no matter what.

Make no secret of what you want to do. Tell everyone; shout it from the rooftops. Not only will that help you tell yourself what it is you want to achieve, but I find that by telling people my plans, I have to stick to them.

We need to make for ourselves, and on our own terms. Persevere in emancipating yourself from the restrictions that you have been given. Work with others to do it.

Berthe Morisot (1841–95), hailed for her rough brushwork and use of glistening white light, captured vividly and intimately the private worlds of bourgeois women in late nineteenth-century Paris society, celebrating their small freedoms.

Source: A letter to her sister Edma, 1869, in Rouart, Denis, (ed), Berthe Morisot Correspondence, Camden Press Ltd, 1987

Create freedom out of control

'I created this daily ritual to make at least fifty drawings in ink, deliberately choosing a medium that defied control. So I think I was after the rigour of that ritual, the act of making hundreds and hundreds of swift, gestural drawings with brush and ink. You know, I kind of was imagining that if I let go of the conscious technique that was innate in my hand and brain, acquired from years of meticulous training and miniature painting techniques, I could come across something very spontaneous between control and surrender.' —Shahzia Sikander

Routines can be very different from each other. What matters is creating one, and finding repetition in it, which leads to freedom to think and to do. No matter if it's one or fifty drawings a day, a week, or a month, or writing 50, 100, 500 words a day, it's good to keep up a regular practice, in order to, as Sikander says, 'let go of the conscious technique'. Doing so keeps us looking, thinking and actively seeking out things in new ways. It also builds in muscle memory, and an inner rhythm. Once we get to know something well, we can take it any way we like. Start at the end, the middle, turn something on its head. Routine and rigour can allow us to achieve freedom in ways we could never have imagined.

Shahzia Sikander (b. 1969) is a Lahore-born, New York-based artist who is widely celebrated for her work that subverts tradition and reclaims narratives – such as of Central and South-Asian manuscript painting – and for launching the form known today as Neo-Miniature.

Source: The Great Women Artists Podcast, *2024*

Take the freedom you deserve

'Nobody will give you freedom; you have to take it.'
—Meret Oppenheim

Reflect on the month that you have been given and what you want to take forward. How will you take freedom for yourself? Will you say no, enable someone else (which will in turn enable you), get into trouble, make a fuck you painting or create a rigorous routine that will give you the freedom to surrender? As Oppenheim says, nobody will give freedom to you. Carve out the space you want, and take it!

Meret Oppenheim (1913–85) was a German-Swiss artist, known for her paintings, sculptures, collages, jewellery designs and more, who was commonly associated with the Surrealists. Influenced by the work of psychologist Carl Jung, Oppenheim kept a dream journal from the age of fourteen, from which she would at times derive her artworks. She is best known for her 1936 *Object* – a fur-lined teacup, saucer and spoon, which thrills as much as it repulses its viewer, and still divides opinion today.

Source: Oppenheim, Meret, 'Nobody Will Give You Freedom, You Have to Take It', acceptance speech for the 1974 Art Award of the City of Basle, 16 January 1975, reproduced in Rosemont, Penelope (ed.), Surrealist Women: An International Anthology, *Athlone Press, 1998*

AUGUST

Beauty

To me, August is like the Sunday of months. A moment to rest and take stock; admire the world outside; travel; swim; sit in the sun. But because it's a month of Sundays, August can also feel slow. This description, from Natalie Babbitt's 1975 children's novel *Tuck Everlasting,* sums it up: 'The first week of August hangs at the very top of summer . . . like the highest seat of a Ferris wheel when it pauses in its turning.'

For many of us, especially those at school or university (or those looking after them), we have long holidays – which are both a blessing and a struggle. They're often a time where we have no imposed structure to help us along.

We ended last month with the idea of creating routines that work for yourself. So this month we are going to be looking at getting ideas from unexpected places; seeking out the beauty that we can get for free; observing things one at a time; placing emphasis on the importance of play and harking back to the fantastical sensibilities we might have had in childhood. We'll look to artists to help us fill our time with activities that enliven rest.

Look to the colour in the world!

'A world without colour would seem dead. Colour, for me, is life.' —Alma Thomas

Alma Thomas painted the world in shards of vivid colour, from the flowers in her garden to how she envisioned the red dust settling on Mars, which together make up her distinct, gestural 'Alma stripes'.

What colours surround you this August, the pinnacle of summer? Look carefully, notice the tonal differences: how does a light red sit against a darker red; how does the sky change its shades of blue? Rather than recording subject or form, record colour this month. Could you make a month-long colour diary, stating which colour sums up each day, or week for you?

Alma Thomas (1891–1978) was born in Columbus, Georgia, and lived most of her life in Washington, DC, where she worked as a high school teacher. It was only after she retired, aged sixty-nine, that she was able to focus on her art career full-time. Within a few years, she was sharing her art in exhibitions, and became the first Black woman to have a solo exhibition at the Whitney Museum of American Art.

Source: Quoted in press release, Columbus Museum of Arts and Sciences, 1982, for an exhibition entitled 'A Life in Art: Alma Thomas 1891–1978', Vertical File, Library, National Museum of American Art, Smithsonian Institution, Washington, DC

Find beauty in unexpected places

'It is not generally known, and certainly I have never before this realised, that scattered about even the most cancerously urban districts of London, there exist patches and stretches of wild marshy land of heath. Of course I don't mean the parks – they are as urban as the buildings. These stretches are different because you can't find them by looking for them – at least it seems to be so, as far as our present knowledge takes . . .'—Ithell Colquhoun

On a walk in London with her friend in the 1940s, the artist Ithell Colquhoun found a patch 'somewhere between Piccadilly and Oxford Street' filled with flowers that 'were of various jewel colours'.

While we can go to the parks and the meadows near our homes or work, sometimes it can be more exciting to discover beauty in unexpected places – especially those that seem densely urban. Look to the cracks in the pavement, the weeds growing on building walls, or the plants entangled in fences. How did they get there? What colours and form do they possess, against the greyness around them? Remember, beauty exists everywhere – even the most densely urban places contain magic – it just might be in a different form, or found in a different place, to how or where you imagined it to be.

Ithell Colquhoun (1906–88) was an occultist and Surrealist artist based in Cornwall for most of her adult life. Drawing from the natural world, she made hypnotising and colourful paintings, often with classically inspired titles, that double up as a landscape and a body – or the inside of a body – depending on the way we look at it.

Source: Colquhoun, Ithell, Goose of Hermogenes, *Peter Owen, 1961. Extract reproduced courtesy of Pushkin Press*

Look for surreality in your daily life

'My studio routine is to consider and reconsider the things around me that are unusual en route to my studio. Sometimes this takes the form of a weathered object or an object that feels out of place – a skyscraper that displaces everything around it in scale, an ironically placed sign that now reads as a defiant statement, a rotten tree growing out of a house, or even a leaf shaking in the wind. The more you practice this, the more you see surreality . . .

Things in the world often present themselves as conspicuously out of place more often than we give them credit for.

But don't take pictures of these experiences! That's just an easy way to shelve those experiences (and pay rent for image storage space on your device of choice). Take it all in. Let your encounter with the world tell you something about itself that you don't already know.

By the time I've gotten to the studio, hopefully I've found one experience in the world that I can share on a canvas with someone else and maybe they will believe me when I say I didn't make this all up.' —Sedrick Chisom

Think of a route you use on a regular basis: now, whenever you're on it, practise seeing 'surreality'. Notice one thing, then share it with someone. Then ask them, what did they notice on their route that day?

Sedrick Chisom (b. 1989) is an American painter whose work, rendered in scorched colour and hallucinatory detail, stages apocalyptic, mythic worlds marked by ideological collapse, imperial decay and haunted futures.

Source: A note to the author, 2025

A day is as long as a year

'When I was a teenager growing up in Beirut, I was always rushing around, staying so busy, trying to accomplish everything all at once. Time seemed to move so quickly. One day, I went to visit my grandmother, who was bedridden at that point. I must have been a bit frantic, because she said, "Mounira, relax, a day is as long as a year." That phrase really stayed with me. I had never before considered how different that time must feel to this wise, elderly woman.' —Mounira Al Solh

Especially when we are young and hungry, it's easy to think that we need to do everything all at once. And it's OK to feel that way. We haven't been on this planet that long, and time can feel short – especially compared to someone who might have been here double, or triple, the time that we have. Every year, or season, might feel like it needs to have 'significance'.

But today, let's think about how we can imagine time from the perspective of those who have been on this planet longer than us – like Mounira Al Solh's grandmother. How would she treat a task, or use a morning? What might we be able to learn about being less frantic, and how can we relish the expanse of a day? What happens when we do? I always think, so much can happen in a day, a week, a month, a year. You never know what's on the horizon, and how much time there is ahead of you.

Mounira Al Solh (b. 1978) is a visual artist who lives and works between Beirut and Amsterdam. Her work explores women's issues and bears witness to the impact of conflict and displacement. Her practice utilises oral documentation, multidisciplinary collaboration and wordplay to explore themes of memory and loss. Motivated by acts of sharing and storytelling, change and resistance, Al Solh strives to craft a sensory language that defies nationality and religion.

Source: Halpert, Juliana, 'Mounira Al Solh: Embroidering a Monument to Women's Stories and Sorrow', Artforum, 3 May 2022

The power of looking at just one image

'I began to visit the National Gallery in London every day during my lunch break and would stand in front of one painting for most of the hour. Every week I would choose a different picture . . . A picture changes as you look at it and changes in ways that are unexpected. I have discovered that a painting requires time. Now it takes me several months and more often than not a year before I can move on. During that period the picture becomes a mental as well as a physical location in my life.' —Hisham Matar

Today's entry is an exercise. Go to a gallery, or find a painting in a book or online. Look at just one painting. And really look. Describe what you see, write down what you think. Then look at it again tomorrow. What do you think now? Do this every day, for the whole of the next week.

Hisham Matar (b. 1970) is an acclaimed American-born British-Libyan author, essayist, memoirist and novelist. In 2017, he was awarded a Pulitzer Prize for his memoir of the search for his father, *The Return*. His most recent novel, *My Friends*, won the Orwell Prize and a National Book Critics Circle Award.

Source: Matar, Hisham, A Month in Siena, *Penguin, 2019*

Hang out; waste time; listen to some bad poetry

'I remember in the poetry world, the ones who became part of the scene were the ones who were willing to hang out. Again, it's like being in front of the canvas, you had to waste time. You had to hear some bad poetry readings, because you knew somebody was going to be there . . .' —Eileen Myles

When was the last time you heard some bad music, or saw a bad film, or art? Was it an entire waste of time, or – thinking about it in another way – did you learn something about yourself, or the person you were with, or the person you were watching? Even if the art is sometimes bad, good things can happen when you keep showing up. You never know what doors will open, or who might be there.

Eileen Myles (b. 1949) is one of the most influential living poets. Born and raised in Massachusetts, and based in New York City since 1974, they have published twenty-two books, from poetry and memoir to plays and fiction, including *Not Me*, *Chelsea Girls*, *Cool for You*, *Skies*, *The Importance of Being Iceland: Travel Essays in Art* and *Inferno: A Poet's Novel*.

Source: The Great Women Artists Podcast, *2021*

Write by hand

'I like the slowness of writing by hand.' —*Susan Sontag*

In an interview with *The Paris Review* in 1995, Susan Sontag stated, 'I write with a felt-tip pen, or sometimes a pencil, on yellow or white legal pads.' She did so because she liked the slowness of writing by hand. Then, she would type it up 'and scrawl all over that'.

What does writing by hand allow for? Not only does it slow you down, but without the busyness of today's computer screens – with tabs opening up every second, leading you astray to another article, video or story – it can also be a way to focus.

Try it. Write by hand. See how it holds your concentration.

Susan Sontag (1933–2004) was one of the most influential American critics, essayists and authors of the twentieth century. She is best known for her works of criticism, such as *Against Interpretation* and *On Photography*, and the essay 'Notes on Camp'.

Source: Hirsch, Edward, 'Susan Sontag, The Art of Fiction', The Paris Review, Issue 143, Winter 1995

Doing nothing is the beginning of something

'By understanding your own body, you understand the world. We never actually put much attention to our body, we try everything else but do that. We are constantly busy: wake up in the morning, you open your emails, you make a phone call, you check your messages, you run away, you speak with friends, you have dinners, you never sit and do absolutely nothing. And, to me, doing absolutely nothing is the beginning of something. Because [only] then when the body starts talking to you – [do you] understand what it is.' —Marina Abramović

How do you start the day? Do you look at your phone, meditate, exercise, call someone, go for a walk? Let's take a moment and plan something different for today, or tomorrow.

When you wake up, choose to spend one, five, or ten minutes doing absolutely nothing. Nothing except listening to your body. Perhaps asking it: how do I feel? What am I capable of? How will I navigate the world today? How does this relationship, or story, or task that I'm trying to tackle, sit with my body?

Doing nothing can sometimes be the most productive thing we can do. As Marina Abramović says, that can be the start of something.

Take one, five or ten minutes today – and do nothing!

Marina Abramović (b. 1946), was born in Yugoslavia (now Serbia) and is considered as a pioneer and 'warrior' of performance art. Since the beginning of her career in the 1970s, Abramović has stretched the limits of the body. Early works include *Rhythm o* (1974), which saw her declare herself as the object, and instruct the audience to use props on her as they wished. She has continued to break boundaries for the last five decades and counting.

Source: The Great Women Artists Podcast, *2022*

Delight at the world

'Love and hate are old. These words are somewhat useless. I prefer delight. Or even euphoria. Unknown but knowable states.' —Dorothea Tanning

I'd love for us to rethink our vocabulary when it comes to what we like or dislike. What if we stopped asking whether we love or hate something, and asked instead: what delights me? Who or what sends me into a state of euphoria? As Tanning says, love and hate can be such polarised extremes; why not use the in-betweens?

Dorothea Tanning (1910–2012) was an American artist who lived in Paris for much of her later life, hailed for her Surrealist-inspired paintings and soft sculptures. She was also a writer and poet, and famously said, 'Don't ask me to explain my paintings.'

Source: Jouffroy, Alain, Dorothea Tanning, *Centre National d'Art Contemporain (C.N.A.C.), 1974*

Receive something

'Something so simple as a bird call can inspire a line of inquiry in my mind about what is the purpose of the bird song, what kind of bird is it and who is it singing to. The bird – just like myself – is compelled to put something of itself into the world. The bird song and my art do not necessarily have the same purpose but we are both living creatures making small or large impacts on our environments.' —Bisa Butler

Butler reminds us that if we choose to receive something, it can have a great impact on our day, or on our lives and work. And, in reverse, if we choose to make or do something ourselves and send it out into the world, who knows the impact it might have? I love the idea that we can be going about our days and, without realising it, be bringing joy or curiosity to someone else through our way of being in the world.

Bisa Butler (b. 1973) is an American artist working in textile hailed for her vivid and vibrant portraits of subjects that weave together personal and historical narratives of Black life. From integrating members of her own family derived from old photographs, to immortalising celebrated figures from Chadwick Boseman to Frederick Douglass or the unknown subjects of Depression-era photographs, Butler's oeuvre aims, in her words, to 'tell the story – the African American side – of American life'.

Source: A note to the author, 2025

Listen to the sea

'When I was a toddler, I would walk into the sea and talk to it, talk talk talk, talking to the sea like it was my friend . . . And now when I go to the sea, I try to listen. Listen, instead of talk to it. And what does it say to you? That we're very small . . .' —Maggi Hambling

Measuring ourselves against nature, or listening to it, can be a great way to start thinking of our place in the world. How do you feel about yourself in comparison to a lake, a river, an ocean?

The sea as a subject has been a source of inspiration for centuries, whether it's J. M. W. Turner's sublime and fiery seascapes from the early nineteenth century; a politically charged Afrofuturist underwater scene by the American artist, Ellen Gallagher; or still, rippling water at twilight, with a glimmer of gold running underneath, as painted by the British artist, Celia Paul.

Take a look at Hambling's painting, *April Wave Breaking* (2009). It gets me to think about the sea's character: how alive but also how violent it can be. What does the sea mean to you, and how might you try to capture that meaning – whether by sketching or painting it, or describing it in words? You could even put together postcards of different seas by different artists for your own mini exhibition.

Maggi Hambling (b. 1945) is a British artist hailed both for her public sculpture, such as the four-metre-high *Scallop* on Aldeburgh beach for the composer Benjamin Britten, the first memorial in London for Oscar Wilde, or her *A Sculpture for Mary Wollstonecraft* at Newington Green, and paintings of people and the natural world that are held in multiple important museum collections. Hambling's work responds to the essence of human life and emotion: the simultaneous presence of chaos and control, life and death.

Source: The Great Women Artists Podcast, *2019*

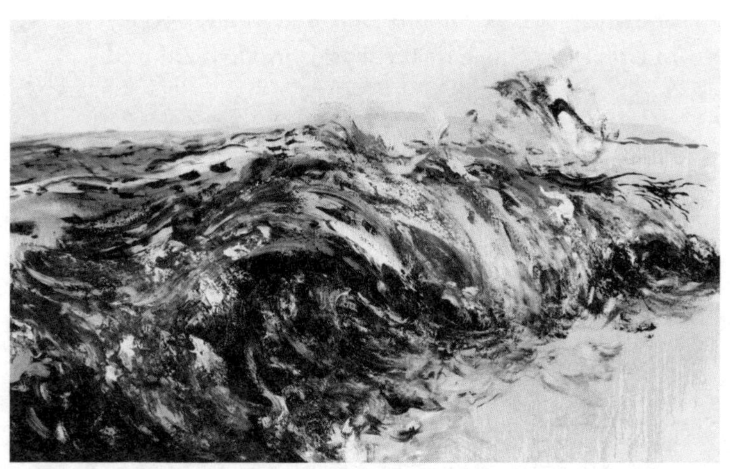

Maggi Hambling, *April Wave Breaking*, 2009

Go slowly

'I have been thinking a lot lately of how many worlds there are contained in very small spaces and how every person is really one world to himself.' —Joy Hester

Take a moment to take stock and think of all the worlds that exist around us. In a month where we are taking time, and going slower, Hester's words are a reminder to look outside yourself and recognise how much is going on – even in the smallest of spaces. So today, think about drawing a face. It could be someone you know or someone you don't. In either case, imagine the worlds inside their head.

Joy Hester (1920–60) was an Australian artist, most prolific between 1939 and 1958, who produced highly emotive, expressive and at times haunting black-ink drawings of faces, with oversized eyes, watery features and fluid-stained marks.

Source: Joy Hester to Sunday Reed, March 1946, Reed Papers, State Library of Victoria, reproduced in Burke, Janine (ed.), Dear Sun: The Letters of Joy Hester and Sunday Reed, William Heinemann Australia, 1995

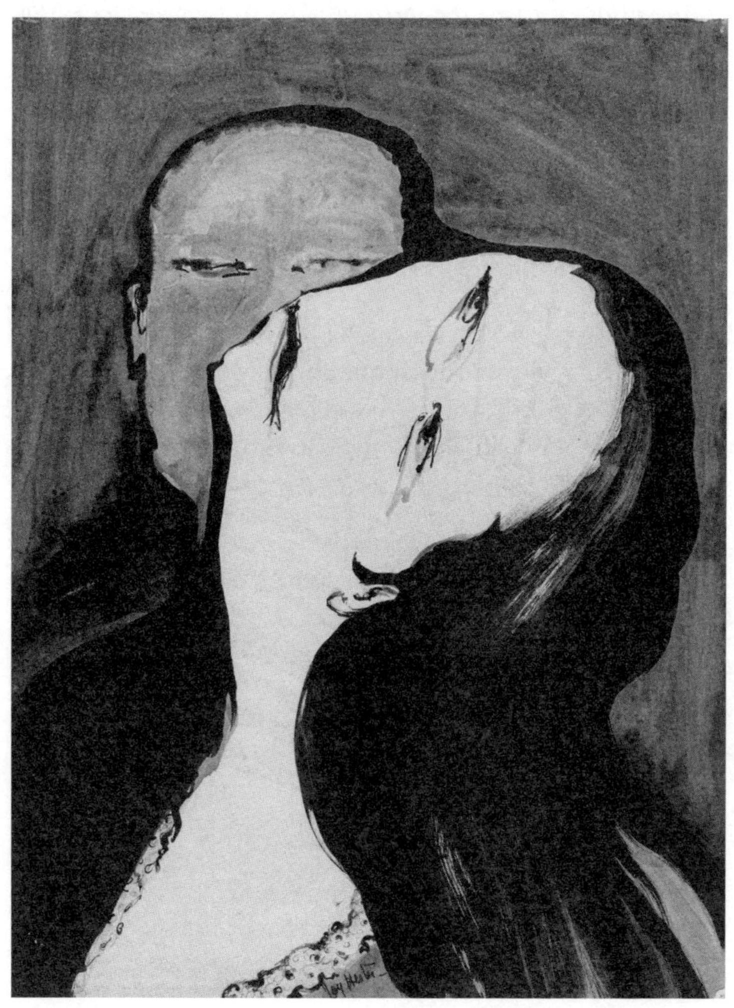

Joy Hester, *Lovers [II]*, 1956

The importance of play

'The twentieth century has begun to realise that most of life's meaning is lost without the spirit of play. In play, all that is lovely and soaring in the human spirit strives to find expression. To play is to yield oneself to a kind of magic, and to give the lie to the inconvenient world of fact, and the hideous edifice of unrelieved utility. In play the mind is prepared to accept the unimagined and incredible, to enter a world where different laws apply, to be free, unfettered.' —Eileen Agar

Eileen Agar was part of the generation of artists who lived through both world wars, who witnessed tumult and violence. In times of trouble and despair, we need to find ways to return to magic. A great way to do this is through play. To play, as Agar says, is to enter an unfettered world.

When was the last time you played something? How much of your day do you spend working, and how much do you spend playing? Make time to play today.

Eileen Agar (1899–1991) was a British artist, born in Argentina, commonly associated with the Surrealists. She is known for her work in assemblage, which devised new conversations within and between objects.

Source: Agar, Eileen, 'Am I a Surrealist?', reproduced in Rosemont, Penelope, Surrealist Women: An International Anthology, *Athlone Press, 1998*

To imagine is to envision

'It's much more fascinating to go for a swim in the sea and imagine mermaids than to say in a rational way that there are no mermaids . . .'—*Marina Warner*

As on 16 July with Jadé Fadojutimi's words about the importance of travelling to our inner worlds, the mythographer Marina Warner also reminds us that we are never too old to apply that imaginative thinking to the real world too.

So much of our world is built on imaginary structures thought up by humans anyway, from the ideas of kingship to all sorts of hierarchies that are kept in place. So why not play with the idea of things that might exist, like mermaids, when we go for a swim?

Also, it's a great way to enliven our day – we can imagine magical creatures in the forest, ghosts in castles – and play a game with our imagination as we go about our daily life. Imagination is a muscle we can strengthen, and by using it, we can perhaps even envision new structures, new principles, of our own.

Marina Warner (b. 1946) is an esteemed writer, lecturer and author of more than twenty books. She is a world specialist on myths, fairytales and ancient stories, and has written indefatigably on how these tales – some thousands of years old – still speak to, and shape, our culture today.

Source: The Great Women Artists Podcast, *2022*

Carry a pencil (or tool) at all times

'I draw daily. I always have a sketchbook . . . a pen or pencil – some drawing instruments. Creativity is not just in the four walls in the studio. It's everywhere.' —Barbara Walker

You never know when something might strike your eye, so carry the tools you need. Whether you're walking along a road, and then noticing, as Walker went on to tell me, 'a crack in the pavement that sparks a discussion in my head', or sitting on a train or bus, drawing to while away the mundane journey, you never know what might come from what you capture.

Walker's words also remind me of something Tracey Emin said – essentially that, for those who don't yet have money for paint, canvases, a studio, there is probably still enough money to buy a biro and a sketchbook, to fill with your thoughts. And later, when you are able to make art, you will have that book to remind yourself of all the art that you wanted to make. If you want to apply for art school, you will already have a portfolio, too.

So, carry those tools!

Barbara Walker (b. 1964) is a British artist who creates works on paper, paintings on canvas and large-scale charcoal wall drawings. They are filled with empathy, depth and emotion, and address the state of Black communities, their experiences and histories.

Source: The Great Women Artists Podcast, *2024; Tracey Emin in conversation with Arturo Galansino, 'Tracey Emin: Sex and Solitude', Palazzo Strozzi, 2025*

Go outside

'You cannot paint with only your little cabinet of knowledge.'
—Barbara Chase-Riboud

Be astounded by what you find beyond the confines of your four walls. Whether it's through travelling into another world and time through a book, looking up to the expanse of the sky, or by talking to people, if you want the ideas, go outside and gather them. Nothing can happen in a vacuum. Trying to figure out a character? Analyse people in the street. Working out how two colours might sit next to each other, or how someone sculpted a mouth? Go to a museum or local gallery and study a work you admire. The answers are out there: in the outside world!

Barbara Chase-Riboud (b. 1939) is an American artist who lives between Paris and Rome. Trained as an architect, Riboud has described herself as a 'poet' who is 'tied up with manufacturing objects', and is hailed for her monumental bronze, silk and wool sculptures that fuse hardness and softness. Riboud is also a celebrated writer, and has said that 'the gesture of writing is like the gesture of drawing'.

Source: Interview with Ursula *magazine, 2024, unpublished segment*

Make the most of what you've got

[On growing up in Margate in the 1960s, and the lack of 'art' available to her:] *'There was absolutely nothing. So it's not like, "Oh yeah, when I was six my mum and dad took me to the Tate for the first time", or "I remember when I went to the National Gallery when I was . . . seven". There was nothing. It was barren. And all that we had was all that we made; all that we saw; all that we created . . .'* —Tracey Emin

It can be easy to think that those who have careers as 'artists' are from a certain place, a certain background, and have a certain 'education'. But it really isn't that way at all. If anything, it's the opposite. An artist is someone who makes do with what they have. If there are cardboard boxes around, they use them. If there's poetry to be written, they grab a piece of paper.

I'm not an artist but my dream was to write about art. I didn't have a book deal or a newspaper column, but I had Instagram, which was free, and I built up my writing there. My next dream was to put on an exhibition, but I didn't have a gallery or a museum. However, I knew someone who worked at an advertising agency, and they let me 'curate' my first exhibition in their foyer. If you're at school or university, and would like to do the same, consider using the corridors, or simply repurpose the walls at home, or make an exhibition on your fridge! Try to use whatever's at hand and make of it what you will.

Tracey Emin (b. 1963) is one of the most influential British artists, looking to her life for primary material, and creating work across painting, sculpture, installation, drawing and more.

Source: Katy Hessel in conversation with Tracey Emin, TKE Studios, Margate, March 2024

Use your body – it might surprise you

'Each time I come to the mirror – drawing rather than making a painting – it's a confrontation . . . I never know what I'll find. You think I'd know myself well. But it's a new journey and I discover something new about what's happening in my body . . . I see my face as a new terrain that I am exploring with line, almost like a mapping exercise.' —Claudette Johnson

You can live in your body for however many years, but every time you come to draw it, paint it, sculpt it, or think about it, it will always be different – growing, decaying, renewing. You can make as many self-portraits as you want, but none will ever be the same. Something will always be new.

Carrying on from yesterday's quote from Tracey Emin about always using whatever is around you, and making something out of what you have – use yourself, like Johnson, who went on to say: 'I come back to myself in the studio because I'm there . . .'

Take the time to notice yourself. What can you do with your image?

Claudette Johnson (b. 1959) is a British artist considered one of the most significant figurative artists of her generation, hailed for her often large-scale, sensitively drawn figures, which range from self-portraits to those close to her. She began her artistic career as part of the BLK Art Group in the 1980s, and in 2024 was nominated for the Turner Prize.

Source: A morning tour of the Turner Prize exhibition, Tate Britain, October 2024

What does a word look like?

'What I also like about painting is, if I say a word, I can make an image that pertains to that word, and that's my ideal version.' —Jennifer Packer

Today's entry is an exercise. Think of a word. Draw it. See what you make. Is it the letters you are accentuating, or is it the sound? Does this word pertain to a certain colour, or is the word that you've chosen an actual colour? What would it look like to draw it? Would you include the letters, or would it be a shape? How would you capture the way it sounds?

If you want to go even further, try drawing a sentence, or the lyrics of a song. The inspiration we can get for our art can exist anywhere. And we never know what will come out of it. As Packer says, we can paint anything and see anything we'd like to see – but also those things that we are not sure we want to, either. See what comes out of it.

Jennifer Packer (b. 1984) is an American painter of portraits – usually of those close to her – interior scenes and still lifes. Imbued with emotion, her figures are often drenched in vivid colouring that adds to the psychological intensity of the scene.

Source: 'Jennifer Packer and Hans Ulrich Obrist Discuss the Meaning and Method of Painting Today', Cultured, 14 June 2021

Make with passion

'There has to be a sense of passion about it. To make an ideal communication, to get close to the truth of anything, you have to be able to address yourself to at least four spirits. There has to be something there for the heart. There has to be something there for the intellect. There has to be something there for sensuality and sensation. There has to be some wit, some things that are direct and clear. If you get the right amount of those vegetables into the broth, then it's satisfying to me, personally.' —Joni Mitchell

This reminds me of the first entry of the year. What makes a work of art, 'art'?

Joni Mitchell (b. 1943) is a Canadian-American singer-songwriter, one of the most celebrated musicians of the twentieth century. She is also a painter, and has designed most of her album covers.

Source: BBC Archive, '1986: Joni Mitchell on how to write good music', clip taken from Whistle Test Extra, *originally broadcast on BBC Two, 1 April 1986*

Shatter stable ideas

'I wanted to shatter stable beauty with my work.' —*Atsuko Tanaka*

Again, we are back to that notion of 'should'. Who gets to decide whether things should be 'beautiful' or not – and what does 'beautiful' in conventional or 'stable' terms even mean? Beauty can come from anywhere, including from ugliness and chaos, disorder and disarray. To fix ourselves to a conventional idea of beauty is to miss the point. Shatter stable beauty; seek out what you think is beautiful.

Write down five things that you find beautiful that shatter 'stable' ideas.

1. ____

2. ____

3. ____

4. ____

5. ____

Atsuko Tanaka (1932–2005) was a central figure of the Japanese avant-garde group, Gutai. Highly experimental, she worked across painting, performance and more.

Source: Quoted in Tiampo, Ming and Katō, Mizuho, Electrifying Art: Atsuko Tanaka, *1954–1968,* Belkin Art Gallery, 2004

Claim back what you love

'In Minas Gerais I found the colors I loved as a child. Later I was taught that they were ugly and rustic. But later I took revenge on the oppression by transferring them to my canvases: the purest blue, violet pink, bright yellow, singing green . . .'—Tarsila do Amaral

Who gets to decide what beauty is? Beauty is in the eye of the beholder. Hold on to that; know it; trust it; use it. Never let anyone tell you that something isn't beautiful. If you believe it is, then it is.

Learn from do Amaral, who accentuated the colours of her region by painting them. Not only was she honouring her region's beauty, but by transferring it into art, she ensured that it lived on – and we can see it now. What could you immortalise?

Tarsila do Amaral (1886–1973) was a Brazilian painter, one of the leading figures in defining a Brazilian modernist tradition in the 1920s. As a young woman, she went to study art in Paris, but she often found herself thinking about the landscape of Brazil.

Source: Quoted in Damian, Carol, 'Tarsila Do Amaral: Art and Environmental Concerns of a Brazilian Modernist', Woman's Art Journal, Vol. 20, No. 1, 1999

Beauty doesn't have to cost much

'Everyone deserves beauty and everyone can make it themselves. You don't have to go out and spend a million dollars, honey.'
—Karon Davis

Davis told me this in the context of the making of the Underground Museum (2012–22) – a set of four converted shopfronts in Arlington Heights, Los Angeles, that she co-ran with her now late husband, the painter Noah Davis. At first, no museum would lend artworks to them. So Noah Davis re-made 'famous' artworks, and called the exhibition 'Imitation of Wealth'. Who was to decide whether these artworks cost ten dollars, or a million dollars? They still made a beautiful space.

What beautiful thing will you make today?

Karon Davis (b. 1977) is an American artist who creates sculptures and installations of imagined and historical figures. Drawing on issues of history, race and violence in the United States, as well as her background in theatre, dance and film, Davis uses a unique plaster method, akin to Egyptian mummification practices, to sculpt entire ballets or recreations of historical events. Her life-size sculptures, covered in white plaster dust, raise questions about Western beauty standards that have been entrenched in our society since classical times.

Source: The Great Women Artists Podcast, *2023/4*

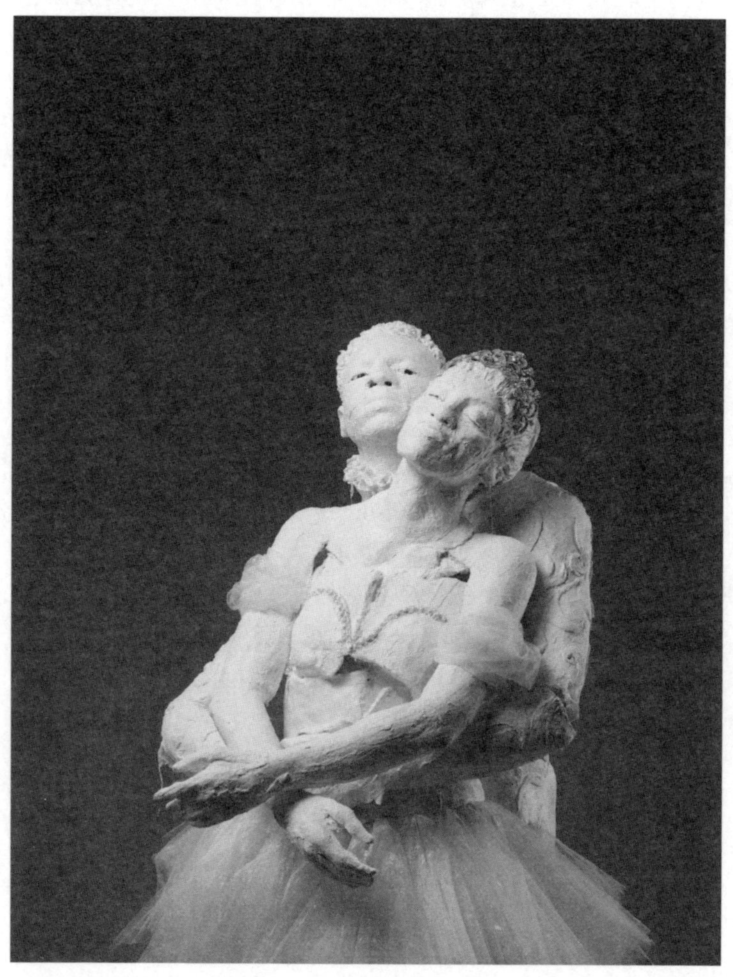

Karon Davis, *Echo & Narcissus: The Embrace*, 2023

Beauty is the mystery of life

'When I think of art, I think of beauty. Beauty is the mystery of life. It is in the mind, not in the eye. In our minds, we have an awareness of perfection that leads us on. The response to beauty is emotion. Sometimes very subtle emotions of which we are almost not aware, and sometimes our most powerful emotions . . . Beauty is very much broader than just to the eye. It is our whole, positive response to life. An artist is fortunate in that his work is the inner contemplation of beauty, of perfection in life. We cannot make anything perfectly, but with inner contemplation of perfection, we can suggest it . . .' —Agnes Martin

Beauty isn't just about what something looks like, but what it feels like, too. Instead of being led by your eye when making up your mind about whether something is beautiful or not – and looking at it purely on a surface level – think about how it makes you feel. Be led by your emotions. Trust your response through feeling. As Martin tells us, beauty is broader than just what it signifies to the eye.

Next time you're figuring out whether you think something is beautiful or not, ask yourself, how does this make me feel? What emotional response does it elicit?

Agnes Martin (1912–2004) was a Canadian-born artist, who lived mostly in Taos, New Mexico. She was known for her six-foot-square canvases made with subtle pencil marks or serene bands of diluted colour.

Source: Martin, Agnes, faculty lecture, Skowhegan School of Painting & Sculpture, 3 July 1987 (audio recording)

Look before it goes

'For 5,000 years, artists of the past have tried to input into their works of art a variety of different qualities. [. . .] But there is one quality they have never used, and that is the quality of love and tenderness that we human beings have for what does not last.

For instance, we have love and tenderness for childhood because we know it will not last. We have love and tenderness for our own life because we know it will not last.

For instance, if someone were to tell you, "Oh, look on the right, there is a rainbow." You will never answer, "I will look at it tomorrow."' —Jeanne-Claude and Christo

Married couple Jeanne-Claude and Christo (who were born on the same day – 13 June 1935) spent their long careers creating spectacular temporary public artworks: from surrounding entire islands with bright pink fabric (see overleaf), wrapping trees in a park in Switzerland, to installing a giant orange curtain across a valley and over a highway in Colorado. I like to think of their works treasuring, protecting or even mummifying the land, dispatching it to a higher place.

Not only did they give prominence to the land, but these public artworks also encouraged a communal way of looking, emphasising the power of what happens when people come together, without hierarchy and as an invitation to all.

Jeanne-Claude (1935–2009, Morocco) and **Christo** (1935–2020, Bulgaria) were a husband-and-wife artist duo acclaimed for their large-scale, site-specific environmental installations that took place all over the world.

Source: Pagliasotti, James, 'Interview with Christo and Jeanne-Claude', originally published in Eye-Level, *4 January 2002*

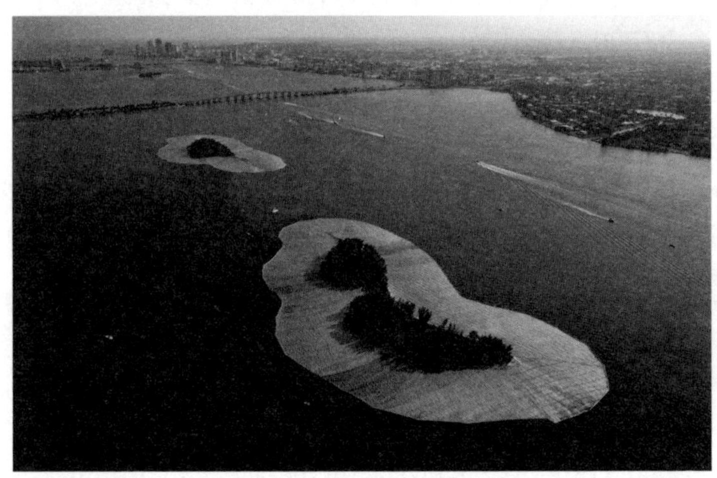

Christo and Jeanne-Claude, *Surrounded Islands, Biscayne Bay, Greater Miami, Florida,* 1980–83

Marvel at nature's beauty

'But I do love how certain aspects of nature are just beyond the most beautiful piece of artwork – fish scales, beetle wings, cumulus clouds, live coral and elephant skin . . .'—*Wangechi Mutu*

The world can look familiar; humans have been looking at it for millennia. But do you ever just stop, and realise the harmony that exists around us, the intricate web of humans, animals, plants? How can we try to grasp the harmonious beauty that nature constantly shows us? In a month like August, take stock. Learn from nature. Take note of its shapes, colours, sounds and forms.

The Kenyan-American artist **Wangechi Mutu** (b. 1972) is hailed for her collages, sculptures and installations, which often fuse an array of features or components to make up a hybridised female figure.

Source: An interview with the author, 2020

Place things with care

'Filling a space in a beautiful way. That's what art means to me . . . I liked to convey to them [her students] the idea that art is important in everyday life. I wanted them to learn the principle: that when you buy a pair of shoes or place a window in the front of a house or address a letter or comb your hair, consider it carefully, so that it looks well.' —*Georgia O'Keeffe*

Just as Jeanne-Claude and Christo show us that art can be displayed anywhere – and Barbara Walker proves that inspiration can come from something as unexpected as a pavement crack – O'Keeffe reminds us that we can live artfully in smaller, everyday moments.

To fill a space in a beautiful way is to fill your day with beauty.

Georgia O'Keeffe (1887–1986) was one of the most significant American artists of the twentieth century and a pioneer of modernism. Her career spanned seven decades and encompassed luminous paintings of New York City skyscrapers, magnified depictions of flowers and the expansive landscapes of New Mexico.

Source: Robinson, Roxana, Georgia O'Keeffe: A Life, HarperCollins, 1989

When should you ask yourself the big questions?

'I ask myself all the big questions, every Sunday.' —*Miranda July*

If it works for Miranda July, then it might just work for you! Which day of the week will you ask yourself the big questions: What is my purpose? How can I make the world a better place? What meal am I going to prepare for someone this week?

Miranda July (b. 1974) is an American filmmaker, artist and novelist. She wrote and directed the 2020 film *Kajillionaire* and wrote the acclaimed novel *All Fours,* published in 2024. Her artworks include *Eleven Heavy Things*, a sculpture garden created for the 2009 Venice Biennale.

Source: Quoted in Crompton, Abigail, Truth Bomb, *Thames & Hudson, 2020*

Take a moment to listen

'I detest a day of no work, no music, no poetry.'
—Barbara Hepworth

Hepworth, in addition to being a great sculptor, was also a pianist. She said that music gave her 'the need for dancing', which 'she linked to the physicality of carving as a means of expression'. How can your creative outputs intertwine in different areas of your life? Even if you might not spend every day 'working' on something creative, make sure you spend part of it listening to a piece of music, reading a poem or whatever works for you.

Barbara Hepworth (1903–75) was a giant of British sculpture. Born in Wakefield, Yorkshire, she carried with her the rhythms of the Northern hills. From 1939, she was based in St Ives, a fishing village in Cornwall famed for its rocky beaches, and the weathered lines and ocean swirls of her surroundings made their way into her highly textured sculptures. Working in an interior and exterior environment, Hepworth interacted with the natural forms of the landscape, as well as analysing the many forms that the human body can take.

Source: Hepworth, Barbara, A Pictorial Autobiography, *Adams & Dart, 1970; revised 1978 (now published by Tate Publishing)*

Get personal

'As for me, I see both the beauty and the dark side of things; the loveliness of cornfields and full sails, but the ruin as well. And I see them at the same time, at once ecstatic at the beauty of things, and chary of that ecstasy.

The Japanese have a phrase for this dual perception: mono no aware. It means "beauty tinged with sadness," for there cannot be any real beauty without the indolic whiff of decay.

For me, living is the same thing as dying, and loving is the same thing as losing, and this does not make me a madwoman; I believe it can make me better at living, and better at loving, and, just possibly, better at seeing.' —Sally Mann

As we near the end of a month thinking about beauty, let's take a moment to reflect upon its meaning with the American photographer Sally Mann. Hailed for her images of nature in the American South, or intimate portrayals of her children, Mann gets me to realise that 'beauty' is something that is alive. While her scenes are of something beautiful – like the youth of a human, or the shape of a tree – they are also of something ephemeral. It seems Mann is trying to freeze a moment so precious, because, by its very nature, it will not last forever. As she wrote: 'for there cannot be any real beauty without the indolic whiff of decay'.

By understanding that something cannot last forever, how can you appreciate its beauty?

Sally Mann (b. 1951) is an American artist who works in photography. Often using an 8x10 bellows camera, she makes dreamlike and hazy images that chime with her interest in memory and decay. A celebrated writer, Mann is the author of *Hold Still: A Memoir with Photographs* (2015) and *Art Work: On the Creative Life* (2025), and is the subject of two documentaries: *Blood Ties* (1994) and *What Remains* (2006).

Source: Sally Mann, Hold Still (Little, Brown, 2015)

Resolutions for the next lap of the year

*'Here are my resolutions for the next 3 months; the next lap of
the year.
First, to have none. Not to be tied.
Second, to be free & kindly with myself, not goading it to parties:
to sit rather privately reading in the studio.
To make a good job of The Waves. [. . .]
To stop irritation by the assurance that nothing is worth
irritation. [. . .]
Then – well the chief resolution is the most important – not to
make resolutions. Sometimes to read, sometimes not to read. To go
out yes – but stay at home in spite of being asked. As for clothes,
I think to buy good ones.'* —Virginia Woolf

The last day of August can sometimes feel like the ultimate Sunday
night. But fear not! It can also be the dawn of the final third of the
year, a chance to pause, reflect and think up new resolutions – or, like
Woolf, have none. What resolutions will you choose for the next lap of
the year? Write them down.

Virginia Woolf (1882–1941) is considered one of the most important authors of the twentieth
century, famed for her nonlinear approaches to narrative. Her acclaimed books and essays
include *Mrs Dalloway* (1925), *To the Lighthouse* (1927), *Orlando: A Biography* (1928), *A Room of
One's Own* (1929) and *The Waves* (1931).

*Source: Diary entry, Friday 2 January 1931, Woolf, Virginia; Olivier Bell, Anne and McNeillie,
Andrew (eds.),* The Diary of Virginia Woolf: Volume 4, 1931–35, *Granta Books, 2023*

SEPTEMBER

Time

September can feel like the world is going back to school – and that can be exciting! It's another moment to take stock, to recognise how much we've changed. But even years after we've left education, the 'September feeling' can still lead to tension and anxiety as well as anticipation. How do we find our way through these moments of pressure and focused energy? Are we doing the 'right' thing at the 'right' age? Where are we supposed to be and where are we actually? Are we supposed to be doing anything at all?

Artists can help us remember our own body clocks, and that we are always on our own paths. They show us that time doesn't have to be linear. Even in the busiest times of the year, we can step outside the daily pressures and release ourselves from too much expectation of what we 'should' be doing – unlike our time at school.

During this month, which can be full of intensity, we're going to look at the many facets of time, discover ways in which to deal with our fears, and remember that we can keep learning at any age. Wonder is a muscle that we must keep exercising: the more we do it, the stronger it becomes.

Reject the idea that time is linear

'Linear time is a Western invention, time is not linear, it is a marvellous tangle, where, at any moment, points can be selected and solutions invented, without beginning or end.' —Lina Bo Bardi

It's liberating to recognise that time is different for everyone and everything. And just look around you: everywhere there will be people, nature, buildings and objects made at different times, tangled together.

The architect Lina Bo Bardi knew this all too well. In 1968, she upended centuries' worth of wall-based exhibition displays in her design of the Museu de Arte de São Paulo (MASP). In a radical move that married the old and the new, she set each historic artwork within two panes of glass then wedged it into a minimalist concrete block, displaying the artworks freestanding in the gallery space – not hung on the walls. Not only did this expose each work's back as well as its front, but allowed for myriad artworks to be seen simultaneously, collapsing all sense of linear viewing and linear time.

If you are ever worried about something happening at the wrong time in your life, or that things aren't happening fast enough, remember that if everything happened to everyone at the same time, the world wouldn't be – as Bo Bardi says – this 'marvellous tangle'.

Lina Bo Bardi (1914–92), born in Italy, was one of the leading architectural visionaries of the twentieth century. She was instrumental in the development of Brazil in the 1950s and 60s, galvanising new ways to display art through time.

Source: Bo Bardi, Lina, 'Annotazioni personali', in Carvalho Ferraz, Marcello (ed.), Lina Bo Bardi, *Istituto Lina Bo e P. M. Bardi, 1994 (p. 327)*

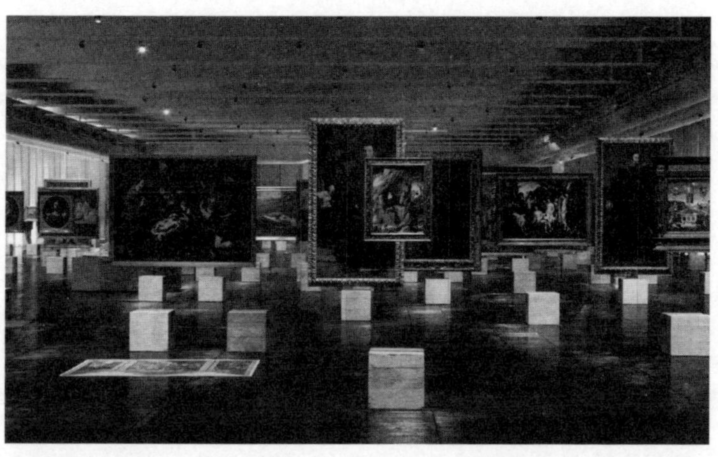

Lina Bo Bardi, interior view at MASP, São Paolo

Forget about age

'I never feel age . . . If you have creative work, you don't have age or time.' —*Louise Nevelson*

The wonderful thing about doing creative work, in whatever field you choose, is that you will always connect to others, despite age, status, or anything.

Say you are a teenager, and you are speaking to someone in their nineties about your shared love of art, or a favourite song or film. In that moment, there is no need to think about the gap in years or what you do or did for a living. How *could* you feel age? You are bonded by something so much greater – something profound. And so art can bring us together in ways that transcend age or time.

Louise Nevelson (1899–1988) was a Ukrainian-born, American sculptor known for her monochromatic, architectural wall sculptures amassed from found, recycled and discarded objects, from bedposts to bannisters.

Source: Charles Osgood interview with Louise Nevelson, CBS News, originally broadcast 6 August 1981

Art doesn't have a retirement plan

'Bankers and dentists can always tell you what they plan to do when they retire, but artists never can . . .' —*Lynn Barber*

An artist's life is not linear, especially when it comes to a 'career'. It doesn't work in the same way as corporate structures, where you are supposed to 'rise' to the top. It looks different – more lateral.

With art there is no handbook, or retirement plan. All you can do is keep going.

This is why the British journalist Lynn Barber loves interviewing artists, because they have no idea of what they'd do if they 'stopped work'.

What role do you have in your life that you will never be able to retire from? What do you love doing so much that time just slips away when you're doing it?

Lynn Barber (b. 1944) is a British journalist who has worked across numerous newspapers and has interviewed the likes of Salvador Dalí and Tracey Emin. Her memoir, *An Education*, documented the affair she had as a sixteen-year-old girl with an older conman in 1960s London.

Source: An interview with the author, Hatchards Piccadilly, November 2024

Keep making, keep dreaming

'As an artist you can go on and on . . . you can just continue to create as much as you want.' —*Senga Nengudi*

Due to women artists being overlooked by the history books and galleries for so long, many were well into their later life before institutions began to give them recognition – but they were still making, still lighting their own fire.

For example, Alma Thomas – a high school teacher for thirty-five years, who always made art – was eighty when she had her first major solo exhibition at the Whitney Museum of American Art in 1972, becoming the first Black American woman to do so.

And the Cuban-born artist, Carmen Herrera, was 101 before she received her first major museum solo show, also at the Whitney, in 2016.

Keep making, keep dreaming; you never know what's ahead. It could even come after you've had an entirely different career.

Senga Nengudi (b. 1943) is an American visual artist, curator and educator. She makes work that challenges what it is like to live in a body.

Source: Senga Nengudi: 'As human beings we're fragile, yet we're so sturdy', *Henry Moore Foundation, 2023 (video)*

Think like an artist, no matter what you are doing

'Be true to yourself. You can be working in a café, or painting and decorating, but if you're still thinking like an artist, it will still come out.'—Rachel Whiteread

'Don't lose hope because things are difficult,' as Whiteread continued. 'Keep enriched and keep a dialogue going . . .' Whatever your profession or situation, you can still think artistically. How can you incorporate artistic thinking into what you are doing?

Rachel Whiteread (b. 1963) is a British artist who works across sculpture and drawing, in mediums ranging from concrete to resin, and in scales from minuscule to colossal. Discussing how her work gives, in her words, 'authority to forgotten things', Whiteread transforms familiar objects and buildings into ghostly replicas in the form of casts. Her sculptures have provided a commentary on social and political changes, reflecting a sense of impermanence and loss.

Source: Artist Rachel Whiteread Gives Advice to Young Artists, *Louisiana Channel, Louisiana Museum of Modern Art, 2022 (video)*

Find a routine that works for you

'Nowadays I try to start at 10.30 in the morning and carry on until 6.30 in the evening. I always have a rest after lunch. I've done that since I was a little girl growing up in Portugal. I eat two rice-cake sandwiches for lunch, full of salad, and a bit of ham or cheese, and an apple. I drink peppermint tea. When I have finished work for the day I enjoy one glass of champagne.' —Paula Rego

Routine can feel restricting, but repetition – and improvements through repetition – can feel uplifting. It is through practice and engagement that we can make our days alive. Create a routine that helps you live, but, like Rego, do something at the end of your day that you can enjoy. The most important aspect of love is to love oneself. What treat will you enjoy today?

Paula Rego (1935–2022) was a British artist, who was born in Portugal. For over seven decades, she made paintings, pastels, drawings and sculptures that dealt with secrets, desires, fears; family dynamics and art history; and, using stories as a framework, upended fairytales, myths, or passages from the Bible. Through her highly political work, Rego fought for reproductive rights and the rights for women, and stood against fascism in Portugal and Salazar's colonial wars.

Source: Rego, Paula, 'Where I work: artist Paula Rego's north London studio', Guardian, 17 December 2014

Do what makes sense to you

'It wasn't like an "I have to succeed" feeling; it was more like an "I have to make this right now". Maybe it's like this for a lot of artists and makers, writers, thinkers; it was how the world would make sense to me. And it always has been, even as a little kid. The experiences were made whole by reflecting on them. And that was a way of sharing it and making it whole for myself.' —Zoe Leonard

One of the most continuously profound works from the last few decades is Leonard's *I want a president* (1992), a statement made at the height of the AIDS crisis, ahead of the then-US presidential election.

What was originally intended to be published in an underground LGBT magazine, but was instead circulated among friends, has resurfaced in recent years. Part of the statement reads:

> *I want a dyke for president. I want a person with aids for president and I want a fag for vice president and I want someone with no health insurance and I want someone who grew up in a place where the earth is so saturated with toxic waste that they didn't have a choice about getting leukemia [. . .] I want to know why this isn't possible. I wanted to know why we started learning somewhere down the line that a president is always a clown: always a john and never a hooker. Always a boss and never a worker, always a liar, always a thief and never caught.*

Sometimes we just have to make work, there and then. You never know how something might speak in years to come.

Zoe Leonard (b. 1961) is an American artist based in New York City, working across installation, photography and sculpture. She often uses repetition and sequencing to trace – and focus on – an image or object through time, and to see meaning in what might at first seem familiar. This can include photographing the same place or entity, whether it be a riverbank damaged by climate change, clouds out of a window, buildings or people. By using subtle shifts in perspective, or the changing of scale, she gets us to look closer and deeper – away from the overwhelming world around us; and to think about the transient nature of our own reality.

Source: Leonard, Zoe, 'Aerials', via Studio International, *2018*

Tap into those magic hours

'I try to get at least two good hours of painting a day. The trouble is there's often several hours' preamble to reach those magic few hours and sometimes you never reach it and the day feels like a dud; but of course it's not, it moves you on somehow, even if the work inevitably goes in the bin.' —*Christina Kimeze*

This resonates with me so much. It's easy to think that you can sit somewhere all day and concentrate, and perhaps occasionally you can. But most of the time, it's those key 'magic' hours that you have, when it's like entering another universe. The work pours out of you. Sometimes the only thing you can do is hold out. You still have to show up for the day to find the hours. There might just be a couple of truly productive hours a day, but when you're in them, there's nothing better.

Christina Kimeze (b. 1986) is a London-based artist known for her figurative scenes filled with vivid colours and lush palm and wing-like forms. Often depicting the partitions to other worlds or thresholds between two places, such as the terrestrial and the celestial, the living and the dead, Kimeze's works are filled with fluidity, but also ambiguity.

Source: A note to the author, 2024

Look at failure

'Dear Obscurity.' —Nicole Eisenman

As we learnt on 1 September, life is not linear. We can find love or success – or whatever it is we are looking for – when we are young or old; we can lose it and regain it; get lost and found again.

We can look to artists to learn how to deal with those moments when we lose, to remind us that we are never the only one – even though sometimes it can feel that way.

Take the American artist Nicole Eisenman. She became very successful (in art-world terms) earlier on in her career in the 1990s, featuring in lots of museum shows, and able to sell her work well. But then, after a few years, that success slipped away.

In that moment of feeling like 'Obscurity' (as if it were a character), Eisenman created a painting called *From Success to Obscurity* (2004; overleaf). It pictures a figure made out of rocks (perhaps representing the permanence of 'Obscurity'), looking sad and worried, hunched over a letter – perhaps from their past self, 'Success'?

Nicole Eisenman (b. 1965) is a French-born American artist working across painting, sculpture, film and installation. Beginning her career in New York City in the 1990s, she has made work that has been an astute commentary on the progression, downfall and chaos of the twenty-first century. Constantly referencing art history in her paintings, she merges characters and scenarios from the past, present and future, to hold a mirror up to the absurdity of current times.

Source: From Success to Obscurity, *painting, 2004*

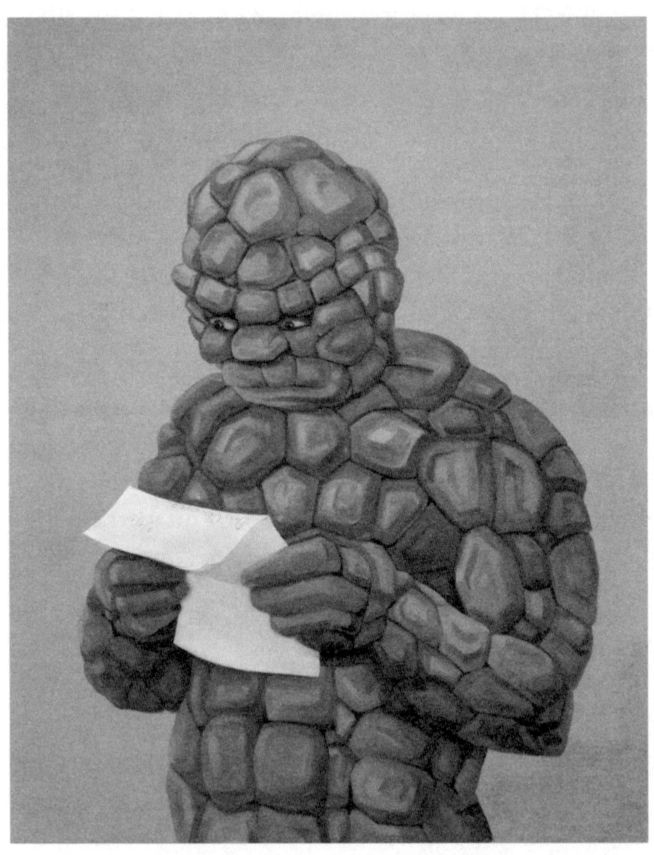

Nicole Eisenman, *From Success to Obscurity*, 2004

How to deal with the pang of jealousy

'I'm a human. So sometimes I see things that other people have done or gotten. I'll have a pang of jealousy. But is it a pang of jealousy? If it sits with me, I ask myself a couple of questions. One is – do I actually want that same thing? If the answer is yes, OK, how do I get that thing? Does that thing feel achievable in XY time? If it does, let's figure out the steps that you need to take to make that happen. Because at the end of the day, for your own self-esteem, for your own heart, you want to be able to be happy for other people's successes. Other people's successes are not taken from yours.' —Michaela Yearwood-Dan

Write down something that gives you that pang of jealousy, and work through it, as Yearwood-Dan suggests.

Michaela Yearwood-Dan (b. 1994) is a London-based artist working across painting and ceramics. She creates lush, vividly coloured works in the language of abstraction that draw on botanical motifs and are infused with meditations through text.

Source: A conversation with the author, 2025

What will you see when you go back?

'I like that quality that, when you look at a work of art, you somehow get an image immediately. And then you have time later, if you have the inclination, which I think maybe only 10 per cent of the world's population has, to look at it later, closer, or to think about it. Different things reveal themselves, depending on what's in your own head.' —Vija Celmins

It's good to continue to take in new things, but what happens when we return to look at something, or someone, again after a period of distance? Celmins reminds us that it's good to look back, to revisit, reread, because when we do, different ideas can reveal themselves.

Vija Celmins (b. 1938) was born in Latvia and moved to Indianapolis, USA, aged ten. As a young girl, she collected comic books and picture playing cards ('because I couldn't speak English'), and looked to images as a form of language. Eventually, photographs, and later scientific images, would become the source material for her art. One of the few women painters associated with Pop Art, Celmins is also hailed for her powers of observation, resulting in the exquisite details of her artworks, usually done in series (spider webs, seas, starry night skies).

Source: Oral history interview with Vija Celmins, Archives of American Art, Smithsonian Institution, 11 February–15 October 2009

Everything changes

'Nothing is absolute. Everything changes, everything moves, everything revolves.' —*Frida Kahlo*

To think that life will stay the same is not to embrace its wonder.

Frida Kahlo (1907–54) was a Mexican artist remembered for her self-portraits imbued with vibrant colours that address every emotion. Although spending much of her life in physical and emotional agony – as a child she had polio; in her teens she was involved in a bus crash that left her body shattered; as an adult she was in a tumultuous relationship with the artist Diego Rivera – Kahlo, through art, transformed pain into beauty, from painting tears like white crystals, to depicting a fluted column that thrusts through her body as a stand-in for a spine, keeping her head held high, queen-like, and alive.

Source: Kahlo, Frida, The Diary of Frida Kahlo: An Intimate Self-portrait, *Harry N. Abrams, 1995*

How do you allocate your time?

'Time is how you spend your love.' —*Nick Laird*

How do you spend your time? With whom, and doing what? Are you doing enough of what you love? In a month of busyness, remember that time is a precious resource to invest in people or projects. Could you take even fifteen minutes less a day on your phone, and fifteen minutes more with something or someone you love?

Nick Laird (b. 1975) is a Northern Irish poet, author, screenwriter and critic.

Source: Laird, Nick, 'The Last Saturday in Ulster' (poem), in To a Fault, *Faber & Faber, 2005*

Refuse the 'signature image'

'In my family, either you went along with what they were doing or you revolted. I felt the most important thing I could do was establish my complexity. If I put a retrospective up twenty-five years ago, it would have looked like a group show to most people. There has always been and maybe there will always be a tremendous pressure on artists to have the signature image. Now they call it the branding image, I suppose. I decided to refuse that as a possibility for me. I needed to have as many different images of myself out there as possible.' —Lorraine O'Grady

In response to someone who made a false and cruel claim that modern art 'doesn't have anything to do with Black people', O'Grady, on a glitteringly sunny day in 1983, rented a giant float with a gold frame, and took her camera to Harlem's African American Day parade. She instructed fifteen performers to hold up gold frames to people's faces in the crowds, to demonstrate that they belonged inside the frame.

Just as her comment tells us, how can anyone define what we are, and where we should belong? Embrace all perspectives, hear from all different voices. They make up much more than just one.

Lorraine O'Grady (1934–2024) was a celebrated artist, writer and critic, working across performance and installation, who used her art to critique systems of power and to make sure everyone felt that they had a place in art.

Source: St Felix, Doreen, 'Lorraine O'Grady Has Always Been a Rebel', The New Yorker, 29 September 2022

How do you see the smaller elements in the bigger picture?

'[I don't] consciously think, if I draw this, it will be that [but then I see] them come together . . . and it's kind of like living a life, right? You live your life and you look back at parts and they kind of accumulate meaning that in moments you won't have known, and then you put it together.' —Somaya Critchlow

It's so easy to think in terms of the big picture but practising art – or any other creative output – every day, even if just by making small, disconnected drawings, is essential training.

When we look back at our life, we might think about it in years, or even decades. But the reality is that every day was different. As Critchlow says, it's like life. How do you measure it? It's not 'one' life – it's made up of thousands – millions! – of different moments, emotions, segments, conversations, journeys. You might not realise that it's one life as you live it. It's only when it comes together at the end that you do.

How can we make the most of the moment to moment? One way would be to record, at the end of a day, the ways in which your day has been unique, building up a picture of time.

Somaya Critchlow (b. 1993) lives and works in London. Working predominantly in oil paint, graphite and ink, she is known for paintings and drawings that often depict the nude or semi-nude female body. Drawing on a wide range of influences, including the Old Master painters, the films of David Lynch and the writing of Angela Carter, Critchlow works at both miniature and large scale.

Source: The Great Women Artists Podcast, *2021*

Face the fear

'I'm frightened all the time . . . Scared to death. But I've never let it stop me. Never!' —Georgia O'Keeffe

Fear can sometimes be the only thing keeping you back. What do you want to do? Why won't you do it? Look to tomorrow for a way to face that fear.

Georgia O'Keeffe (1887–1986) was one of the most significant American artists of the twentieth century and a pioneer of modernism. Her career spanned seven decades and encompassed luminous paintings of New York City skyscrapers, magnified depictions of flowers and the expansive landscapes of New Mexico.

Source: Kotz, Mary Lynn, 'Georgia O'Keeffe at 90', ARTnews, December 1977

Draw the fear

'I paint to give a face to fear.' —*Paula Rego*

Following on from yesterday, Rego knew the power of art to help us process and exorcise demons. When I spoke to her son, Nick Willing, he told me that, as a kid, when he was scared or suffering, his mother would get him to draw his fear: 'She'd say to me, paint a picture of it. I want to see what it feels like.'

Paula Rego (1935–2022) was a British artist, who was born in Portugal. For over seven decades, she made paintings, pastels, drawings and sculptures that dealt with secrets, desires, fears; family dynamics and art history; and, using stories as a framework, upended fairytales, myths, or passages from the Bible. Through her highly political work, Rego fought for reproductive rights and the rights for women, and stood against fascism in Portugal and Salazar's colonial wars.

Source: De Lacerda, Alberto, 'Paula Rego nas Belas-Artes', Diário de Notícias, *25 December 1965*

Embrace the failure

'Failure is such a great territory to learn because if you don't risk, you will never go anywhere.' —*Marina Abramović*

Risk! Fail! Risk again. Fail again. Name one artist who didn't make a mistake.

No one gets everything right all the time, not even your heroes. The best thing we can do is acknowledge that something we did was a mistake. By learning from it, something better will come.

Marina Abramović (b. 1946), was born in Yugoslavia (now Serbia) and is considered as a pioneer and 'warrior' of performance art. Since the beginning of her career in the 1970s, Abramović has stretched the limits of the body. Early works include *Rhythm 0* (1974), which saw her declare herself as the object, and instruct the audience to use props on her as they wished. She has continued to break boundaries for the last five decades and counting.

Source: Abramović, Marina; Warsh, Larry (ed.), Abramović-isms, *Princeton University Press, 2024*

Crash the system

'The early challenge was getting somebody to show my work, because nobody would. The way I solved that was that I finished my degree at San Francisco State, but I didn't finish it in the art department. I did my master's thesis on art criticism. In order to do art criticism, I created three different fictional critics and they each had different names. [. . .] These three critics would write in varying styles for very different kinds of magazines [. . .] But one thing that they had in common was that they would write about Lynn Hershman and Lynn Hershman's work. So, I finally had all these reviews about my work, which I took to galleries, and that's how I got my first show.' —Lynn Hershman Leeson

Sometimes, like the American artist Lynn Hershman Leeson, a little imagination is required to get our work out there.

Take heart from the fact that traditional ways of doing things are not the only routes available through life.

Lynn Hershman Leeson (b. 1941) is an American multimedia artist and filmmaker, known for pushing all boundaries with her innovative media work that investigates the relationship between humans and technology, identity and surveillance.

Source: Turner, Christine, 'Lynn Hershman Leeson couldn't give up on being an artist', Art21, November 2023

Don't take no for an answer

'WHEN YOU HEAR "NO", WORK LIKE HELL UNTIL YOU HEAR "YES"!!!!!' —Judith Bernstein

What the legendary artist Judith Bernstein said. Keep knocking down those doors! Sometimes persistence over time is what the situation requires.

Judith Bernstein (b. 1942), a pioneer of feminist art in the 1970s, is a New York-based artist hailed for her provocative, larger-than-life phallic drawings and paintings. She lives in her downtown Manhattan studio which is full to the brim of her collected items, from stickers to stuffed toys, which she has acquired over the last few decades.

Source: A note to the author, 2025

Interrogate greatness

'I mean, what constitutes greatness? What is that thing?'
—Barbara Kruger

Society's assumptions about what greatness is, might not equal what 'greatness' can actually be – especially when we think about how many histories have been erased while others have been prioritised. As Kruger continued, 'This is not to devalue extraordinary abilities, skills, intelligence, whatever, but to just talk about the inflationary rhetoric that really works to make some people visible and others not.'

Essentially: don't be put off by somebody else's idea of what 'greatness' means. What is/was considered 'great' can be changed. And know that it's never too late to question something. No matter your age, you always have a right to call something out. The idea of timelessness can sometimes be used to keep certain boundaries up – or certain people out.

Barbara Kruger (b. 1945) is an American artist who works within an iconic visual language, made up of words and images, that is graphic, bold and easily identifiable, and borrows from advertising and other media.

Source: The Great Women Artists Podcast, *2024*

Pass it on

'A quote that I saw in a museum some years back, I think it was by Edgar Degas. He said that art is not what you see, but what you make others see. And so I think to me, what it means is, we see quilts and other people see art.' —Mary Margaret Pettway, Gee's Bend Quiltmakers

The Gee's Bend Quiltmakers have made dazzling and jazzy quilts from all sorts of materials for four generations (see overleaf). They see their work as practical; other people see them as 'art'. What do you see?

Mary Margaret Pettway (b. 1963) is a fourth-generation Gee's Bend quilter. She has taught quilting workshops throughout the American southeast and is a regular instructor at Black Belt Treasures Cultural Arts Center in Camden, Alabama. She is a member of Gee's Bend Quilting Collective – an all-female, Black American group based in Alabama, USA, to promote and market quilts from the community of Gee's Bend. They make their colourful quilts for a multitude of reasons.

Source: The Great Women Artists Podcast, *2021*

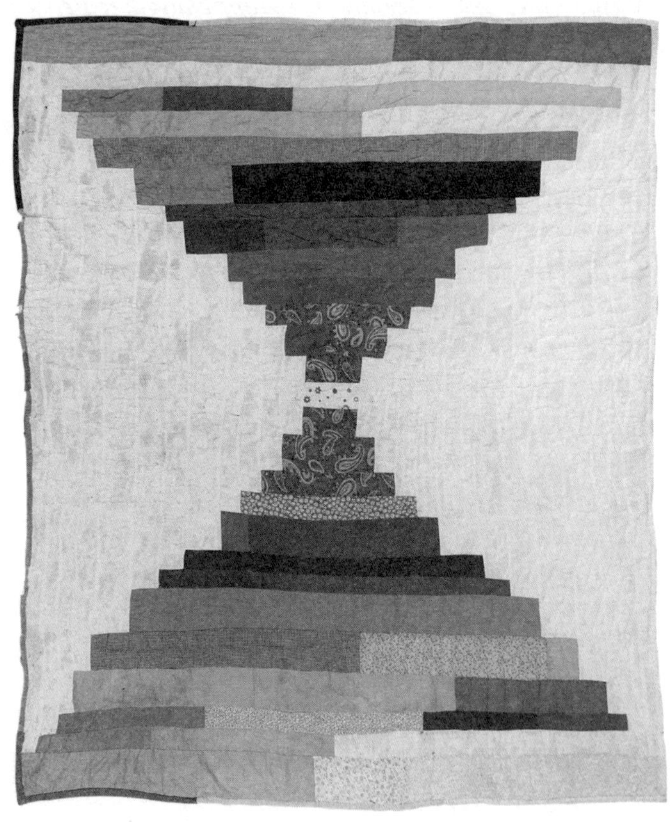

Loretta Pettway, *Log Cabin – Single Block 'Courthouse Steps' variation (Local Name: 'Bricklayer')*, 1959

Find your voice

'I initially painted because I had no voice, or didn't know where to find it.' —Christine Sun Kim

Christine Sun Kim was brought up in a signing household. Discouraged from pursuing a career in art, she initially studied graphic design and when she inquired about taking studio art classes, she was told she had to join classes that already had Deaf students in them. Eventually, she did enrol in an MFA programme, where she began to explore what kind of artist she would be. Sun Kim initially painted, and began by borrowing from other artists' narratives, motifs, styles. 'I wanted to know how they found their voice,' she said. Eventually she focused on sound.

How do any of us know how to find our voice? We start by looking to others, and eventually we might find our own. Take the time to discover your own inspirations.

Christine Sun Kim (b. 1980) is an American artist based in Berlin. Her practice explores the role and politics of sound in society, looking at how oral languages operate as social currency. She creates drawings, large-scale murals, videos, installations and performances, employing musical notation, written language and infographics, American Sign Language (ASL), and the body.

Source: Sun Kim, Christine, 'On what listening looks like', The Gentlewoman, *Autumn/Winter 2021*

Be in sync with your space

'The time of the studio, in which I move most often, is mysterious for me. It's not linear time. It's made of accelerations, visions, but also times of slowing down, which can last weeks, months, years. Time can be light and heavy. The time of exhibitions is in opposition to studio time, and requires artworks to leave the studio on a specific date. I fight against outside time to stay in my magical time, that of the studio. It's essential to always be in tune with studio time.' —Claire Tabouret

What is your equivalent of Tabouret's studio? From a bedroom to an office – all our spaces have both heavy and light time. We operate in them in different ways, but the best thing is when we're in sync with them. Being in a space which is operating at a different speed to the one we're in is like wearing a glove that doesn't fit – or being with someone we have outgrown.

Think about what you could do to be in sync with your space: how can the space help you be present; could you change the placement of the furniture, put quotes on the wall?

Claire Tabouret (b. 1981) is a French artist known for portraits of figures executed in her distinct washy style. Not existing in a specific place or time, Tabouret's scenes, whether portrayed in daylight or in the depths of night, are full of mystery.

Source: Claire Tabouret in conversation with Théo de Luca, in L'urgence et la patience, *Almine Rech Editions, 2021*

Stop time

'What I am sure of is that we seek out ways to make time stop. That only happens in moments of total attention, which is why we pursue them . . . My only interest in dealing with time is to find ways to make it stop. Because when it doesn't stop, you're in boredom.' —Anne Carson

What could you be so absorbed by, that time stops?

Anne Carson (b. 1950) is a Canadian poet, essayist, professor of Classics, and celebrated translator of the ancient Greek poet Sappho, as well as the writers Euripides, Simonides, Sophocles and more.

Source: Dwyer, Kate, 'Throwing Yourself into the Dark: A Conversation with Anne Carson', The Paris Review, 17 April 2024

Rest

'I always forget how important the empty days are, how important it may be sometimes not to expect to produce anything, even a few lines in a journal. I am still pursued by a neurosis about work inherited from my father. A day where one has not pushed oneself to the limit seems a damaged damaging day, a sinful day. Not so! The most valuable thing we can do for the psyche, occasionally, is to let it rest, wander, live in the changing light of a room, not try to be or do anything whatever. Tonight I do feel in a state of grace, limbered up, less strained . . .' —May Sarton

September is an intense month. Always remember that rest is key. We must be able to take things in. If we are on a constant treadmill then we won't have enough energy to go forward.

Although our brains might always be thinking creatively, let's learn about the importance of rest from the Belgian-American author May Sarton. To take a break is key; to 'live in the changing light of a room', as she says. It's not possible to go on and on. It's like the life cycle of a tree: it wouldn't be possible to regrow its leaves in spring if it hadn't already shed them in autumn.

So take time. When will you factor in an empty day?

May Sarton (1912–95) was a Belgian-American novelist, poet and diarist celebrated for her introspective and candid writing. Her bestselling *Journal of a Solitude*, written as she neared her sixtieth birthday, is a poignant account of the experiences of a female artist, showing Sarton grappling with ideas about ageing, sexuality, solitude, nature and more.

Source: Diary entry, 18 January 1971, Sarton, May, The Journals of May Sarton: Journal of a Solitude, *W. W. Norton & Co., 1993*

What is the future of the past?

'The future of the past is full of women.' —Ramie Targoff

In a month where we are thinking about time, I want to explore how we might go about rethinking time – in particular, the past. History has so often been written in a particular way, charting and prioritising the same types of voices, stories and perspectives, but it doesn't have to stay that way. Ramie Targoff wrote a book, *Shakespeare's Sisters*, which changed how I thought about the Elizabethan and Jacobean ages by introducing me to four women authors who were all new to me. Our understanding of the past can change in the future.

Ramie Targoff (b. 1967) is an American professor of English and Italian literature at Brandeis University in Massachusetts. In *Shakespeare's Sisters*, she examines the life and work of four of the most prominent Elizabethan and Jacobean female writers, from the diarist Anne Clifford to Elizabeth Cary, author of *The Tragedy of Mariam*, the first original play by a woman to be published in English.

Source: Targoff, Ramie, Shakespeare's Sisters: Four Women Who Wrote the Renaissance, *Riverrun, 2023*

All time is art time

'[In Italy] I thought everything was a painting – so it wasn't just the fresco per se that was inspiring me, but it was the way that the facades were painted with all these different layers of ochre or washed away again from the rain here or there [. . .] And everywhere there were little Madonnas and little signs of an image that was restored, or somebody scribbled something somewhere. So everything was almost as if it was a painting. So that was my reality I lived in.' —Katharina Grosse

Grosse, who constructs all-engulfing painting installations, gets us to think about how, in places like Italy, painting is everywhere. For example, the chapels entirely covered with frescos, or the external walls that change colour depending on the weather. Once we realise these possibilities, whole worlds can open up.

But it's not just in Italy. Paintings, stages and performances can exist anywhere, fusing elements – such as characters, scenes, words and more – that were created over a whole range of periods. Be curious, or you might not notice the range of art – from the ancient to the contemporary – in front of you right now.

Katharina Grosse (b. 1961) is a German artist hailed for her wall paintings that explode with luminous colours, as well as her site-responsive paintings which she spray-paints onto rocks, walls, landscapes and architecture.

Source: The Great Women Artists Podcast, *2024*

What questions are you asking?

'The core questions of my life, and probably of your life, are fairly consistent. What changes over time is simply how you enter the discussion now; how you frame the work now; how you frame your point or reference now. But the core question, I think, is always the same, which is actually a sort of existential idea, but one that is true.

My core question revolves around the question of dismantling power: How do you unlock it? How do you unpack it?' —Carrie Mae Weems

Through which lens are you looking at something? How is your perspective shaped by your age, your gender, your culture, your family, your nationality? As Weems says, 'We are always negotiating levels of power, no matter how you shake it.' And positively, your lens can change as you age, or move, or educate yourself to other points of view. Questions should always be asked, even after the supposed period of education comes to an end. Time is not linear; we are constantly switching around our frames and references.

Carrie Mae Weems (b. 1953) is an American artist who – through photographs, text, fabric, audio, installation, video and more – investigates history, identity and power.

Source: Crystal Bridges Museum of American Art, 'Carrie Mae Weems on Identity, Relationships & More', Crystal Bridges Distinguished Speaker Lecture, 8 December 2017, via Ostende, Florence et al. (eds), Carrie Mae Weems: Reflections for Now, *Hatje Cantz Verlag, 2023 (p. 75)*

Be curious

'Active, informed, iron-willed wonder is a skill, not a gift: you have to work at it. And you cannot remain in awe of that which is familiar, so the only way to maintain wonder is to learn: learn, and keep learning.' —Katherine Rundell

Being able to learn, which means being able to be amazed, as Rundell informs us, is not a gift, but a skill. We must keep exercising it. The more we look, the more we see; the more we read, the more we know.

Think of wonder as a muscle. Keeping working it. What exercise will you do to keep yours active?

As we close the month, remember that you can keep learning even after the back-to-school period is done, and that wonder can keep us connected to that sense of time we had when we were young, even when we're grown up.

Katherine Rundell (b. 1987) is an award-winning writer of children's fiction and adult non-fiction, including the *Impossible Creatures* series, and *Super-Infinite: The Transformations of John Donne.*

Source: Rundell, Katherine, 'Why children's books', London Review of Books, 6 February 2025

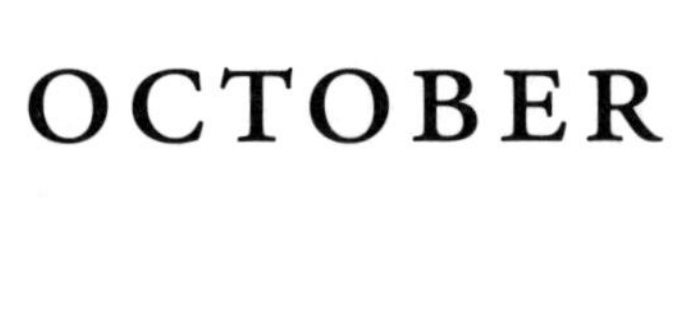
OCTOBER

What is a month like October if not a time of transitions? Days which begin as late summer and end on the cusp of winter, a shift in shades as we leave behind bright, dazzling colours and enter a palette of browns, yellows, oranges and purples.

Agnes Pelton's painting, *Departure* (1952; overleaf), depicts this perfectly: two circular shining orbs dislocating from each other atop a serene, desert-like horizon. While you could read it as lightness coming out of darkness, I like to read it as darkness saying goodbye to lightness, and falling back down towards the ground before it blooms again in spring, just like the month of October itself. As Pelton said of her cosmic paintings: 'They are records of inner visual experiences, bringing light out of darkness, or serenity out of oppression.'

This month, let's focus on the idea of transformations – in nature, in art and in our daily lives: from transforming the mundane into the sacred, to understanding the possibilities of learning new skills and ways of working.

Agnes Pelton (1881–1961) was an American artist, working mostly in solitude in Palm Springs, known for her cosmic paintings of the spiritual world. Infused with biomorphic shapes and recurring motifs such as moons, stars and clouds, Pelton's works show her quest for a world beyond the physical.

Source: Pelton, Agnes, 'On Abstract Painting', c. 1930–40, Agnes Pelton Papers, Archives of American Art, Smithsonian Institution, Box 1, Folder 18

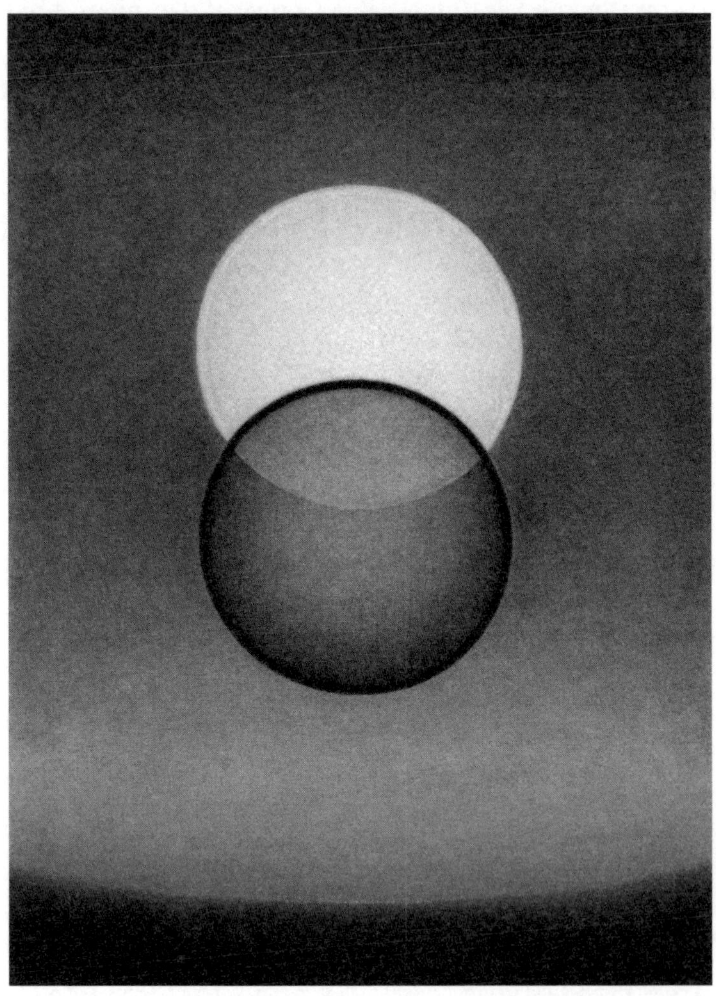

Agnes Pelton, *Departure*, 1952

What is a true autumn day?

'Is not this a true autumn day? Just the still melancholy that I love – that makes life and nature harmonise. The birds are consulting about their migrations, the trees are putting on the hectic or the pallid hues of decay, and begin to strew the ground, that one's very footsteps may not disturb the repose of earth and air, while they give us a scent that is a perfect anodyne to the restless spirit.' —George Eliot

On the first of the month, take stock of what is around you. How does the air smell, what is the thickness of the clouds; how high is the sun? Have the leaves fallen yet – are they thin and damp, shrivelled and crisp?

What does a true autumn day look, feel, smell and taste like for you?

George Eliot (1819–80), born Mary Ann Evans, was a British novelist, poet, journalist and translator. She is recognised as one of the most important writers of the Victorian era. Her novel *Middlemarch: A Study of Provincial Life* (1871) is considered her masterpiece.

Source: Eliot, George, letter to Miss Lewis, 1 October 1841, in Cross, J. W. (ed.), George Eliot's Life Vol. I, William Blackwood & Sons, 1885

Dream this fine October

'I will cut adrift – I will sit on pavements and drink coffee – I will dream; I will take my mind out of its iron cage and let it swim – this fine October.' —Virginia Woolf

What will you do this fine October? What do you want to make happen this month?

Write down five things:

1. ____

2. ____

3. ____

4. ____

5. ____

Virginia Woolf (1882–1941) is considered one of the most important authors of the twentieth century, famed for her nonlinear approaches to narrative. Her acclaimed books and essays include *Mrs Dalloway* (1925), *To the Lighthouse* (1927), *Orlando: A Biography* (1928), *A Room of One's Own* (1929) and *The Waves* (1931).

Source: Diary entry, Wednesday 15 October 1930, Woolf, Virginia; Olivier Bell, Anne and McNeillie, Andrew (eds.), The Diary of Virginia Woolf: Volume 3, 1925–30, *Granta Books, 2023*

Continue to look around and through

'A sculptor's landscape embraces all things that grow and live and are articulate in principle: the shape of the buds already formed in autumn, the thrust and fury of spring growth, the adjustment of trees and rocks and human beings to the fierceness of winter – all these belong to the sculptor's world.' —*Barbara Hepworth*

Hepworth's sculptures (see overleaf) are a great guide for closer looking. Not only are her sculptures beautifully rendered organic forms, but they also allow you to see the landscape (whether a seascape or an architectural building) through them, or from a different angle – as if framing the environment for us.

This month, think about how you could embrace change by looking 'through' or 'around' what surrounds you, just like a Hepworth sculpture.

Barbara Hepworth (1903–75) was a giant of British sculpture. Born in Wakefield, Yorkshire, she carried with her the rhythms of the Northern hills. From 1939, she was based in St Ives, a fishing village in Cornwall famed for its rocky beaches, and the weathered lines and ocean swirls of her surroundings made their way into her highly textured sculptures. Working in an interior and exterior environment, Hepworth interacted with the natural forms of the landscape, as well as analysing the many forms that the human body can take.

Source: Hepworth, Barbara, Drawings from a Sculptor's Landscape, *Praeger, 1966, reprinted in Bowness, Sophie (ed.),* Barbara Hepworth: Writings and Conversations, *Tate Publishing, 2015*

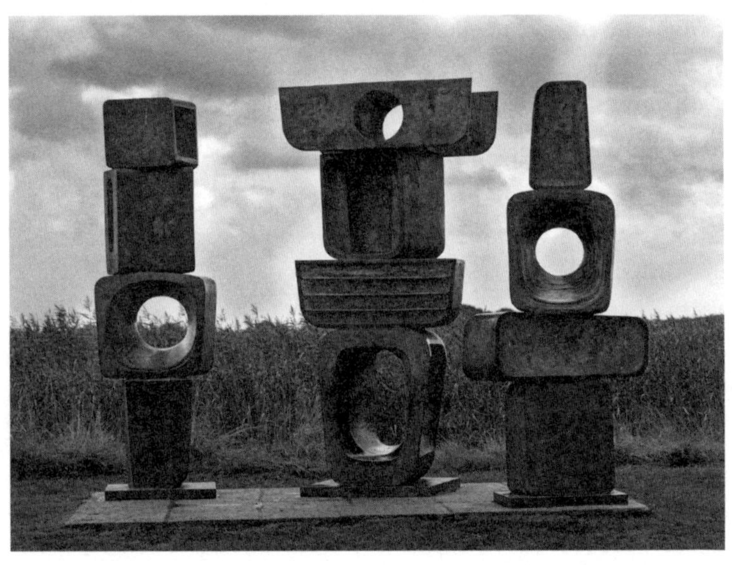

Barbara Hepworth, *The Family of Man*, 1970

Make a carpet out of leaves

[Talking about her studio that she's had for over fifty years:]
'I have a large pile of newspapers, and [it] builds up on the floor. What happens then? It's soft to walk on. It's like walking on fallen leaves in the studio. And I love fallen leaves. I have trees close up to my house, and [the leaves] come into the dining room and blow across the floor . . .

I like the colour of them. I like the feel of them when you walk on them . . . Anyway, the newspapers are like that. They pile up and it's soft to walk on. You sometimes hear artists saying that they get backache because of the concrete floor under their studio, but in my case, because of the newspaper – and I mean, really, there's a lot of it – it makes a kind of carpet.' —Rose Wylie

In autumn, the leaves start to fall from the trees. They change colour, crunch up and, in some cases – like Wylie's – blow into the house. Not only can artists guide us to look upwards, but they can also help us pay close attention to what lies beneath our feet, too.

Rose Wylie (b. 1934) is a British painter based in Kent. Her recognisable painting style is filled with text and image, referencing film, sports stars, mythology and everyday life.

Source: The Great Women Artists Podcast, *2025*

Watch the change

'You have to be slower than change to see change.' —*Rebecca Solnit*

What can you do to be slower than change to see change? How can you trace time? Could you analyse the view outside your window – such as sketching it, writing about it, or taking a picture of it – at different times of day for a set number of days, or every month, year, or more? How, by looking at one thing – multiple times and over an extended period – can you notice and capture change?

Rebecca Solnit (b. 1961) is an American writer, historian and activist, and the author of twenty books on subjects that span feminism to the environment.

Source: Zoe Leonard in Conversation with Rebecca Solnit, *Whitney Museum of American Art, 10 April 2018 (video)*

Transform the everyday

'The ancient meaning of sacred is "to set apart" – to take out of the flow of everyday life. Within the tumult of my life, where studio and home blur, plaster cast limbs and real moving children's limbs feel entangled, I attempt to make moments of the everyday sacred. Shopping lists are poems, 5pm dinners "Last Suppers", tax returns autobiography . . .'—Clementine Keith-Roach

On 18 March, we learnt from Sarah Sze about reflecting on what it is to be alive at any given moment, and the power of being a conduit for our time. While shopping lists today might seem dull, in years or decades to come, they could be seen as 'poems'. So why not see them like that now?

How can you make the everyday feel special? How can you transform – or as Keith-Roach says, 'set apart' – the mundane? Turn the page to see how Keith-Roach elevates body parts.

What everyday tasks do you involve yourself in – cooking, shopping, caring, washing up – and how can you fill these with wonder? Everything is what we make of it; there is no limit to the beauty that we can impose on our lives.

Clementine Keith-Roach (b. 1984) is a British artist. She is an art historian by training and a former set designer, whose practice is imbued with these different approaches. Merging antique vessels with plaster casts of body parts – hands, feet, breasts – she draws on both Surrealism and the ancient world. While her sculptures might appear archaeological, their surfaces aged and weathered, they are in fact illusionistically painted, blurring the boundaries between vessel and body, terracotta and skin.

Source: A note to the author, 2025

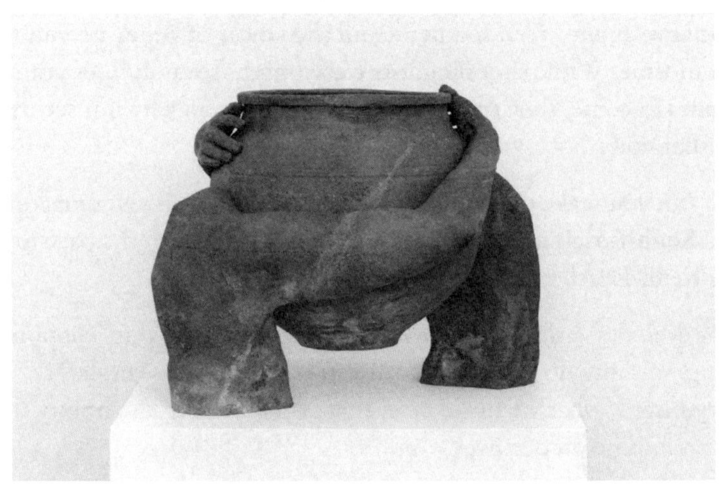

Clementine Keith-Roach, *Tide*, 2023

Find music that transports you to different places

'I listen to music while I'm working – pretty much the whole time. Sometimes I use it like fuel to give me energy, other times I'll seek out an album that transports me to a particular emotion or period of time in my life, as if to access a mood just out of sight . . .' —Gabriella Boyd

Music is powerful. In an instant, it can unlock moods or memories; take you back in time, transport you to a place where you can creatively thrive. What song takes you to your youth, the person you love most in the world, or someone no longer around? How can you use music as fuel for your work and to transform your mindset? For Liza Lou (26 May), it was the operatic energy of Maria Callas.

Like yesterday's entry, about tax returns being like an autobiography and shopping lists seen as poems, what song or collected playlist captures a mood for you? Put it on, and take yourself there.

Gabriella Boyd (b. 1988) is a Glaswegian-born, London-based painter known for her light-filled works, often set in surreal-like architectural settings, that are imbued with memories. Full of symbols and objects that stem from different moments in her life, Boyd's works are explorations into the real, imaginary and remembered.

Source: A note to the author, 2025

Transform what you already know

'He [László Moholy-Nagy] came in and taught us one day. The drawing class really released me from the feeling I couldn't draw. He said, "You can all write your name, can't you?" And we said, "Yes." So, he had this big board. He said, "Write your names," so we wrote them down of course. Then he said, "Next week I want you to draw your name as you've written it." . . . This was a very freeing thing. Then he also held up a string and he dropped the string and we were all to do that and draw what happened . . .' —Lenore Tawney

It's easy to think that we are not capable of doing certain things, or working in a particular creative practice. But just as Tawney was inspired by a class with the Hungarian photographer Moholy-Nagy at the Chicago Institute of Design in the 1940s, try taking something that is familiar to you, and – in small steps – transform it into something entirely new.

Lenore Tawney (1907–2007) was an American artist working in postwar New York City. She was known for her monumental textiles and installations made from linen thread, as well as collages and graphic drawings.

Source: Oral history interview with Lenore Tawney, Archives of American Art, Smithsonian Institution, 23 June 1971

Pass on passion

'She [my art teacher] was, I mean, greatness beyond words because what she had was passion. And my memory of how passion can be infectious is so clear [for me] at the age of fourteen, [for] a student that had no concentration, that was not a scholar, that daydreamed. It just showed that a great teacher can arouse, sort of, excitement in a student.' —Tina Barney

What are you passionate about? How can you pass it on? We have all been shaped by teachers – whether they were at our school or university, or whether they were our friends, parents, children, cousins, neighbours, or even artists and writers from afar. We have also most likely been teachers ourselves.

Think of passion as a sacred and invisible gift, working its way down to every generation.

When I was sixteen years old, I changed schools. I remember going to the open day and learning that you could 'study' history of art. A teacher called Mr Street was leading a session, and – just by watching him teach – I was convinced that this was what I needed to do. Full of passion for the subject, he made it feel exciting, welcoming, accessible, relatable – worlds away from anything stiff and elitist.

As a result, every time I discuss art history, I want to do it with as much excitement as Mr Street did that day. I'm sure you have a similar moment.

What is your passion? Pass it on. It's free to do so!

Tina Barney (b. 1945) is an American photographer known for her large-scale photographs that observe the repetition of traditions and rituals across generations of families.

Source: Oral history interview with Tina Barney, Archives of American Art, Smithsonian Institution, 10 December 2009

Copy

'I remember I really learned figure drawing from Esquire *magazine and Vargas girls . . . I had drawn them and copied them. And I think I cheated. I think I used tracing paper to trace them and then I would develop sneaky ways to get it off the tracing paper onto good white paper so that nobody would know that I had traced them. And then I would say very proudly that I had done it, never mentioning that I had traced it. And then of course I would paint them. And they really were good. They were copies but they were good. So I learned some forms of anatomy that way.' —Emma Amos*

There are so many routes to learning a skill. Trace! Copy! Develop sneaky ways!

You can apply it to any part of your daily life. Copying is a great creative tool. It gets you looking, closely, and then after a while, you get the hang of it. From there, you can form your own language.

One way Joan Didion taught herself how to write was by typing out Ernest Hemingway's sentences 'over and over again', looking for 'how they worked, because they appeared to be so simple,' as she told Charlie Rose in 1962. What did she learn? 'There was withheld information in these sentences . . . it had to do with the rhythm.'

Who and what can you copy, and then transform into your own?

Emma Amos (1937–2020) was an American artist, acclaimed for her feminist paintings that referenced – and twisted – a patriarchal art history. A founding member of the Guerrilla Girls, Amos also worked with warm, vibrant colours for her scenes of daily life that addressed both political issues and personal experiences.

Source: Oral history interview with Emma Amos, Archives of American Art, Smithsonian Institution, 3 October 1968

Embrace the mystery

'Don't try to push the work into the realm of understanding. Let it remain a mystery even to you.' —Arlene Shechet

It's not always possible to know where you're going, to be able to see the outcome when you begin. We live in a world that's often more interested in 'what is' than in 'what if'. Artists can help us retain that sense of unknowing, of working with 'what if' and staying open to what comes, whether in a piece of creative work, or in the shape our life takes.

Arlene Shechet (b. 1951) is a sculptor widely recognised for her use of colour as language in both monumental, welded sculptures and intimate, tactile ceramics. Her pioneering works fuse seemingly disparate elements to create precarious and provisional arrangements and boundary-collapsing visual paradoxes.

Source: A note to the author, 2025

Notice the space you have – or you and others could have

'My images are portraits, so if my work is being exhibited, someone else's existence is also being affirmed. What matters is having a dialogue – with people, with institutions and with history. It's a collective project of reclaiming space.' —*Zanele Muholi*

Zanele Muholi is a South African artist who uses photography in myriad ways, including giving precedence and visibility to queer communities in their country of birth, especially those who have been subjected to violence. Their work brings these stories to the realm of the museum, helping to make these voices part of history, too. Muholi also takes self-portraits of themselves adorned in different household objects (pegs, plugs, hair combs, ropes) that form crowns and other regal embellishments – to suggest that anyone can be royalty in their own way.

Telling your own story can be about telling someone else's. Affirming your own existence can affirm someone else's. Entering a space can bring others in with you, too.

Zanele Muholi (b. 1972) is a South African artist and 'visual activist' known for their powerful work celebrating the lives of LGBTQI+ communities.

Source: Abel-Hirsch, Hannah, 'Zanele Muholi: art and activism', British Journal of Photography, *24 November 2021*

Make your own memorials

'I made witch sculptures because I was asked to make a proposal for the Irish famine memorial in downtown Manhattan. I didn't get the commission but thought, "I have to make my own memorials – nobody's going to give me a memorial to make."

[. . .] Many of the witch trials had secret motives. In some cases it was land grabbing by neighbours done with the help of the Church. I made witch memorials and I thought, "People need witch memorials in their towns." No one ever wanted them, but I made them anyway.' —Kiki Smith

We live in a world full of erased histories. While poignant memorials are rightly erected across our towns, cities and villages, often they are only telling a particular history. For example, in Scotland, UK, it was recorded in 2020 that there were more statues of men called 'John' than there were of women.

What could you see that isn't as visible, how could you bring it into the frame, as Lorraine O'Grady did in 1983 (as we learnt in the entry on 14 September), and as Kiki Smith has done here by telling a story of those – mostly women – accused of witchcraft in the sixteenth century? How can you pay homage to erased histories? How can you honour the people of the past who weren't given their dues? Make your own memorial, no matter the size: put up a postcard on your wall, keep a spirit alive by writing about it in your journal. And as Smith says, you don't need permission – or a commission. Do it yourself!

Kiki Smith (b. 1954) is an American multidisciplinary artist known for her tapestries and sculptures that often address themes of mortality and decay, the body and the earth, what it means to be human, and our relationship to nature.

Source: A conversation with the author, 2024

Learn to see the endless possibilities in something

'We are fibrous structures.' —Magdalena Abakanowicz

In 1978, Abakanowicz gave a lecture at a symposium at Berkeley about fibre, which – like us humans – has endless possibilities. Before you go to a machine to do something, remember all the things you are capable of doing, too, as a 'fibrous structure' that can go in any direction. We live in a world that is becoming increasingly reliant on technology to think and imagine for us, but remember that AI lacks the emotion of a hand and heart – the 'fibre' of our bodies.

Take words. While an AI bot can write a sentence or give you answers in an instant, when you have language as a tool, and you put words together, side by side, line by line, anything can happen, and it happens to your body too. Writing is a physical act.

Magdalena Abakanowicz (1930–2017) was a Polish artist hailed for her colossal-scale and malleable sculptures made from woven fibre. Called 'Abakans', they came in dazzling tones of orange, red, yellow and black.

Source: Magdalena Abakanowicz's lecture at the Fiberworks symposium at the University of Berkeley, 1978

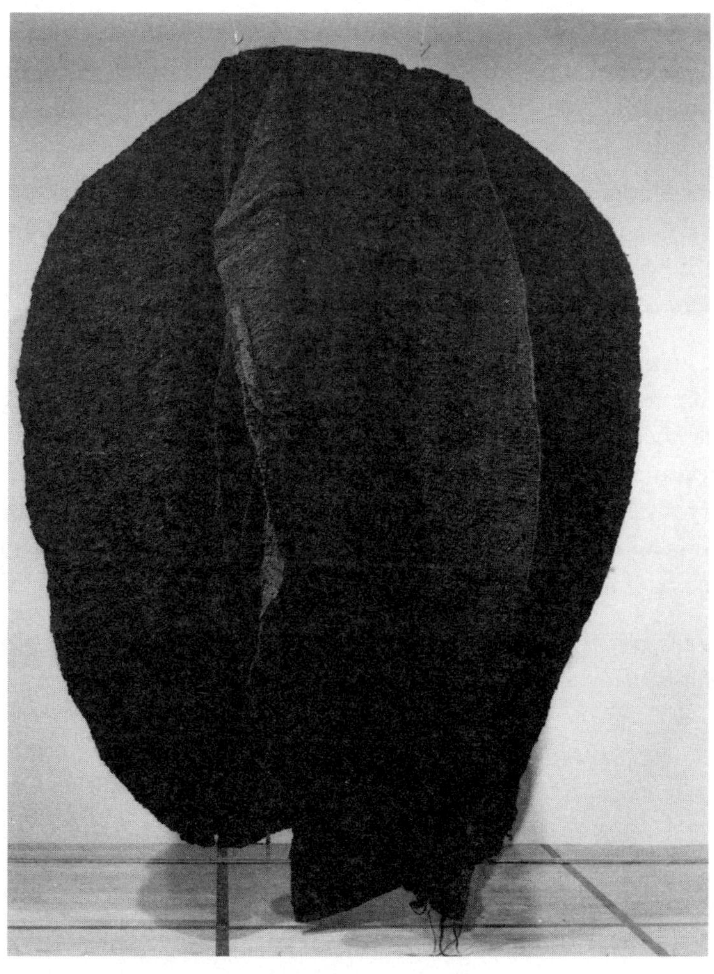

Magdalena Abakanowicz, retrospective exhibition at the Museum of Contemporary Art (Musee d'Art Contemporain) Montreal, 1983

Painting is forever

'Painting is the only art form except still photography which is without time. Music takes time to listen to and ends, writing takes time and ends, movies end, ideas and even sculpture take time. Painting does not. It never ends, it is the only thing that is both continuous and still . . .' —*Joan Mitchell*

Mitchell, the pioneering postwar artist who transformed paint into gusts of light and colour, once said that painting is the only art form that is 'without time'. 'Music takes time to listen to, and ends . . . movies end', whereas painting is forever . . .

This is especially the case for Mitchell's painting *Iva*, 1973, a colossal six-metre-long triptych and a theatre in itself that sees brushstrokes fly, wither, dance and descend. Its blocks of colour conceal as well as reveal pockets of paint. *Iva* lives in London's Tate Modern, and every time I visit it I see something new – such as the helix of reds and yellows on the right, or the flickers of oranges at the bottom akin to a flame, as if forever alive.

Has any painting that you've seen remained strongly lodged in your memory? How can you keep being surprised by it?

Joan Mitchell (1925–92) was an American artist hailed for her often large-scale abstract paintings that pulsate with colour, paind are full of action and intensity. Associated with the Abstract Expressionists, a group of artists working in downtown Manhattan in the 1940s and 50s, as well as the New York poets (with whom she collaborated in her pastel works), Mitchell settled in France in 1959. In 1968, she moved to Vétheuil, near Giverny, and adopted a palette evocative of the late nineteenth-century Parisian painters.

Source: Joan Mitchell interview with Yves Michaud, 12 January 1986, in Joan Mitchell: New Paintings, *Xavier Fourcade, 1986*

Seek empathy

'I find staid and true definitions or forms . . . very dull . . . Even if you might believe a certain principle or think you're a certain type of person, transformation is like a gateway to empathy, a gateway to thinking about different ideas.' —Toyin Ojih Odutola

So often society drills it into us that we should be X or Y, one thing rather than multiple. I love this quote by Ojih Odutola, which reminds us that mutability is desirable. Art can encourage us to open our minds to other possibilities.

Ojih Odutola creates extensive mythical worlds, often with meticulously rendered characters dressed in sumptuous clothing, or set in utopian landscapes. They feel cinematic, and more like stepping into a novel, or play, than looking at a series of flat surfaces. However, on closer inspection, it's clear her worlds are not real, but full of impossible narratives and uneven perspectives that distort the characters' surroundings.

Art can be great tool and 'gift', as Ojih Odutola told me, 'because it gives you time to think'.

How can you look to artworks to show you different perspectives, stories and experiences? Don't just let an artwork tell you something; be an active participant when viewing it, too.

Toyin Ojih Odutola (b. 1985) is a Nigerian-born, American artist working across pen, pastel, charcoal and chalk. As much a storyteller as she is a visual artist, Ojih Odutola sees the 'pen' as a writing tool first, as she embarks on her episodic narratives that can present alternative histories. At times, she joins in the story herself – taking up fictional roles such as a private secretary, or the director of a research initiative.

Source: The Great Women Artists Podcast, *2020*

Be an alchemist

'I think of oil painting being a transformative medium. It's alchemy at its highest. To make this coloured mud – essentially – actually look like something else, is the ultimate sense of the transcendence and transformation. It's utterly religious, I think!' —Louise Giovanelli

Giovanelli's words remind me of seeing the possibilities in what we find around us. While she is specifically focusing us on all the beauty that can flow from what she calls 'coloured mud', we can apply her words to the magical nature of transformation in general.

Whether we consider the alchemy of food in cooking, the pencil lines that make a picture, the bulbs that grow to make a garden, or the friendships we have (how incredible that a stranger can become someone whose continued presence shapes our life!), Giovanelli's words encourage us to focus on how we might go about making such transformative encounters deeper by recognising the power of that process of change.

Take a look at what surrounds you and take the time to see it as not fixed but changeable, something that you can work with to transform aspects of your day-to-day existence.

Louise Giovanelli (b. 1993) is a British painter known for her luminous canvases of curtains, film or music-video stills, metallic shirts, classical sculptures and architectural details. Giovanelli's paintings fuse art history – harking back to the techniques employed by Renaissance painters – with the modern, pop culture-filled world, referencing music videos and cultural figures. Her delicately painted works are explorations into the dazzling and enchanting transient nature of light, solidifying something that is fundamentally ephemeral.

Source: The Great Women Artists Podcast, *2022*

Get out of your comfort zone

'If you do only things you like, you never change. There is nowhere to go, you are always doing the same things again and again.' —Marina Abramović

Everything, in order to grow, has to evolve, change, decay and evolve again. Take the seasons. If they stayed the same, there would be no mesmerising moment when new flowers come out each year, surprising you every time. Or, when the leaves of a tree wither, inviting light in and making way for something else.

In order to progress we need to feel uncomfortable, and it's a reminder that change is a process, and not always easy. Today, take a moment to reflect on the last time you got out of your comfort zone, and what happened as a result of that. See if you can reframe your thinking about something being hard, or new, or unfamiliar, by embracing those feelings as part of a creative process. Change can be good. It can let things in, and bring about beauty in ways you might never expect.

Marina Abramović (b. 1946), was born in Yugoslavia (now Serbia) and is considered as a pioneer and 'warrior' of performance art. Since the beginning of her career in the 1970s, Abramović has stretched the limits of the body. Early works include *Rhythm 0* (1974), which saw her declare herself as the object, and instruct the audience to use props on her as they wished. She has continued to break boundaries for the last five decades and counting.

Source: Abramović, Marina; Warsh, Larry (ed.), Abramović-isms, *Princeton University Press, 2024*

Set something free

'Art within the confines of any tradition is like an animal in a cage.' —*Grace Pailthorpe*

Working within a rigid structure can be stifling – whether it's the professional hours we have to abide by, the institutions we must attend, or the formats that we have to work within. While structure can also be freeing, the excitement lies in playing around with it. If you are caught in a rigid structure at work or school, can you still find ways to play inside it? Or can you bring that sense of flexible rigidity into other parts of your life, the ones private to you?

Let's take Grace Pailthorpe, born in England in 1883, who trained in medicine, serving as a surgeon in the First World War, and was later a medical officer in Australia. Upon her return to the UK, she studied psychological medicine, publishing numerous articles and books, before turning to art as a tool to explore the mind. Breaking free of conventional ideas of analysis, Pailthorpe, together with the artist Reuben Mednikoff, experimented by using art as a way of interpreting childhood trauma.

Whatever your job, how can you invite in something new, and release the animal from the cage?

Grace Pailthorpe (1883–1971) is known for her Surrealist-style paintings of fractured faces within objects, and hybrid figures that meld animals, seashells, cells and more.

Source: Pailthorpe, G. W., 'The Scientific Aspect of Surrealism', published originally in the London Bulletin, *No. 7, December 1938–January 1939*

How can we let in hope?

'Action is the antidote to despair.' —Joan Baez

How can you not let the bad energy win? It can be very difficult to see hope in times of despair, especially when it feels like the world is falling apart and on the verge of destruction. Not only can it exist if you let it in, but the more you do, the more it will impact other people, too.

One of the most powerful essays written in this century is Toni Morrison's 'No Place for Self-Pity, No Room for Fear' for *The Nation* (2015). In this, she discusses the importance of making in times of despair and dread: to beat the enemy who seeks to erase the beauty, magic and imagination that art gives us.

Strive to create and spread hope where you can. We need art more than ever.

Joan Baez (b. 1941) is a legendary American singer-songwriter, as well as an activist for social justice.

Source: Joan Baez speaking at the United Nations, Geneva, July 2023

Don't be afraid to go underground

*'That summer, I was taught by a man called Elmer Bischoff . . .
He got us started by letting us make a lot of mistakes, and
I realised I didn't have to draw academically. I decided
in 1965 that I was bored with what I was doing and there
was a lot more to be learned, so I stopped painting heavy
Expressionistic paintings and became my own teacher, and a
student of myself . . . and I said, "To hell with it!", and went
underground for three years, exploring and studying different
areas, painting new pictures . . .'—Joan Brown*

Brown's words are a reminder that you don't always have to work in the ways you've been taught: be your own teacher, and your own student. And when you want to change direction, don't be afraid to take that time and go underground.

You can't always be 'on'. Despite the images given to us by social media, of people constantly producing, the idea of never-ending creative production is a myth. It is not how creativity works. Don't be afraid to take time out. How else will you protect and conserve your artistic spirit? Keep your ideas safe. Try them out. Make mistakes. Then do the talking.

Joan Brown (1938–90) was an American painter known for her luminous palette, bold brushstrokes with thick scratchy textures, and jazzy patterns that feel almost rhythmic. She became something of a legend in the fifties and sixties' Bay Area Figurative movement – an art scene which rivalled the East Coast's Abstract Expressionism.

Source: 'Joan Brown', VHS archival interview from 1979, via San Francisco Museum of Modern Art

Wake up your energy

'People take coffee, they take speed, whatever. I take rosemary. My company is called Ciné-Tamaris, which is rosemary. That's my speed. Hot water and herb. But it's nice to think that we have in ourselves the energy. It's somewhere, but it's sleeping sometimes. I try to wake it up when I need it.' —Agnès Varda

What do you take to get your creative practice going? Perhaps it isn't about anything more than what you choose to drink to get you going. My drink of choice is Yorkshire Tea with milk, unlike Varda who favours hot water with rosemary (great for boosting your mood and improving concentration). Maybe I'll give hers a go, too!

Agnès Varda (1928–2019) was a Belgian-born French film director, screenwriter and photographer, considered the 'grandmother' of the French New Wave. Both playful and political, she is best known for her films *Cleo from 5 to 7*, *Vagabond* and *Le Bonheur*. She coined the term 'cinécriture' (cine-writing) to describe her innovative storytelling method.

Source: Heti, Sheila, 'An interview with Agnès Varda', Believer, 1 October 2009

Enliven your brain with Surrealist tools!

'Surrealism always existed, like the original one-celled sea creature, like an anthropological secret.

Absent from physical vision, it must be viewed with eyes closed.

And I, with my pencil ready under the pillow I never use, awaken with my brain in my hand.' —Maruja Mallo

Surrealism is a movement which saw artists find the unfamiliar in the familiar (hence 'sur', meaning 'more than' real). If we look closely at the world, we can see that Surrealism is everywhere. It has always 'existed', as Mallo says. It just takes us to notice it, and twist something we thought we knew so well on its head – like the idea of a brain in our hand!

Is that not what all artists do: transform what has always been there – whether it be the minerals that become paint, or the trunk of a tree that turns into a wooden figure – so that we can see the dazzling possibilities in what we've been given?

It's a reminder we should always have our tools ready to transform what we encounter into something new – and to remember that we might already be carrying those tools around with us now: from our brains to our hands, our eyes to our ears. We have been made as creative beings, always ready to be awakened!

Maruja Mallo (1902–95) was a Spanish-born painter who worked in the traditions of Surrealism. Hailed for her complex and vibrantly coloured paintings, she drew inspiration from theatre, masks and costumes as well as the natural landscape, often populating her works with shells, cacti and fantastical flowers.

Source: Maruja Mallo, *Guillermo de Osma Galeria, 1992*

Do something truly unusual

'Put everything in the studio on wheels. Tables, chairs, shelves, your palette. I find reconfiguring the space with ease can help with shifting ideas and spaces in your head. It can literally give you a new perspective on your work and alters your physical interaction with it.' —Mary Stephenson

What can you do to ease your creative space, switch things up, and be as mobile as possible? Putting everything on wheels is one option, or why not create different working environments for yourself in different corners of a room? One for reading, one for listening, one for making and another for dancing!

Mary Stephenson (b. 1989) is a British artist, based in London, known for her serene, dreamlike paintings, often drenched in dazzling hues of greens, yellows and blues, and frequently punctuated by architectural-like forms and structures. They draw from art history, personal memories and family experiences.

Source: A note to the author, 2025

Let your imagination run wild

'Elizabeth [Catlett] taught me when I was an undergraduate. She used to take me outside and we'd look at the clouds and the sky, and she'd tell me about what was up there, and more than I could see, and all kinds of things . . . My imagination went wild when I was with Elizabeth, because she had such an imagination herself. . .' —Samella Lewis

Are you looking for a story, or the clue to the next step in your creative process? How can you transform the elements of nature that you see every day into a place full of fantasy? Use your imagination to dream up the worlds that exist beyond the clouds.

Samella Lewis (1923–2022) was an American artist, art historian and educator known as the 'Godmother of African American Art'. Lewis published magazines, founded a museum, and is the author of the still influential *African American Art and Artists*, first published in 1978 as *Art: African American*.

Elizabeth Catlett (1915–2012) was one of the foremost artists of the twentieth century. Involved in the Harlem Renaissance movement, and a key contributor to the civil rights movement of the 1960s, Catlett taught Lewis at Dillard University in New Orleans.

Source: Samella Lewis: Pioneering Visual Artist and Educator, *a film by Eric Minh Swenson, 2018*

Find the painter behind the painting

'It was a breakthrough for me when I realised, looking at the [Cézanne] painting one day, at how he was putting the paint on . . . I realised it was very sensual, and clumsy in a certain way. And he was a real person. All of a sudden, I realised . . . that . . . the joy of looking at a painting was finding out who the person was inside the painting.' —Elizabeth Murray

When the American artist Elizabeth Murray studied a Cézanne painting of apples and a basket, at first she wasn't quite sure what she was meant to be looking for/at. She had been told by her teachers that looking at art was an 'intellectual exercise'. But it didn't feel intellectual to her. When she really looked, though, she discovered something more physical and human. She noticed how Cézanne's application of paint – 'sensual and clumsy' – stood in for who *he* was as a human being.

It's common to intellectualise art, but how could you look at an artwork, the way it was made, and find the human behind the work? Look at how the paint was applied, the sculpture was carved, the words or colours that were chosen, finding the artist through the artwork.

Elizabeth Murray (1940–2007) was an American artist who, in 1967, found herself at the centre of the New York art world. Working primarily in painting, Murray defied all traditions by upending the rigidity of the four corner-canvas (her paintings took shape in a variety of multi-panelled structures) and fusing cartoons with Cubism, to reference both art history and popular culture.

Source: Elizabeth Murray: Finding the Artist Inside the Painting, *San Francisco Museum of Modern Art (undated video)*

Look to the spark

'Art speaks of who we are at our very best. It speaks of our heart. And you go into a museum, and you can see that, over and over again, that divine spark, that humanness, that heart.' —Kay WalkingStick

Think of museums as places that contain hundreds, or thousands, of sparks. Every piece – just like every human – has a magic to it. Spend time with as many or as few works as you like, but don't forget about that spark. Imagine a tiny firework going off in each work (or person) . . . Notice how someone spent time making something; think about what they saw in the object, or the person they captured. When we begin to notice these things, something magical unfolds in front of us. As we close the month, let's think not just about the transformation of an object, but how our minds can look at something in a new way, too.

Kay WalkingStick (b. 1935) is a Cherokee painter who paints the beauty and expanse of the American landscape and its spiritual and metaphorical significance to both Native Americans and US citizens. 'The landscape sustains us physically and spiritually. It is our beautiful corner of the cosmos,' as she writes.

Source: Meet the Artist: Kay WalkingStick, Smithsonian American Art Museum, 2023 (video)

Work with others

'The good thing about painting with other people outside is there's somebody else there, and the other thing is you make a date and you do it. Because by yourself you can think of reasons not to, like, I don't want to go out, it's too cold, it's too something. But you go do it when there are others, it's a very good support system.'—Lois Dodd

Lois Dodd is famed for her seemingly solitary scenes of both urban and rural environments. They are devoid of people, or depict views through a window that look out onto an electrically lit city (see overleaf).

But behind the canvas she was engaged in conversations, laughter and friendship. As the spectator, knowing that about Lois Dodd brings about a new dimension to what we're looking at. As she went on to say in the same interview: 'When you hear what the circumstance was, it's often shocking.'

Creative work can be a lonely business. It can also be hard to motivate yourself when it's just you, and easy to make excuses because not doing something won't affect or disrupt anyone else. So, go schedule yourself an art date! Take your brushes or pencils, notepads or mood boards, and hold each other accountable to art. Surprise us with your circumstances.

Lois Dodd (b. 1927) paints her immediate surroundings, such as natural landscapes or urban cityscapes. Her paintings are devoid of people, and often take the form of her view through a window (as a framing device) from her home and studios in New York City, the Delaware Water Gap and Maine.

Source: 'In Conversation: Lois Dodd with John Yau', The Brooklyn Rail, February 2011

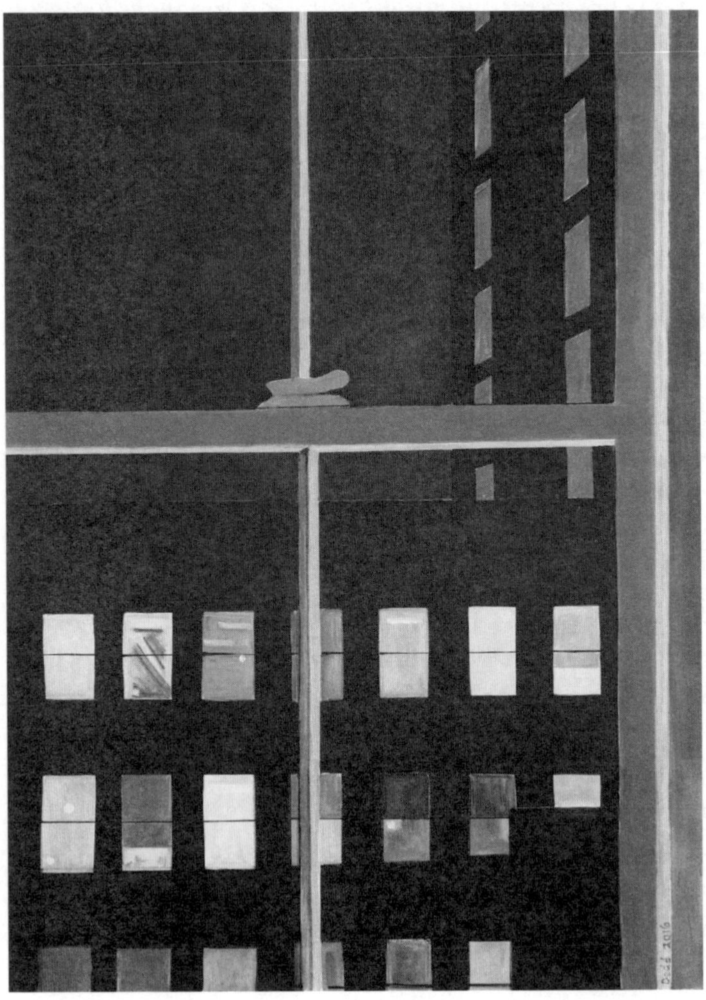

Lois Dodd, *Back of Men's Hotel (from My Window)*, 2016

Fuse heritage and modernity

'I attempt to follow a colour palette that mirrors Riyadh's landscape or go back to traditional textiles and motifs that give an ode to all the traditional artisans that I grew up admiring . . . Engaging with individuals you have always respected, despite their artistic practices differing from yours, will highlight the motivation behind your work.' —*Alia Ahmad*

Bring the past into the present, and fuse the manmade with nature, heritage with modernity. Pay homage to those you respect, and bring that language into the now.

Today, think about those you grew up around whose lives inspired you. Think about your home, its colours and its patterns. Take the time to pay homage to those you respected in your youth, and think about the qualities you admired in them, the textures that remind you of home that you would like to live with now. Bring the past into your present time and see both differently.

Alia Ahmad (b. 1996) is a Saudi Arabian painter known for her large-scale, vividly coloured paintings which draw from both her country's desert and verdant landscapes, as well as its cultural and artisanal traditions.

Source: A note to the author, 2025

Embrace change

'I make paintings really slowly because I change them and change them and change them and change them and change them. I don't really know how to not do that.' —*Amy Sillman*

As we come to the end of a month in which we've been learning ways to look differently at what's around us, let's think about how we tell the stories of our own lives. We're constantly redrafting who we are, and we can allow ourselves to do more of that, from changing what we eat to what we wear, the music we listen to, or the tales we tell others about ourselves.

Sillman's words are a reminder that the fundamental nature of creative work, an artful life, is change. Embrace it. Let change happen, make it a mantra: change, change, change!

Amy Sillman (b. 1955) is an American artist known for her process-based and layered paintings that bridge improvisation and structure, figure and form, erasure and accumulation. In addition to painting, Sillman writes, curates and makes zines, animations and site-specific drawing installations.

Source: Mullen, Matt, 'The playfully troubled art of Amy Sillman', Interview Magazine, *25 January 2018*

Play at being someone else

[Recalling dressing up as a child:] *'Probably more than other kids . . . There are pictures of me dressed up as an old lady . . . I was more interested in being different from other little girls who would dress up as princesses or fairies or a pretty witch. I would be the ugly old witch or the monster.'* —*Cindy Sherman*

Today is Halloween, which, for many people across the world, means transforming into different (sometimes spooky) guises. On this last day of October, we are encouraged to change into something completely different, even if just for one day. But beyond tonight, how might you, like Sherman, keep that energy of play and possibility with you every day?

Cindy Sherman (b. 1954) is an American artist who, since the 1970s, has transformed herself into – and photographed herself as – an array of unsettling and humorous identities, from women in Hitchcock films and horror movies to the strange figures in Old Master paintings, as well as clowns, housewives and fake-tanned, prosthetic-filled society women.

Source: Vogel, Carol, 'Cindy Sherman Unmasked', The New York Times, 16 February 2012

NOVEMBER

Memory

Suddenly the clocks are going back and, as we go into November, everything gets that little bit darker, quieter, more enclosed. It's not quite the end of the year – we still have the glittering lights of December to go – but the nights are drawing in. So how should we treat this month of gathering dark, without the moments of celebration in the month to come? I like to think of November as a month for reflection, of thinking of times past and telling the stories of those who came before us.

So after a month of change, and before a month of celebration, let's take time to look at loss and memory, but also reflection and repair.

Embrace being indoors

'The quiet transition from autumn to winter is not a bad time at all. It's a time for protecting and securing things and for making sure you've got in as many supplies as you can. It's nice to gather together everything you possess as close to you as possible, to store up your warmth and your thoughts and burrow yourself into a deep hole inside, a core of safety where you can defend what is important and precious and your very own. Then the cold and the storms and the darkness can do their worst. They can grope their way up the walls looking for a way in, but they won't find one, everything is shut, and you sit inside, laughing in your warmth and your solitude, for you have had foresight.' —*Tove Jansson*

On the first of the month that sees autumn transition into winter, and before we start to look at what we have lost and how it can be remembered, let's take a moment to recognise what we can gain from a time of year when we often start to retreat inside. Who or what do you already have near you? Who or what do you want to keep safe over this winter? It might be certain relationships, memories of what you have done this year, meals you know you can make that help you keep warm. Let's build that core of safety.

Tove Jansson (1914–2001) was a Swedish-speaking Finnish writer, artist, painter, cartoonist, novelist, illustrator and children's book author, best known for creating the wondrous world of the Moomins: the tales of Moominmamma, Moominpappa and Moomintroll, and their adventures in Moominvalley.

Source: Jansson, Tove, Moominvalley in November, Ernest Benn Ltd, 1971

Be enchanted by the dark

'My most inventive time to paint is winter. I find the cold weather very invigorating, given that I did not grow up with strong winters in Mexico City; I love the change of seasons, winter being one for going inwards, and for discovery. It's a time for hibernating, letting intuition lead, and for taking bigger risks with my work. Especially when there is snow outside, the view is beautiful. I can spend a very long day in my cozy studio with a particular song on repeat until I lose myself in painting.' —Aliza Nisenbaum

As someone who grew up in Mexico City but now lives in New York, Nisenbaum is still enchanted by the magic of what winter can bring.

Think of the aspects of winter that enchant you: is it the change in the light, the clothes you wear, the food that is in season, the long nights for those of us who are nocturnal souls? What are the benefits of hibernation, of a cosy environment that envelops you? What can this season allow for, that no other can?

Write down five things that enchant you about this time.

1. ____

2. ____

3. ____

4. ____

5. ____

Aliza Nisenbaum (b. 1977) is a figurative painter who uses the genre to honour professionals and people from under-represented communities, such as nurses, teachers and construction workers, as well as friends with other occupations. Full of vivacity and vibrancy, Nisenbaum's figures are made up of a whole spectrum of colours to evoke their multifaceted personalities.

Source: A note to the author, 2025

Look elsewhere

'Sometimes words guide me – it's the rhythm of the language – but, at other times, it's images. And I just follow them.' —*Elif Shafak*

The Turkish-British writer Elif Shafak reminds us that no matter what art form we choose to engage with, we can use other forms as a guide. For example, when beginning to write, Shafak has found that something wordless – like an image – can inspire a whole novel. As she told me:

> *One of my earlier novels is called* The Bastard of Istanbul. *The opening scene came to me as a picture: this young woman in Istanbul, wearing high-heeled shoes, but one of the heels is broken. So, she carries that broken heel, almost like a wounded bird. And she's walking under the rain. Meanwhile, there are cars passing by pedestrians, and she's experiencing harassment . . . it came to me as an image. I loved what I saw. And I felt what I saw. I wanted to know, who is this woman? So I followed her story.*

What might you look at to help spark a creative project? Could it be an image that you saw in a dream or something from real life that has stuck in your memory? Where does it take you, why has it stayed with you? What does that inspire? Or, if you are a visual maker, what can you find in the written word, in someone's diaries or the images of a novel?

Elif Shafak (b. 1971) is a celebrated French-born, Turkish-British author. To date she has written nineteen books, twelve of which are novels, and has been instrumental in her work as an advocate for women's and LGBTQ+ rights and freedom of expression.

Source: The Great Women Artists Podcast, *2023*

Collect words

'Words, English words, are full of echoes, of memories, of associations – naturally. They have been out and about, on people's lips, in their houses, in the streets, in the fields, for so many centuries. And that is one of the chief difficulties in writing them today – that they are so stored with meanings, with memories, that they have contracted so many famous marriages.' —Virginia Woolf

As we move further into a month focused on remembrance, let's begin by thinking about the memory of language. Each word in whatever language you speak is weighted with significance. Not only in its etymology, its history, its meaning, but in how it has been used, as Woolf says, 'in the streets, in the fields, for so many centuries'.

What bank of words have significance to you, and why? Perhaps they remind you of a certain place, a song, a book, a cultural moment, or something someone once said to you. While words naturally have fixed meanings, they can take on very personal definitions for all of us, full of memories and associations.

Imagine a memory palace of words – which words would you put in there? Take a moment to write them down.

Virginia Woolf (1882–1941) is considered one of the most important authors of the twentieth century, famed for her nonlinear approaches to narrative. Her acclaimed books and essays include Mrs Dalloway (1925), *To the Lighthouse* (1927), *Orlando: A Biography* (1928), *A Room of One's Own* (1929) and *The Waves* (1931).

Source: Woolf, Virginia, 'On Craftsmanship', BBC Talk, 29 April 1937

Find the artists already inside you

'I think the beauty of being a painter is that the paintings that have come before you, live inside of you.' —*Cassi Namoda*

Sometimes we forget what we've already got inside us – we think about the external things, but not the inner. Whatever your profession or your creative output, your inner world is in part a place of memory, an accumulation of all the things that you've seen, read, tasted, witnessed and marvelled at. Think of it as having infinite Matryoshka dolls inside of you. So how can you remember what you already know, and cherish that knowledge?

One way might be through visual reminders: try printing out photographs of meaningful people, placing meaningful books by your bed or having an inspiring artwork as the wallpaper on your phone.

If you like to look at paintings, which ones exist inside of you? If you like to read poetry, whose words live within you?

Cassi Namoda (b. 1988) is a painter and performance artist from Mozambique, who, as a former student of cinema, lets narrative inform her atmospheric paintings, populated with her imagined named characters that hark back to her childhood.

Source: The Great Women Artists Podcast, *2020*

Look for the answer in what you've already done

'Staying connected to a practice or knowing what to do next in a piece is never easy. [The American painter] Carroll Dunham once said the clue to the next piece exists in what you've already done . . .' —*Doron Langberg*

Following on from yesterday, visual reminders can help you connect to the roots of who you are. As we gather energy into us this month, look to the last thing you made and see how it could be a springboard to the next.

You can also apply this idea more broadly in life, especially when it comes to figuring out what you want to do next. Think deep into your memories and reflect on what you've done this week, this month, this year, this decade. What threads can you follow into the future?

Doron Langberg (b. 1985) is an Israeli-American painter based in New York City, who paints himself, his family, friends and lovers. His luminescent and hazy scenes, blending intense colouring with different textures of light, focus on the physicality of touch.

Source: A note to the author, 2025

Keep the past alive

'When you're an artist, you're kind of living with the ancestors who have made art, like they're alive today . . . It's almost like they made [their work] right in front of me, because what you're looking at is how the work is being made. It becomes like a performance that's happening in front of you. It becomes almost contemporary, because you see "oh, you made this decision, and then you made that" . . . The past becomes really present.' —Alvaro Barrington

What are you looking at when confronted with an object, or artwork? Is it the full image as one, or – if taking Barrington's approach – can you think about it as a series of decisions, as something crafted and worked out over time? It might be easy to think that the final product appeared as you see it, but remember: this painting was once a clean canvas; that book was once a blank page.

There are many ways to look at art. But if you think about it like this – with one thing informing the next – suddenly, the artist, as Barrington says, becomes present. All those decisions that were made in the past are revealed, playing out in front of you now. In this way, we can keep the past alive.

Alvaro (cadet) Barrington (b. 1983) is a painter. He was born in Venezuela, raised between the Caribbean and New York, and now lives in London. He has said: 'Art is about learning how to be. Painting is about what's in front of you, it's about learning to see.'

Source: Alvaro Barrington in conversation with Allison Katz and Dorothy Price, 'When Artists Curate: Noah Davis and the Artist-Curator', Barbican Centre, London, February 2025

Pay homage

'Sometimes it's almost like giving homage to everyone that you've been, or felt, related to.' —*Marlene Dumas*

The artist Marlene Dumas, who has painted highly emotive and, at times, ghostly portraits of the likes of Oscar Wilde (overleaf) and Amy Winehouse, as well as friends, family and anonymous figures, has spoken about her hope for people to be 'touched by her hand'.

In one way, this book pays homage to the artists, makers, thinkers and writers who have shaped me. But we can all take stock of all those who have helped to shape the person we are, or are becoming, from friends and family members to writers and artists. Take a moment today to say thank you.

Marlene Dumas (b. 1953) is a South African-born painter, based in Amsterdam, who often paints figures from 'second-hand images', such as films, postcards, magazines and more. Picturing the famous and infamous, anonymous faces and states of being, Dumas creates portraits that aim to trigger every sense in the body.

Source: 'Barbara Bloom in conversation with Marlene Dumas' (July 1998), in Marlene Dumas, *Phaidon, 1999*

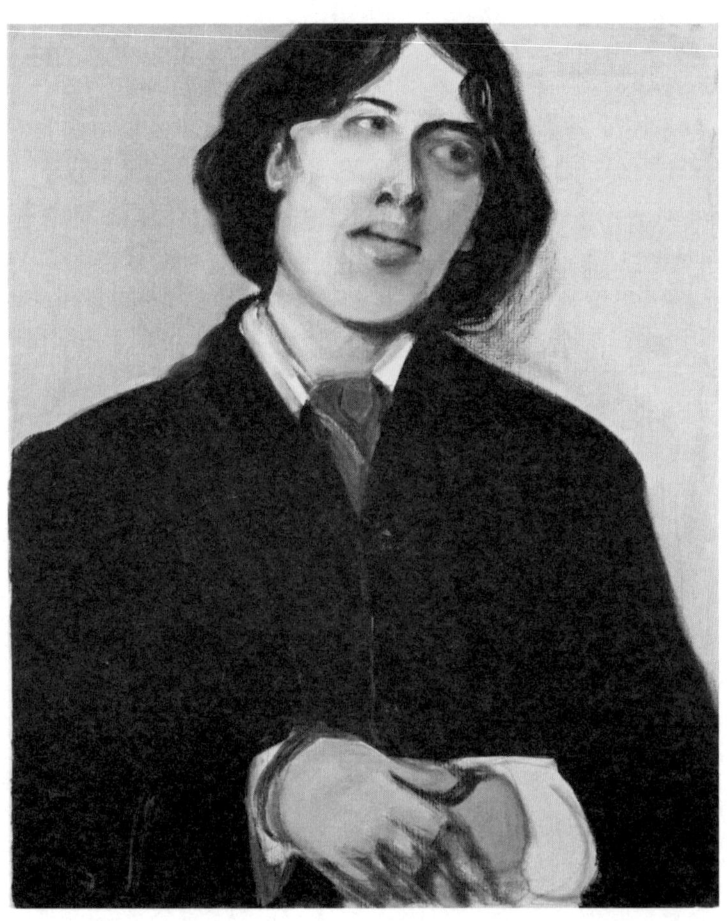

Marlene Dumas, *Oscar Wilde*, 2016

Art as grief

'My friend George Melly always said I'd go down in art history as Maggi "Coffin" Hambling, because of drawing people in their coffins or going on painting them after they're dead . . . I've always felt it's very lucky to be an artist, to have this positive way of grieving. Of course you're cut up, you're sad, you're in the depths of depression about somebody dying, but it does help . . . Henry Moore said the whole thing is therapy and I agree with him, whatever kind of artist you are . . . As W. H. Auden said, making art is like breaking bread with the dead, and it's a very clear example of that, to go on painting someone after they've died . . .'—Maggi Hambling

How do we get to grips with death and loss? How can we use artistic portrayals as a means of comfort? Hambling's drawing, *Cedric February 8th 1982* (overleaf), pictures Morris, her former teacher, embracing the moment of death, with a guiding hand leading him to another world. Notice how she's drawn him, in 'our world', with much fainter pencil marks (as if fading from view), whereas the hands are much fuller, as if to signify that it's time for him to leave us and enter into a new life in whatever form exists beyond this one.

Maggi Hambling (b. 1945) is a British artist hailed both for her public sculpture, such as the four-metre-high *Scallop* on Aldeburgh beach for the composer Benjamin Britten, the first memorial in London for Oscar Wilde, or her *A Sculpture for Mary Wollstonecraft* at Newington Green, and paintings of people and the natural world that are held in multiple important museum collections. Hambling's work responds to the essence of human life and emotion: the simultaneous presence of chaos and control, life and death.

Source: The Great Women Artists Podcast, *2019*

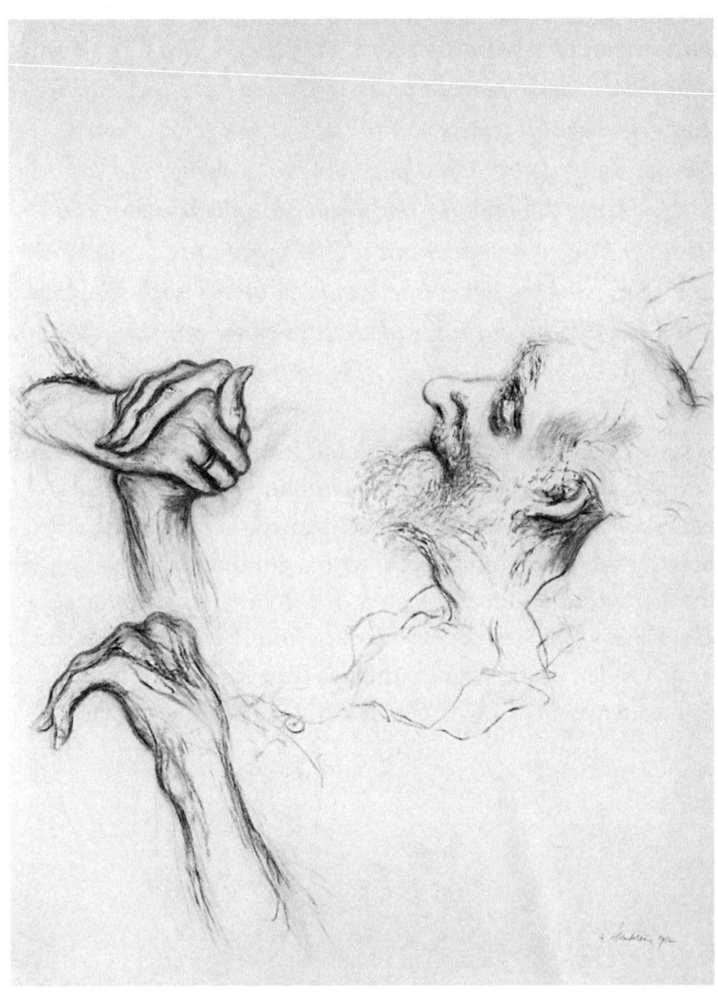

Maggi Hambling, *Cedric February 8th 1982*, 1982

Document

'I don't ever want to lose the real memory of anyone again. I always thought that if I photographed anyone or anything enough, I would never lose the person, I would never lose the memory, I would never lose the place. But the pictures show me how much I've lost.' —Nan Goldin

In 1985, Goldin exhibited *The Ballad of Sexual Dependency* – a slide-show of 700 photographs, complete with a soundtrack – that presented her life in a diary-like form. From beginnings to ends; passion and pain; lovers in AIDS wards sharing one final kiss; an elderly couple still infatuated; and young people sitting carefree by the water, untouched – perhaps only for a moment – from the brutal judgement of the outside world. (Look up one of my favourite of her photographs, *Picnic on the Esplanade, Boston*, 1973.)

It's a portrait of a life, and lives lived; everything laid out in its raw state.

Goldin photographed much of *The Ballad* throughout the AIDS crisis. Looking back now, it shows us the communities that were lost, but it also shows us something magic, too: the beauty and rawness of when they were alive. These people were not to be defined by their death, but how they lived: that's what Goldin captures.

Nan Goldin (b. 1953) is an American artist who has transformed photography in contemporary art. Her work addresses the human experience with themes of love, loss, sexuality, violence, beauty, addiction and mortality. As an activist, Goldin continues to stand up to injustices committed by governments and global conglomerates.

Source: Goldin, Nan, The Ballad of Sexual Dependency, Aperture, 1986

Remember those we love

'I once read a phrase by Liliana Segre [an Italian senator and survivor of Auschwitz] who urged us not to forget the horrors of the past because, once forgotten, they will be repeated. I would not want my children to find themselves living in a world full of violence and I want to believe that they have felt loved . . . To quote another phrase from Segre: "I resisted because I was loved".' —Anna Maria Maiolino

Today is Remembrance Day, a day to honour those no longer here. But it's also a time that we can take to reflect how to not repeat the violence of the past. What is a power and force stronger than all of this? As Segre says, it's love. How can you spread love today?

Anna Maria Maiolino (b. 1942), born in Italy, is one of the most significant artists working in Brazil today, where she has lived since the mid-1960s. With a practice spanning drawing, printmaking, performance, poetry, installation, sculpture and more, Maiolino has addressed and confronted resistance through the turmoil of living under a dictatorship, and contributed to a new abstract language in Brazilian art history.

Source: Epps, Philomena, 'Anna Maria Maiolino, Making Love Revolutionary', The White Review, December 2019

Find a stream of consciousness

'Back in the nineties, when I was in my mid-twenties, I discovered an exercise, 'Morning Pages', via Julia Cameron's book, The Artist's Way. *It involves filling three sides of paper with words. The instruction was to write in a stream-of-consciousness style, without paying attention to syntax or grammar – as that will only distract from what you are writing – first thing every day.*

What's important is that you get the words, which the voice inside your head is expressing, out onto the page . . .

Often the first page of my Morning Pages contains a lot of my anxieties, occasional rants and diatribes, banal thoughts, and eventually the writing opens up to more creative thinking. I think Morning Pages allows me to have breakthrough ideas.'
—Victoria Cantons

Morning Pages is one of the more famous exercises from Julia Cameron's *The Artist's Way*, a groundbreaking book, published in 1992, that helps guide anyone in need of freeing themselves creatively. How can you get your internal voice to manifest itself outside your head? This reminds me of Susan Sontag's entry on 7 August, explaining how writing by hand, away from the technology that is constantly seeking to distract us, allows us to let loose. Sometimes those 'breakthrough ideas' only happen when we relinquish self-consciousness/control.

In a month of reflection and repair, how can you use exercises such as these to help you make sense of what is going on inside your head? While you can use it for your work, it's also a way to work through relationships and other situations in your life, too.

Victoria Cantons (b. 1969) is a British artist working across painting, poetry, performance and more, who creates autobiographical and confessional works that speak to – and confront – the many journeys she has experienced in life.

Source: A note to the author, 2025

Be the keeper of history

'I think as an artist, I think part of my mission – or what I think artists should do – is capture history. Be a storyteller. Because especially nowadays, with our books being banned, our history not being taught in schools, we are the keepers of the history . . . We make the works and they end up in museums, and they show it like that as a way to preserve our history. When I did No Good Deed Goes Unpunished, *I was surprised about how many people didn't know that this happened.' —Karon Davis*

One of the ways we can remember the past is in places like museums, where what we keep is a reflection on what we choose to remember. In this way, museums are keepers of history, and artists are the makers of history.

The work Davis is referring to is *No Good Deed Goes Unpunished* (2021), an installation she made depicting the 1969–70 Conspiracy Seven (originally Conspiracy Eight) trial in Chicago. This was a politically motivated trial in which the US government led charges against figures involved in US counter-cultural race and anti-Vietnam protests, including Bobby Seale, co-founder of the Black Panther Party. Most of the judgements were later overturned. Davis's artwork depicts the physical reality of the trial itself, with Bobby Seale gagged in a courtroom, loomed over by Judge Julius Hoffman.

Karon Davis (b. 1977) is an American artist who creates sculptures and installations of imagined and historical figures. Drawing on issues of history, race and violence in the United States, as well as her background in theatre, dance and film, Davis uses a unique plaster method, akin to Egyptian mummification practices, to sculpt entire ballets or recreations of historical events. Her life-size sculptures, covered in white plaster dust, raise questions about Western beauty standards that have been entrenched in our society since classical times.

Source: The Great Women Artists Podcast, *2024*

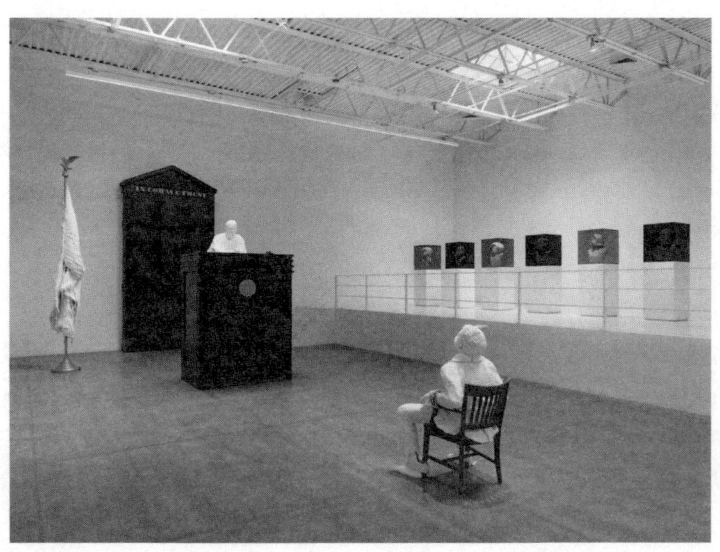

Installation view of Karon Davis, *No Good Deed Goes Unpunished*, 2021

The meaning, and memory, of belongings

'She [my mother] didn't expect to die, but she died, and she left many things behind. I really wanted to talk much more with her, but she died so suddenly. And because of that, I talked to the things she had left behind.' —Ishiuchi Miyako

Managing grief can take so many forms. After loved ones die, we can feel bereft and lost. If we are close to them, there's also the practical job of sorting out their belongings which, although often worthless to the outside world, are still impinged with meaning.

After her mother died, Ishiuchi Miyako photographed her belongings – a used hairbrush, a worn chemise – in a series she called *Mother's* (2000–2005). Not only was it a way to have an intimate conversation with her, but it was also a means of maintaining her presence, by creating a portrait not of her image but of what she held, carried and used each day.

Today, note down a conversation you've had with a loved one that contains something important to you, something true. How will you remember them after they die/go? Like Ishiuchi, how can you keep alive a conversation, or keep discovering who they were?

Ishiuchi Miyako (b. 1947) is a Japanese artist who uses photography as a way of tracing time, from capturing people in myriad ways – whether it be their image or their belongings – to recording places that have sentimental value to her, such as her childhood town of Yokosuka.

Source: Ishiuchi Miyako: Photography Makes History, *Louisiana Channel,*
3 September 2020 (video)

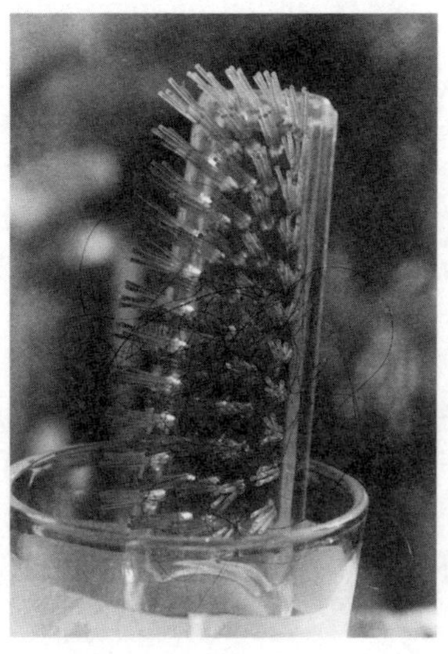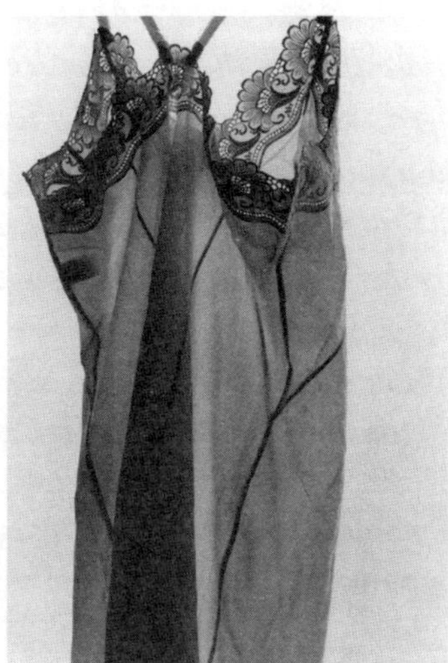

Ishiuchi Miyako: (left) *Mother's #19*, 2001; (right) *Mother's #49*, 2002

What will you pass on?

'I sat for a long while in one of the rectangular courtyards listening to the fountain. Feeling the artists all around me, I slowly took an unassuming place (for two of my own sculptures were somewhere in the museum) among the people whose lives . . . had been distilled into objects that outlasted them. Quilts, pincushions, chairs, tables, houses, sculptures, paintings, tilled and retilled fields, gardens, poems – all of validity and integrity. Like earthworms, whose lives are spent making more earth, we human beings also spend ourselves into the physical. A few of us leave behind objects judged, at least temporarily, worthy of preservation by the culture into which we were born. The process is, however, the same for us all. Ordered into the physical, in time we leave the physical, and leave behind us what we have made.' —Anne Truitt

Thinking about the lives and memories of others can lead us to thinking about our own mortality. As we continue to gather up our experiences through this month, take a moment to think about how you would like to be remembered. What will you pass on? Will it be something in the physical realm, and/or something you instil in others?

Anne Truitt (1921–2004) was an American sculptor celebrated for her large-scale minimalist sculptures.

Source: Diary entry, 3 September 1975, Truitt, Anne, Daybook: The Journal of an Artist, *Scribner, 2013*

Take inspiration from deep time

'Ephemerality has been a topic for art for centuries: a memento mori [memory of death], a still life, even a photograph . . . are always about impending death, impending disappearance.'
—Naomi Beckwith

What are museums, filled with objects that can span up to thousands of years, if not places to think about deep time? How can we use them to think about our place in the world?

As Beckwith notes, artists have often been drawn to subjects or images that make us think about deep time, and our own mortality, in forms that will – almost ironically – outlive their creators, showing us a snapshot of worlds past while also resonating in the present.

Looking at art, and visiting museums, can be a reminder to appreciate everything still alive in this world, and the precious time we have on this planet.

Naomi Beckwith (b. 1976) is an American art historian and curator, who has played an instrumental role in shaping a new vision for The Solomon R. Guggenheim Museum in New York. She has curated groundbreaking shows, such as by artists Howardena Pindell and Lynette Yiadom-Boakye, and is celebrated for her collaborative approach to exhibition-making – fusing visual arts with music, performance and community. In 2027, she will curate Documenta 16, a highly influential 100-day exhibition that takes place in Kassel, Germany, every five years, showcasing contemporary art to the world's stage.

Source: The Great Women Artists Podcast, *2024*

What can give you a new lease of life?

*'From the first moment I handled my Lens with a tender ardour &
it has now become to me as a living thing with voice & memory
& creative vigour.'* —*Julia Margaret Cameron*

There are all sorts of ways that art can guide us. Julia Margaret
Cameron was forty-eight years old in 1863 when she first used
a camera, a present from her daughter. Cameron chose portrait
photography as her focus, developing a distinct style that saw her
photograph bohemian-looking women in a hazy sepia glow, in images
that still feel contemporary today.

An upper-class woman living in Victorian England, Cameron had
particular restrictions on what she could do with her time, though of
course she had the benefits of class too. But the camera, as her words
attest, gave her new creative life. Today, no matter what stage you are
in life, think about what you could do that will make you feel
more alive.

Julia Margaret Cameron (1815–79) was an English photographer. A pioneer of portrait
photography, she was working at a similar time to the Pre-Raphaelite painters, whose style
chimed with her soft-focus lens and ethereal-looking, mythical subjects.

*Source: Cameron, Julia Margaret, 'Annals of my Glass House', 1874, via the Victoria & Albert
Museum, London*

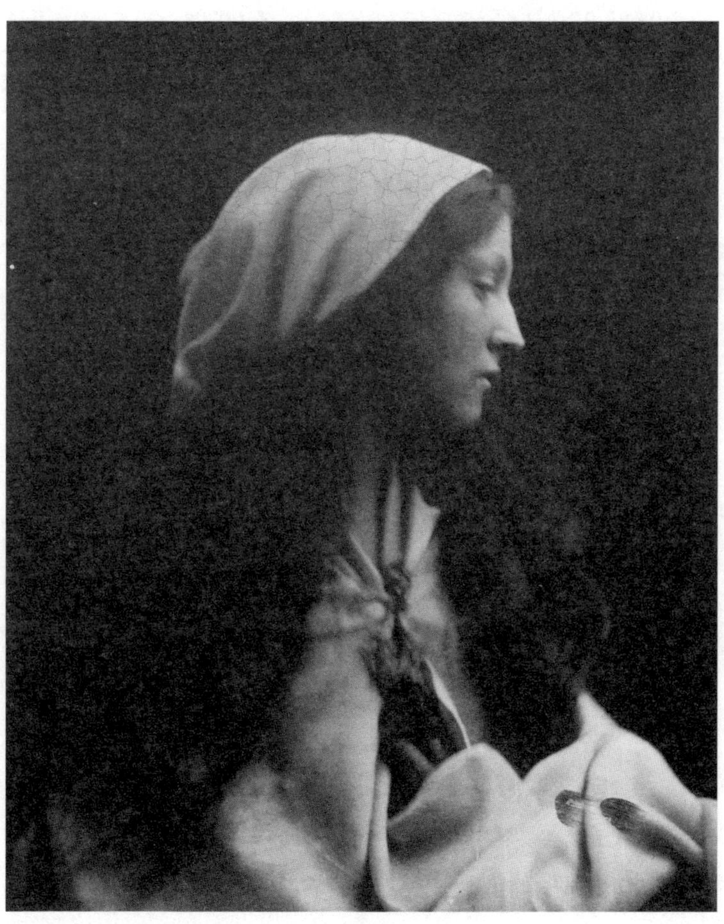

Julia Margaret Cameron, *The Dream*, 1869

Build up your layers

'Painting is like a room, in that if a painting takes a long time, it's like a room that has been quietly lived in. There are layers of silence built into the layers of paint . . . Whereas, if a painting takes a short time, it's like a room that you've just moved into that has been recently decorated. The echoes are completely different.'
—Celia Paul

You could liken this to a life – the more years you have in this world, the more you know and understand. This is all the more reason to be excited for getting older! But it's also a reminder that, no matter how old you are, your opinion always matters.

Celia Paul (b. 1959) is a British artist, born in India. She paints intimate portrayals of those close to her, from her sisters to past lovers, whom she cloaks in a hazy glow.

Source: The Great Women Artists Podcast, *2019*

Deal with the wreckage

'You have to think about Europe too and the Second World War . . . Here we had gone through this Holocaust and for what? What is there left? What was left was a private conscience, an individual searching his or her feelings, and making a move into an unknown. One could only move as honestly and closely toward oneself as possible. For the painters the unknown was a blank area or space. That was all there was. There was no structure, nothing interwoven. A lot of the music, dance, and poetry also had this as an underlying philosophy.' —Grace Hartigan

Grace Hartigan was an American painter known for her bold, ambitious and large-scale canvases. She was part of the New York School who worked in downtown Manhattan in the postwar era, in a style known as Abstract Expressionism.

Like the poets and dancers of the same period, the painters working in this style rid themselves of all traditions in their work. When they had experienced something as horrifying as the Second World War, how was it possible to return to how things used to be? Out of this collapse of what had come before, they began to find exhilaration, a reawakening.

When we hit rock bottom, or experience traumatic events on both a macro and micro level (from collective global events to the varying forms of grief in our personal lives), it can seem as though there is nothing left. But as Hartigan says, sometimes all we can do is search for that unknown – the 'blank area or space'.

Grace Hartigan (1922–2008) was celebrated for her all-encompassing, brightly coloured and gestural paintings. She drew from art history, as well as pop motifs, for her work.

Source: Grace Hartigan in conversation with Cindy Nemser, 1976, from Nemser, Cindy, Art Talk: Conversations with 15 Women Artists, *HarperCollins, 1995*

Make something beautiful

'I focus on the small, individual, particular experience of a human being. I'm trying to extract that and put it in the work. The memories of anonymous victims are always being obliterated. I'm trying to rescue that memory, if it could be possible. But of course I don't succeed. My work lives at the point where the political aspect of these experiences is appearing and disappearing. We are forgetting these memories continuously. That's why my work does not represent something; it's simply a hint of something. It is trying to bring into our presence something that is no longer here.' —Doris Salcedo

In 2016, Doris Salcedo covered Plaza de Bolívar, Bogotá, with 7,000 metres of white fabric. Along with hundreds of others, she inscribed in ash the names of 2,000 war victims lost in Colombia's fifty-two years of civil war.

Titled *Sumando Ausencias* ('Adding Absence'), it was a way to visualise the scope of human loss, which was even further emphasised by the fact it represented just 7 per cent of the total number of victims of the war.

Salcedo said, 'The important task for an artist here is to try to give society tools of mourning . . . Art cannot explain things, but at least art can expose them.'

Doris Salcedo (b. 1958) is a Colombian artist who works with public – at times participatory – installation, and found objects, such as chairs, roses, tables. While her work draws on her experiences of Colombia's violent political history, it can also speak to wider and timeless global issues.

Source: Doris Salcedo in 'Compassion', *Art in the Twenty-first Century Season Five*, Art21, *2009 (video)*

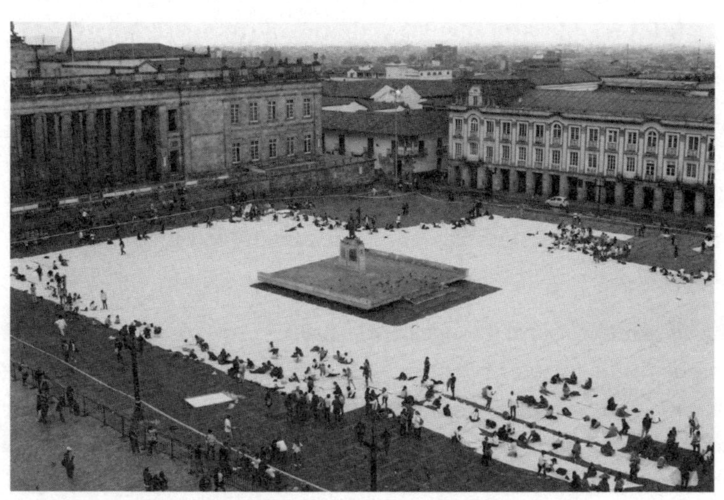

Doris Salcedo, *Sumando Ausencias*, Plaza de Bolívar, Bogotá, Colombia, 2016

Have a mission

'At a certain point I realised what my mission was. And that was, to help women. To stress the importance of equality.' —Sylvia Sleigh

The Welsh-born painter Sylvia Sleigh, who was based in New York City for most of her adult life, painted men and women in poses that reworked art-historical compositions from a feminist viewpoint. She said: 'I liked to portray both man and woman as intelligent and thoughtful people with dignity and humanism that emphasised love and joy.'

Our missions in life can range from what we set out to do in our creative practices, to who or what we choose to champion, or give a platform to. They can be interwoven into our daily routines, or touched upon once a week, month or year, in ways that are small or large.

What is your mission? How can you execute it? Could you work towards fulfilling your purpose by having a conversation with someone about it, or putting on an event in your living room, or elsewhere, and begin by inviting your friends? Is it to spark a debate, or play beautiful music? Executing our missions can begin anywhere, and at any time.

Sylvia Sleigh (1916–2010) was known for her Neo-Realist paintings of men and women often set in vibrant interiors. She was an instrumental figure in the Women's Liberation movement of the 1970s.

Source: Sylvia Sleigh – Equality, University of Chicago, 15 July 2011 (video)

Use art as a way to repair

'The spider is a repairer. If you bash into the web of a spider, she doesn't get mad. She weaves and repairs it.' —*Louise Bourgeois*

Bourgeois first drew the 'spider' in two small ink and charcoal drawings in 1947. Several decades later, the motif famously reappeared in her monumental spider sculptures. She also employed it across drawing, printmaking, textiles and more, up until her death in 2010. Bourgeois used the spider both literally and metaphorically. She likened the act of art-making as a means of psychological repair to the spider's physical act of weaving and repairing its web.

She was born in Paris in 1911 to a family with a tapestry restoration business. Bourgeois titled her largest spider sculpture *Maman* ('mummy' in English; overleaf) after her mother, a skilled weaver who ran the restoration atelier. She saw the spider as a symbol of protection, which becomes evident when you stand under the sculpture, look up, and see its white eggs bundled up in its sac. Suddenly, the spider shifts from being a symbol of terror to one of care.

Bourgeois's work demonstrates how art can be a way towards psychological and physical repair.

The French-American artist **Louise Bourgeois** (1911–2010) was best known for her sculptures, prints, installations and fabric works, featuring motifs such as the spiral and the spider.

Source: Quoted in Frances Morris (ed.), Louise Bourgeois, *Tate Publishing, 2007*

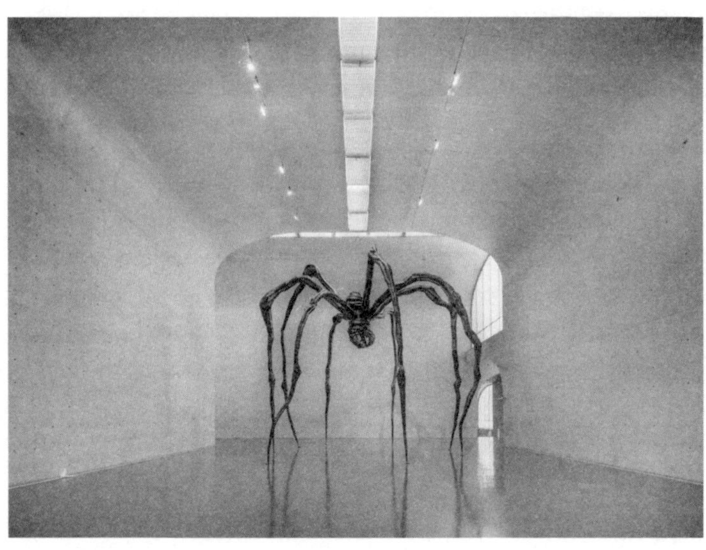

Installation view of Louise Bourgeois's *Maman*, 1999, during the exhibition
Louise Bourgeois: The Eternal Thread, Long Museum, Shanghai, China,
2 November 2018 – 24 February 2019

Find that spark

'In David Lynch's Wild at Heart, *it takes getting his lights punched out for Nicolas Cage's character to wake up to an essential revelation about his life: namely, that he would be a fool to "turn away from love". I wouldn't suggest anything so extreme. But I do think that particular cinematic intervention works well as a metaphor for how I reach revelations in my own life and – just as importantly – in my work as a writer.*

For me, every truth, every reckoning, every epiphany is borne out of an encounter with another person. Sure, we tend to write alone and make art alone. But the substance from which we draw our inspiration is the spark generated by ordinary human interactions. [. . .] I come away from them feeling newly alive to the world around me. And then I go home to my desk and let these sparks and conversations make my writing breathe again.'
—Lamorna Ash

Our interactions with our fellow humans, whether they be about love or grief, don't just shape us as people, but can fuel all sorts of avenues for our creativity. How can you reflect on recent interactions with people, and transform them into creative outputs? So many of my most creative moments have been sparked by human interactions – whether it be a past relationship, my experiences with love, but also forms of grief, a conversation I had, a mood someone was in, or a dismissal implying that I wasn't good enough. Be alert to always draw something from both the good and the bad – be lit by human interaction as fuel for your creativity.

Lamorna Ash (b. 1994) is a British writer, critic and editor. She is the author of *Dark, Salt, Clear,* an exploration into the Cornish fishing industry, and *Don't Forget We're Here Forever,* which looks at young people in Britain's search for Christianity.

Source: A note to the author, 2025

Remember to remember

'I had this very weird, interesting thing as a kid, which was that there were photographs and I didn't want people to be forgotten, so I would write down dates and names of people on the back of pictures. I guess that was one of my first curatorial efforts. I think that it was about memory for me in some way; I didn't want people to be forgotten, and there was this visual information or clues to who these people had been in a photograph . . . And now that I'm telling you this, I realised that, as a queer kid, I didn't want to be forgotten . . . It was an act of saying I didn't want to be forgotten, too.' —Hilton Als

As the Als quote reminds us, keeping stories and people alive helps us find ourselves in the past, too. We wouldn't know about half the people in this book if it wasn't for the efforts of others.

This speaks to why I wrote *The Story of Art without Men*. Not only did I want to see ideas and artworks made by women from the last 500 years, but I wanted to find my own story there, too.

Is there a story, history or person whose memory you keep alive, that reminds you of something essential about yourself?

Hilton Als (b. 1960) is an American writer, critic and curator, known for his non-fiction books and contributions to *The New Yorker*.

Source: The Great Women Artists Podcast, *2023*

Be aware of time

'When you are experiencing the threat of death, you become so aware of time. That's really a gift. I had to become so sick early in my life because it made me value the time I had, and the fact that you can't really waste time. It made me value what you do with time, and that making things that had resonance and importance were vital to completing your life.' —Lynn Hershman Leeson

Time is a gift. It is the most precious thing we have, and something that we can give to others. But we live in a world where we are consumed by social media and doom-scrolling. Sometimes it feels impossible to get ourselves out of our phone. When we are in it, time can pass like quicksand.

To help me monitor my time – and make sure I concentrate on what brings me joy – every morning I write down, by hand, what I want to achieve with my time that day. It can be as little as making sure I text or call someone, making time for a film I want to watch, or a walk I want to take.

It's not to say don't engage with apps, just be wary of how much time they are taking up. As we edge towards the end of the month, reflect on how you've spent your time, and, when entering a new month, look ahead to your day, week, month. Think of your future time: how do you want to spend it? Time is precious. Use it wisely.

Lynn Hershman Leeson (b. 1941) is an American multimedia artist and filmmaker, known for pushing all boundaries with her innovative media work that investigates the relationship between humans and technology, identity and surveillance.

Source: Turner, Christine, 'Lynn Hershman Leeson couldn't give up on being an artist', Art21, November 2023

Work indoors

'Above all else, protect your creative time. An artistic life is heavy on distractions: paid work, caring, subsistence – beware of situations and people that impinge on it. It's not always possible to show up creatively every day, but consistency matters. I wrote my first book by getting up (often reluctantly) at 5 a.m., before work, before my children woke, before the world and emails crowded in. There's something about those quiet hours – that hazy seam between sleep and waking – where I work things out on the page. Years later, I discovered a line that David Hockney had painted on a chest of drawers in his room. "Get up and work immediately." He's right.' —Sinéad Gleeson

My favourite day to do creative work is a Sunday; 11 a.m.–1 p.m. are my favourite hours. It's a time, for me, free of distractions and emails. In a month like November, seek out the quiet moments. Sometimes the sleepiest hours for others might be the most energising for you. And as Gleeson says, be consistent. Carve out that time, and stick to it, even if it means getting up reluctantly – something that may be even more true as the nights draw in.

Sinéad Gleeson (b. 1974) is an Irish writer of fiction and non-fiction. Her debut novel, *Hagstone* (2024), follows the evocative life of Nell, an artist who lives on a wild and rugged island.

Source: A note to the author, 2025

Find reflective rituals to support your work

'My artistic process is straightforward. I begin by sitting in quiet reflection, allowing myself to pray and find tranquillity before I start creating. This practice helps me eliminate the distractions of the outside world and ground myself before approaching the canvas. Next, I focus on establishing the right atmosphere; I often play calming music from artists like Sade, Cocteau Twins, or Yebba while I mix colours. Alternatively, I enjoy browsing through old photographs, which transport me back to moments when life felt simpler.'
—Danielle Mckinney

What are the rituals that you perform before approaching a piece of work? Think of this like a warm-up: you wouldn't not stretch before going on a run. Art is the same. How can you prepare? Like Mckinney, does it take the form of a reflection, rather than something active?

I love knowing what artists listen to in the studio or to get going, especially those who make atmospheric and evocative paintings. And some of the best exhibitions I've been to – such as 'Soul of a Nation' at Tate Modern, or 'Black American Portraits' at LACMA – provided a playlist to listen to when walking around.

A few things to take away today: what can you listen to that will allow you to get in the mood to capture the atmosphere of what you want to create? If you're stuck in terms of who you're painting, or a fictional character you are building, ask yourself: what do those people listen to?

Why not provide your audience with a playlist? People's music choices are just as much of a portrait of them as anything else.

Danielle Mckinney (b. 1981) is an American painter. She is celebrated for her atmospheric and enigmatic scenes of women often caught in moments of solitude (see overleaf).

Source: A note to the author, 2025

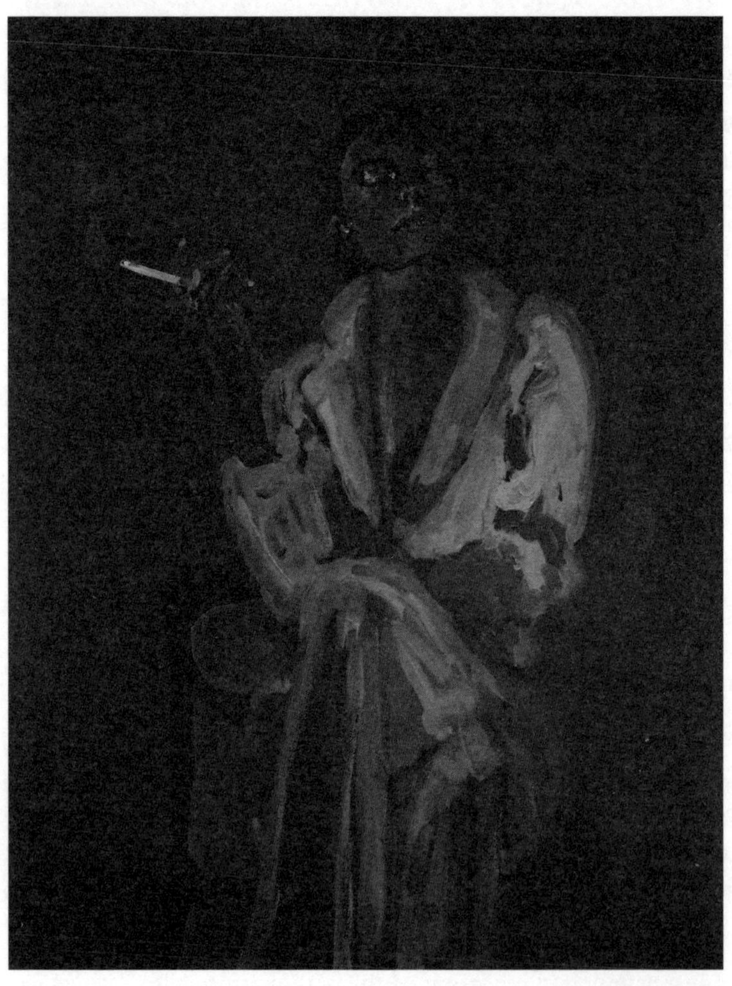

Danielle Mckinney, *Hold your Breath*, 2024

Switch up your creative space

'I have now turned a bedroom here into a studio, as I found it rather difficult to work in the barn, which was nearly always too cold, even at this time of year. This room is rather nice, though not very big, and I have painted all the chocolate paint white and put marbled papers on some places, which makes rather interesting colour.' —Vanessa Bell

Are you needing to change direction, as a means of repairing and resolving whatever you might be stuck with? Do as Bell did and switch up your working space, whether it's moving your desk or easel to catch a different light, working in a new room, or changing the route you take to work. See how it can spark new ideas.

Another thought here: for those who don't have a designated 'studio space', it's a reminder that so many famous artists worked in their bedroom – you're not alone. Make the best of what you've got, even if it's just a corner. And use it to your advantage. I often think about the great artist Lee Krasner (1908–84) who, at the time of being married to Jackson Pollock, worked in the cramped spare bedroom while he had the sprawling barn. Although she didn't have much space to work, Krasner made some of her most dazzling, jewel-like works there, which she called 'Little Images'. It was only after his death that she was able to work in his much larger studio space, and create the breathtaking canvases – filled with expressive, somersaulting shapes – for which she is celebrated.

Vanessa Bell (1879–1961) was a British artist and core member of the Bloomsbury Group, along with her sister, the writer Virginia Woolf (whose dust jackets she designed). Bell was primarily a painter, but never restricted herself to just the canvas, painting ceramics and furniture as well as making textiles. Her style is often composed of simple mosaic shapes, and executed in loose brushstrokes.

Source: Bell, Vanessa, letter to Roger Fry, June 1916, in Marler, Regina (ed.), The Selected Letters of Vanessa Bell, *Bloomsbury, 1994*

No one is born an artist – or everyone is

'I love the idea of not being born an artist . . .'
—Christina Quarles

There's a common mythology that often characterises artists as having a 'mystical genius' sent from the gods above. But, as Quarles encourages us to ponder: are people 'born' into these roles, or can they seek out that role, spending (part or all of) their life figuring out and experimenting? Reflect on who you think can be an artist – could it be you, too?

As Quarles went on to tell me, being an artist 'is something you do over a lifetime'. It's something you have to work at, and it can also feed into your life in any way that suits you. Don't let history tell you otherwise. None of us are born as anything. The best thing we can do is make in a way that is true to ourselves. We are in a constant state of becoming.

Want to be a writer? Write. Want to be an artist? Make!

Christina Quarles (b. 1985) is an American painter of bodies that stretch, condense, tangle and meld into shapes that range from fleshy to stringy. Her paintings elicit a visceral reaction with their fluorescent colouring, limbs that dismantle from the body, and faces devoid of detail that exist between reality and surreality.

Source: The Great Women Artists Podcast, *2023*

Make for your future self

'*I really think of art, and certainly literature, as being collaborations through time.*' —*Ruth Ozeki*

Remember, whatever you are making doesn't just exist in the time in which you are making it. What keeps art continuously alive is the fact that it can be seen, viewed or read by people across the years. As Ozeki went on:

> *I make a book, and I put it out there. And it's a time-being. It is something that I can only make at that particular time, that particular moment in my life. It's an expression of the time-being that I am during however long it takes to make it.*
>
> *Then I take this thing, and it's an object: it's one novel. And then it's picked up and read . . . at that point, it ceases to be a singular object. It becomes a collaboration between me and every single person who reads it. This is what brings it to life . . . it is simply this moving, changing, dynamic process.*

I think it's important to reflect on the idea that art isn't simply finished once it leaves the studio. It keeps living – moving and enchanting people wherever it goes, long beyond the life of its maker – and changing, moulding and constantly evolving, depending on who and what interacts with it, and the context in which it exists.

Ruth Ozeki (b. 1956) is an American-Canadian Zen Buddhist priest, and author of the novel *A Tale for the Time Being*, as well as several other fiction and non-fiction books.

Source: The Great Women Artists Podcast, *2023*

DECEMBER

Joy

December: you got here. The last month of the year. A time of celebration, light and beauty; a time to spend with family and take part in festivities; to relish in the delights that the gift of art can give, and to take stock in everything you've discovered, learnt, tried and tasted this year. You've drawn your fears, found beauty in the mundane, made new routines and experimented with getting lost, and found, and lost again. This month, let's focus on joy, on doing, as Laurie Anderson puts it, whatever makes you 'feel free and really good'.

As we embark on this month, before we start again in January, think of December – like art – as a gift that has been given to you, full of work yet to be written, painted, sculpted and more; people whom you have yet to meet, talk to or fall in love with.

Have fun

'Whatever makes you feel free and really good – that's what to do. It's really simple.' —*Laurie Anderson*

Let's kick-start our month of joy with this very simple quote from the pioneering American artist Laurie Anderson.

Think of the last time you felt like this, really free and really good. Was it while playing sport, with a particular person, immersed in a book, in a particular place? We can live our lives by what we 'should' do or what 'looks' good, but the way you feel never lies.

While it's always good to step out of your comfort zone and try to understand the things you don't like, relish what *you* like, what brings *you* joy and makes *you* feel free and really good. Whatever you engage in, make it work for you.

Laurie Anderson (b. 1947) is an American multimedia artist and creative pioneer. She is hailed for her experimental and unpredictable performances, and has spent her extensive career working across – and breaking new ground in – visual art, poetry, vocals, music (from violin to keyboard), writing, directing, theatre, opera and more.

Source: Laurie Anderson Interview: Advice to the Young, *Louisiana Channel, 31 May 2016 (video)*

There is no reason not to do things artfully

'A definition of the word art is the application of new knowledge to ordinary, everyday objects. There is no reason not to do things artfully. You could equally say that a peasant who improves his wheelbarrow has made a work of creation. Art is everything. It is wonderful.' —*Charlotte Perriand*

So much creativity exists in what you already do. You are living it without even realising it – from how you wear your clothes to how you arrange your furniture, or place food on a plate, or plant some flowers on a sill.

If you find it hard to carry out such creative love for yourself, perhaps think of it as doing it for your younger self. If something was broken, how would you fix it for them? If they were feeling sad, how would you take care of them? If they were bored, where would you take them, or what would you read to them? What beauty could you bring into their world?

Charlotte Perriand (1903–99) was a French architect and designer who was acclaimed for her Modernist furnishings, such as the steel cradle-like *Chaise longue basculante*. She was instrumental in the avant-garde movement of the early twentieth century, transforming the aesthetic of modern living.

Source: Perriand, Charlotte, Charlotte Perriand: A Life of Creation, *The Monacelli Press, 2003*

Everyone should make art

'Everybody should paint. It's good for the soul. I think the world would be a better place if everybody made some sort of art. If not painting, something, you know?' —Kay WalkingStick

Sometimes life can get so busy it's difficult to remember what we really love. This applies to where you spend your time, too. Where makes you feel good: is it the park, or the pub, a museum or a library? Where do you connect with people the best, or have your greatest ideas? Are you walking, sitting, dancing, standing? Where is good for your soul?

December, while a time of family and festivities, busyness and beauty, can also be a time of increasing loneliness. Thinking of the past three days, remind yourself of where, what and who makes your soul feel good. Write them down here, and say why, too.

1. ____

2. ____

3. ____

4. ____

5. ____

Kay WalkingStick (b. 1935) is a Cherokee painter who paints the beauty and expanse of the American landscape and its spiritual and metaphorical significance to both Native Americans and US citizens. 'The landscape sustains us physically and spiritually. It is our beautiful corner of the cosmos,' as she writes.

Source: Meet the Artist: Kay WalkingStick, *Smithsonian American Art Museum, 2023 (video)*

Get a kick out of looking

'It's such a kick, really, seeing things.' —*Lois Dodd*

For Dodd, who paints landscapes through windows, empty staircases through doorframes, houses bookended by trees, reflections on glass – her works are about seeing the things that pass others by (see overleaf).

We all notice things that others don't. Artists make that looking tangible. But we can all pay more attention to what it is that *we* notice, what or who we find worthy of our gaze. Bring what you notice to the front of your mind.

Without making a piece of art, you can still tell someone about what captured your attention. Today, take a picture of what it is that holds your gaze, or send a voice note to someone describing what you saw. Give them something that they get a kick out of, too!

Lois Dodd (b. 1927) paints her immediate surroundings, such as natural landscapes or urban cityscapes. Her paintings are devoid of people, and often take the form of her view through a window (as a framing device) from her home and studios in New York City, the Delaware Water Gap and Maine.

Source: Conversation with Lois Dodd, *interview with Bill Maynes, 9 January 2007 (video)*

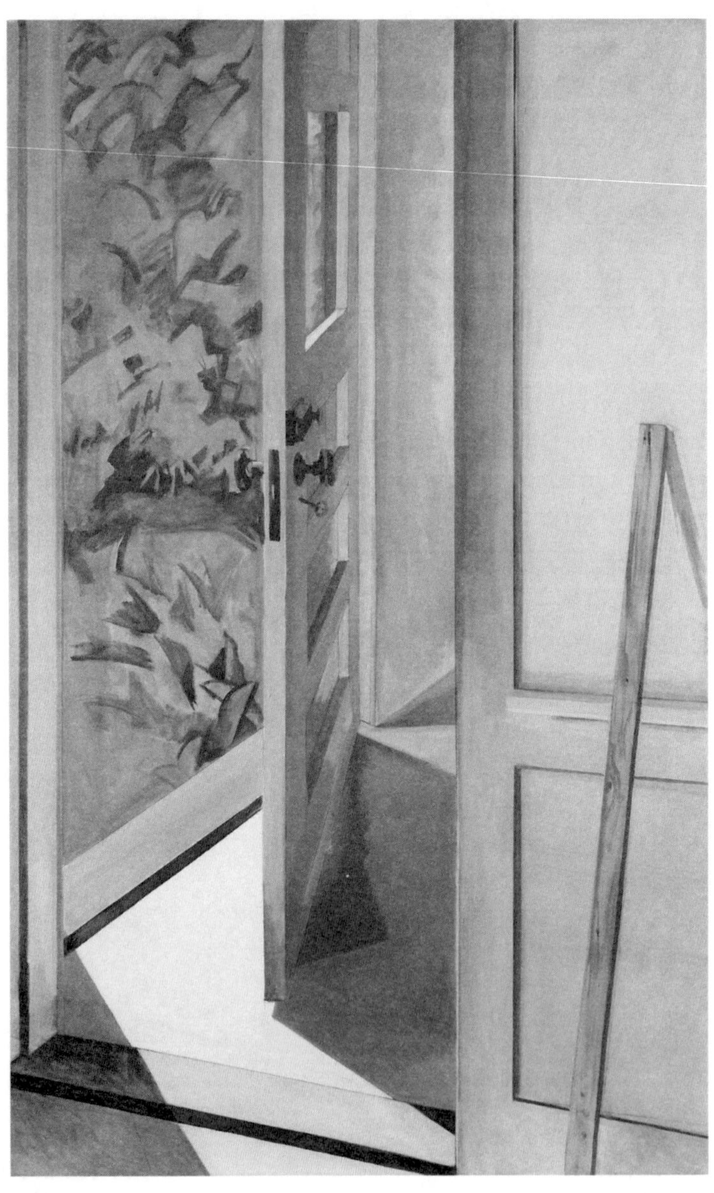

Lois Dodd, *Front Door Cushing*, 1982

Dream together

'A dream you dream alone is only a dream. A dream you dream together is reality.' —*Yoko Ono*

The Japanese-born artist Yoko Ono makes dreams reality by bringing people into participatory artworks that centre on the power of collaboration and human relationships. Take her *Wish Trees* – trees that she transforms into artworks by providing her viewers with a piece of paper, string and a pen, and the instruction to make a wish and tie it around the branches until the trees 'are covered with wishes'. Or *My Mommy Is Beautiful* (overleaf) – where she asks her participant to 'write your memory of your mother and/or paste a photograph of her on the canvas' to make a collective portrait of motherhood. Ono's works show the universal ways in which humanity can unite rather than divide.

Isn't the joy of life to be found in being with others, working collaboratively, seeing what they do and dreaming together?

Yoko Ono (b. 1933) is a Japanese-born artist, musician and activist, hailed for her participatory performances and conceptual artworks.

Source: Ono, Yoko, Grapefruit, Sphere Books, 1970

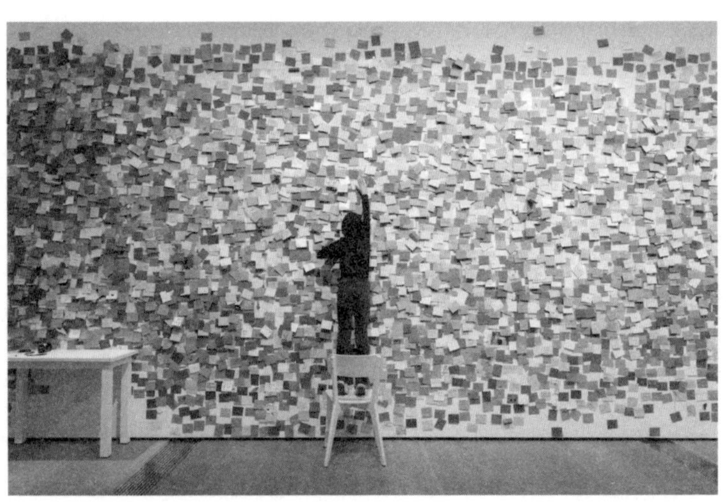

Yoko Ono, *My Mommy Is Beautiful*, 2004

Art gives you life

'Living with art stops one wilting!' —*Maria Lassnig*

I have interviewed hundreds of artists, and while they might be famous now – and surrounded by real art objects – many of them tell me that the pictures they grew up around were in the form of posters, postcards or printouts of their favourite artworks. Living with art doesn't have to cost much and can invite endless readings of close looking and inspiration, feeding into your life in ways you won't even imagine.

So, how to do it? Create your own mini art collection through posters and postcards, old book covers and pages from magazines; stick them on your wall, your fridge, doors and pinboards; make your own work (or copy your favourite artist!) and hang them up or put them in cheap second-hand frames. They are guaranteed to bring you joy, and stop you wilting.

Maria Lassnig (1919–2014) was an Austrian artist known for her self-portraits, drenched in an often acidic-like palette, based on her theory of 'body awareness'.

Source: Obrist, Hans Ulrich, Pakesch, Peter and Poschauko, Hans Werner (eds.), Maria Lassnig: Letters to Hans Ulrich Obrist: Living with Art Stops One Wilting!, *Walther König, 2020*

Create from a place of joy, always

'I'm a really silly, playful person. There's so much pleasure to be taken in small things, something we embrace as children but often lose as we grow up. So, I'm committed to maintaining a level of silliness and to creating my work from a place of joy.' —Rachel Jones

As we get into the swing of the festive season, reflect on what it was about this month that brought you joy when you were a child. What were your traditions, what did you make or bake or sing? Often these get lost as we get older. Bring them back – no one is ever too old to relish the magic of this time. Light up that spark and bring back that joy.

Rachel Jones (b. 1991) is an artist working across painting, installation, sound and performance. Her practice is rooted in an ongoing exploration of identity and selfhood, particularly in relation to Black culture and community. Her work is held in major public collections including the Tate, Hammer Museum, ICA Miami and Stedelijk Museum among others. In 2024, she designed the BRIT Awards trophy, joining a lineage of artists including Zaha Hadid and Tracey Emin.

Source: Lander, Anastasia, 'Rachel Jones – A Place of Joy', Puss Puss, 4 July 2024

Seek the small joys of daily life

'I just live every day. I don't seek for my inspiration. I just take a walk and I read books and I meet people and I just want to live fully and that's all . . .' —*Han Kang*

It's that simple. The small things. You don't have to seek far and wide. Ask yourself: what do we have here? Maybe that's the secret to living life, fully.

Han Kang (b. 1970) is a South Korean writer, best known for her surreal and subversive novels, including *The Vegetarian*, for which she was awarded the Nobel Prize in Literature in 2024.

Source: Via Nobel Prize (video)

There is no end to creativity

'The wonderful thing about being an artist is that there is no end to creative expression.' —*Loïs Mailou Jones*

While we all finish work and move on, everything we do can be seen as feeding into a larger web of creativity that, as Mailou Jones states, has no end. Creativity is a constant.

There's a line in an essay by the Italian philosopher and activist, Franco 'Bifo' Berardi, which reads: 'This place we don't know is the place we are looking for.'

Being an artist, or being creative, you're always looking for that place you don't know. For me, that looking is the 'wonderful' that Mailou Jones is referring to. Once you understand that, you're ready to begin. Because the only way to figure it out is to see where it takes you.

I often liken it to a vision I have of swimming underwater, a stream of light ahead of me. I'm trying so hard to reach it, to touch it, but there's nothing solid there. Rather than being frustrated, I have to remember that just by swimming in it, I'm already living it. What's beyond 'doing', I will never know. The best thing we can do is revel in the 'doing' not the 'done'.

Loïs Mailou Jones (1905–98) was an American artist, working across painting and textiles, whose extensive career stretched from the height of the Harlem Renaissance through to the late twentieth century. Constantly reinventing her painting style, Jones took inspiration from trips to France, Haiti and the African continent, creating tender, intimate portraits and fractured images of masks.

Source: Benjamin, Tritobia Hayes, The Art and Life of Lois Mailou Jones, *Pomegranate Artbooks, 1994*

Make with love

'When people try to live up to an image of success that is not them, they are trapped and unhappy. I see many wonderful and beautiful people and some are happy and many are not. The difference between them is mainly this: To do. To work. With love. This means to have an interest in something fine – anything – to be involved and to put the whole personality into this thing that you love. To love is to be engaged is to work is to be interested is to create. This is to love. When someone gets caught in the imagery of success they are trapped.' —*Lina Wertmüller*

If I ever need to be reminded about the fundamentals of success, or happiness, I turn to one of my favourite poems: 'Happiness' by Raymond Carver, written in 1985. It's written from the perspective of a person who, sipping his morning coffee, sees two paperboys contentedly doing their round together as the light is rising for the day. Look it up! Whatever you do, if you do it from and with love, you are doing it successfully.

Lina Wertmüller (1928–2021) was a director, screenwriter and pioneer in Italian cinema, who was best known for her arthouse films of the 1970s.

Source: Winter, Nina, Interview with the Muse: Remarkable Women Speak on Creativity and Power, *Moon Books, 1978*

The only way to see it is to build it

'You see, what is it that we do? We want to create works of art of joy and beauty, which we will build because we believe it will be beautiful. The only way to see it is to build it.' —Jeanne-Claude and Christo

The more joy and beauty you build, the more people can build on that. Think of making as building foundations of joy. Whatever you make today – a cake, a card, a decision – see if you can imagine it as building a foundation of joy.

Jeanne-Claude (1935–2009, Morocco) and **Christo** (1935–2020, Bulgaria) were a husband-and-wife artist duo acclaimed for their large-scale, site-specific environmental installations that took place all over the world.

Source: Pagliasotti, James, 'Interview with Christo and Jeanne-Claude', originally published in Eye-Level, 4 January 2002

Leave something behind

'If I can inspire one of these youngsters to develop the talent I know they possess, then my monument will be in their work.' —Augusta Savage

We tend to see monuments as buildings or statues, something tangible and big. But a monument can be thought of as a spirit that lives on in people. If we think of it this way, then who *we* are is a monument to all the people who have shaped us in some way – whether it be with their personality, their courage or their work. And we may pass on that spirit, too.

Augusta Savage was an American artist known for her busts of locals and notable Black Americans. Part of the Harlem Renaissance movement, she was instrumental to the neighbourhood's community: as an educator, the owner of a gallery, and as director of the Harlem Community Arts Center.

As a teacher and mentor to many students who became groundbreaking artists in the mid-to-late twentieth century, such as Jacob Lawrence and Gwendolyn Knight, Savage and her legacy continue to live on today, due to the impact her students had on the current generation of artists.

Is there anyone whose 'monumentally' inspiring spirit lives on, inside of you?

Augusta Savage (1892–1962) was an American sculptor known for her life-size figures and plaster portrait busts, which she often painted with shoe polish for a bronzed effect.

Source: Poston, T. R., 'Augusta Savage', Metropolitan Magazine, January 1935

Commemorate

'So much of our precious heritage as women – our artefacts, our painting, writing, needlework, music – have no homes. As long as we do not provide permanent places for the treasures women create, we will continue to tread water and repeat ourselves.' —Judy Chicago

I want to pick up the thought from yesterday. Although the spirit of Savage lives on through contemporary artists, it's important to acknowledge how many people have missed out on knowing about her due to the meagre number of places that gave a permanent home to her work.

For the World's Fair in 1939, Savage was commissioned to make a sculpture to commemorate the contribution to music by Black American people. She made a sixteen-foot-high artwork of choristers singing in the shape of a harp, or the palm of God's hand (overleaf). While it attracted huge attention, the original was destroyed after the fair due to lack of storage and funding costs.

A small maquette remains. The only time I've seen it was in 2023, at Judy Chicago's show at the New Museum in New York City, titled 'Herstory'. On the fourth floor, Chicago curated an exhibition within the exhibition that she called 'The City of Ladies' (referencing the poet Christine de Pizan's book of short biographies of accomplished women, believed to have been finished in 1405). 'The City of Ladies' featured 500 years of work by women and, while it was an extraordinary collection of artworks, it was also a stark reminder that hardly any museums in the world present this as their 'canon'.

Judy Chicago (b. 1939) is an influential American artist whose wide-ranging oeuvre, consisting of sculptures and installations, painting, drawing and more, is concerned with feminism and feminist histories.

Source: Speech for 'The Women's Dinner', published in the Women's Art Register Bulletin, *Vol. 1, No. 1, April 1988*

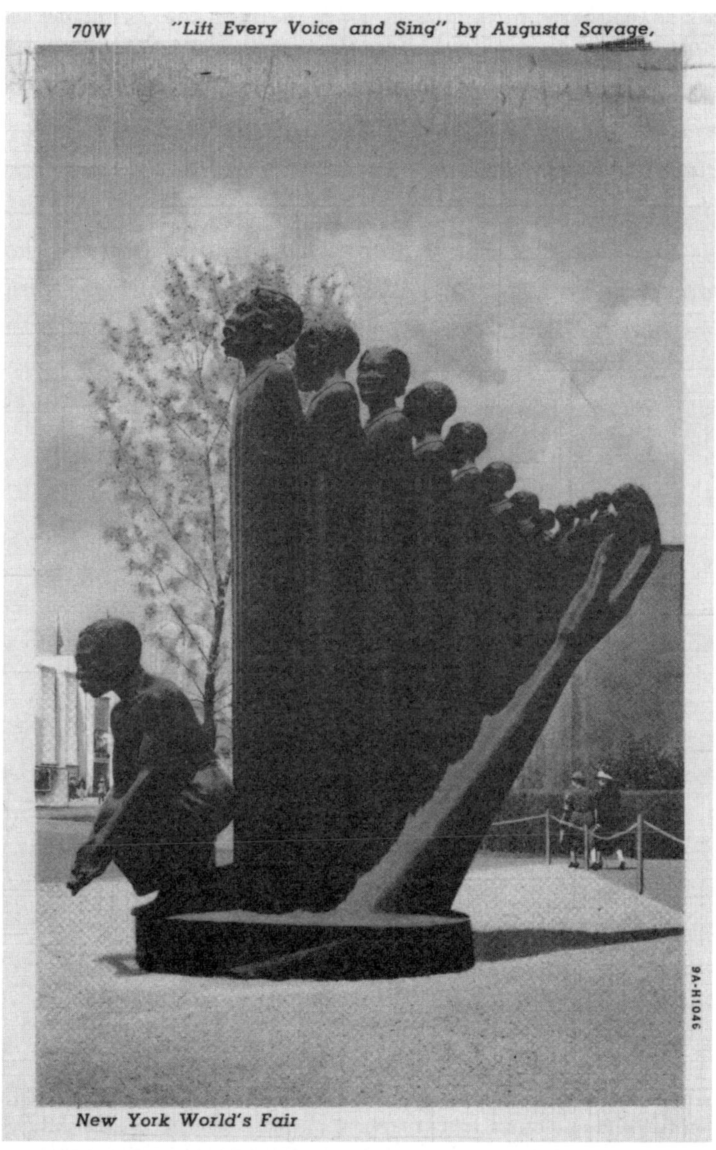

Augusta Savage, *Lift Every Voice and Sing*, 1939

Take a moment to see beauty

'Beauty is just an accident. Beauty is just a happenstance. Beauty is the remainder of being a painter. The work becomes pretty because I wouldn't be able to look at a work about something as grotesque as what I'm thinking about and as grotesque as projecting one's ugly soul onto another's pretty body, and representing that in an ugly way. I have always been attracted to the lure – work that draws a viewer in through a kind of seductive offering: "Here's something to look at. Stay a while".' —Kara Walker

Today, find something beautiful. Stay with it a while.

Kara Walker (b. 1969) is an American artist who, through sculpture, painting, printmaking, silhouettes, performances and large-scale public artworks, addresses the violent histories of the past. Her work sparks discussion around race, oppression and sexuality, as well as the power dynamics of a capitalist and imperialist world.

Source: Interview with Kara Walker, 'Projecting Fictions: "Insurrection! Our Tools Were Rudimentary, Yet We Pressed On"', Art21, November 2011

Trust

'You will never run out of ideas.' —*Tali Lennox*

I remember watching Lubaina Himid in conversation at the Tate Modern a few years ago. She spoke about the (occasional) frustration of making art because of how every artwork asks a new question, which only invites the answer of making more. Each creative act you do opens the door to another – even if you do not realise it. It can be hard to trust this, though, especially as we all experience frustration at times, get stuck in our work or bored in our thoughts. At times like that, we might need something to lift us out of our rut.

The visual cue that I turn to is *Birthday* (1942; overleaf) by Dorothea Tanning, a painting she made to mark her 'entrance' or 'birth' as an artist. She stands before us bare-chested and in a skirt made up of green, fantastical figures. Behind her are flurries of slightly ajar doors with worlds all yet to be discovered. Although it's a self-portrait of the artist created nearly 100 years ago, I see it as capturing the joy of being about to set out on an adventure, delighting in what's about to happen, and a portrait of uncharted ideas yet to be unleashed. What do you see?

Tali Lennox (b. 1993) is a British artist who paints fragmented, Surrealist-inspired bodies and faces set in imaginary landscapes. Jewel- and relic-like, her shimmeringly textured oil paintings bridge the ancient and the futuristic.

Dorothea Tanning (1910–2012) was an American artist who lived in Paris for much of her later life, hailed for her Surrealist-inspired paintings and soft sculptures. She was also a writer and poet, and famously said, 'Don't ask me to explain my paintings.'

Source: A conversation with the author, 2024

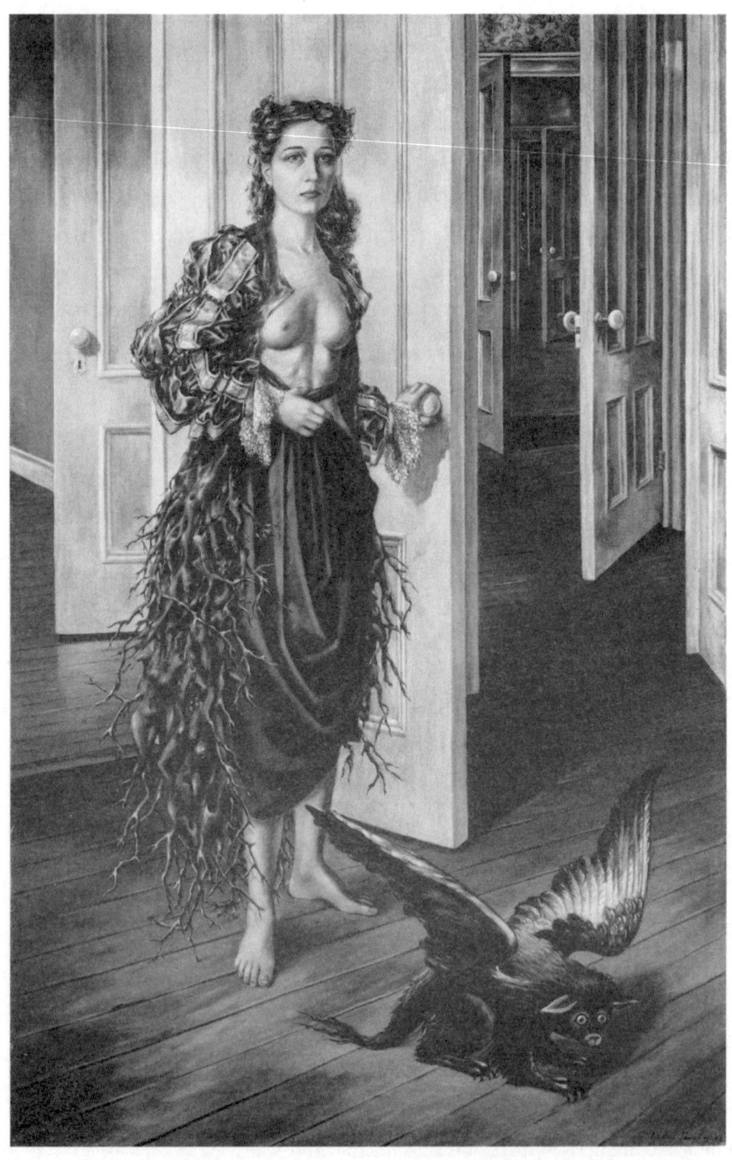

Dorothea Tanning, *Birthday*, 1942

Write about everything

'And by the way, everything in life is writable about if you have the outgoing guts to do it, and the imagination to improvise. The worst enemy to creativity is self-doubt.' —*Sylvia Plath*

Imagine if Sylvia Plath hadn't had the guts to be honest. Who gave her permission to speak so honestly? If she hadn't had the guts to apply pen to paper, then we wouldn't have Plath. But the truth is, we're not given that permission, it's up to us to give it to ourselves, to show our vulnerabilities. Try not to make fear your enemy – use it, surrender to it, and squash it!

Sylvia Plath (1932–63) was one of the most acclaimed American poets and authors of the twentieth century. She is admired for her confessional style, full of honesty, such as her poem 'Daddy' that deals with the troubled relationship she had with her father. Her only novel, *The Bell Jar*, follows the semi-autobiographical life of a young girl who dreams of being a poet.

Source: Plath, Sylvia; Kukil, Karen (ed.), The Journals of Sylvia Plath: 1950–1962, Faber, 2014

Give yourself the gift of reading

'I was writing seriously by the time I was in high school, and I knew it was something that I would always want to do. But how was I to earn a living? I didn't especially want to teach. I did want to give other people that kind of joy that I found from books, and libraries were the places I knew and felt good in, so it was natural enough that I should become a librarian.' —Audre Lorde

There can be nothing better than losing yourself in a book, discovering a different world. This festive season, think about what gift you can give yourself, what book you might read in the dark but cosy evenings.

I often think about this passage by the novelist Elizabeth Hardwick, from an interview with *The Paris Review* in 1985: 'The greatest gift is the passion for reading. It is cheap, it consoles, it distracts, it excites, it gives you knowledge of the world and experience of a wide kind. It is moral illumination.'

Audre Lorde (1934–92) was an American writer, teacher, philosopher, poet and civil rights activist. A self-described 'black, lesbian, mother, warrior, poet', Lorde is renowned for her writing – including the books *Sister Outsider* (1984) and *The Cancer Journals* (1980), which fearlessly explored race, gender, sexuality and identity.

Source: Winter, Nina, Interview with the Muse: Remarkable Women Speak on Creativity and Power, *Moon Books, 1978*

Stay indoors!

'The sun is your enemy
It will waste your time
Stay indoors if possible
With a book as protection from it.'
—Jeremy Deller

Deller has a point. No matter what season we may be in, to make art requires sacrifice. While one can enjoy the sun, to be immersed in one's work means sometimes we have to stay indoors. But he also reminds us, what better way is there to spend the winter season than to be protected by a book? Books are almost always guaranteed to bring you joy.

Jeremy Deller (b. 1966) is a British artist known for his highly broad, collaborative and conceptual art practice that has seen him inflate Stonehenge in a work called *Sacrilege*, organise a brass band to play acid house, and produce films about rave culture or the Brexit protests. As he wrote in his book, *Art Is Magic* (2023), 'Art is a way of staying in love with the world. It is also a form of magic.'

Source: A note to the author, 2025

Look for the lights

'The discovery of color was probably the most important thing that happened to me. I live color, it's like a language for me. I'm not conscious about it, it's just something that lives in me.' —Olga de Amaral

One thing I love most about this festive season are the lights: strung up on buildings, trees, lampposts and balustrades, accentuating the natural world, or on objects and furniture in our houses, or out on the streets.

Olga de Amaral is a Colombian artist renowned for her intricate weavings made from coloured fibres. Her works often resemble shimmering fields and frequently incorporate gold leaf, evoking the dazzling luminosity of the December season. (I like to think of them as being akin to the craquelure – the network of fine, natural cracks on aged surfaces – found on a medieval icon painting.)

But de Amaral has also frequently talked about how the colours of the Colombian landscape are deeply ingrained in her, and therefore her work. Today, when the lights are shining bright, think about what colours exist inside you.

Olga de Amaral (b. 1932) is a Colombian artist who creates fibre art that spans both small and monumental scales, moving fluidly between two- and three-dimensional forms. Her practice bridges the precision of traditional craft with the immersive qualities of installation art.

Source: A note to the author, 2025

Sit by the fire

'Because I didn't have a foundation in art, I was drawn to, let's say, someone like Rothko. His work glows, as you say. There's an inner light. He's not interested in directional light, in showing where the sun or the lamp is hitting something. I never painted that way [either]. And I kind of stumbled on a way to make my paintings luminous, and so I kept repeating it. And I think it comes from admiring a painter like Mark Rothko. It's an inner light. And you know, I think it might come from fire. When you're sitting by a hearth, the light is coming from that fire from somewhere. And all my time in Maine, we would sit by a wood stove that was glowing with heat, which we needed very much.' —Katherine Bradford

Bradford's words and painting, particularly *Couples Swim* (2015) (overleaf), remind me of the inner lights that people carry, too. When I think about the people I love, they glow in my eyes – as if they have an inner light. Who do you know who carries that glow? At this festive time, whose inner light could you seek out?

Katherine Bradford (b. 1942) is an American artist. Translating the freedom she felt after leaving the life of being a woman in stifling 1960s Connecticut and swapping it to be an artist in New York City, Bradford paints luminous paintings of swimming pools and cosmic skies, ballet dancers and bicycle riders. Looking at Bradford's paintings is like being transported into another world, whether it be outer space or in cosmic waters. It's like they are lit with a glow akin to a blanket of stars.

Source: The Great Women Artists Podcast, *2024/5*

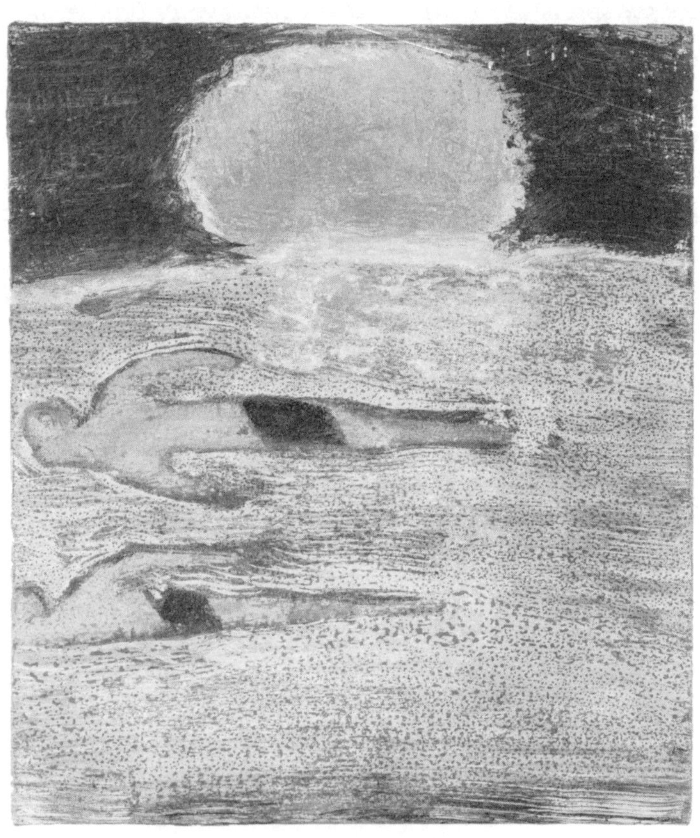

Katherine Bradford, *Couples Swim*, 2015

Embrace the solstice

'I write every day, and each morning I sit at my desk and try to picture a world otherwise.

That is, a world beyond hierarchies of power and order . . . that takes fellow feeling between humans and other living creatures . . . as the basis by which to live a shared life on this planet . . .

That process involves nothing more than trying to feel, anew, the texture of the everyday. I find I glimpse this most readily at those liminal times of day, the rise of the sun or the gathering of dusk, when all is uncertain and anything seems possible . . .

But the liminal can be a place too. A last strip of land before the earth gives way to the sea.' —Ekow Eshun

In the Northern Hemisphere, today is the winter solstice: the shortest day of the year, when the Earth is tilted furthest away from the sun. It's a time of balance, of a world about to change: tomorrow it won't be so dark, and light will continue to grow in our lives until the summer solstice in June.

The year is not yet over, but today it hangs in the balance. Take a moment to remember: what moments of happiness have you found this year, what sorrows have you lived through? How do you hope your year will start to move towards the light that grows from tomorrow?

Ekow Eshun (b. 1968) is an acclaimed writer, journalist, former magazine editor and museum director, curator and trailblazer in British culture. He has curated numerous exhibitions and authored books, such as *The Strangers: Five Extraordinary Black Men and the Worlds that Made Them* (2024).

Source: A note to the author, 2025

Celebrate

'Isn't it wonderful that we can admire something? Isn't it wonderful that we desire it?' —*Rose B. Simpson*

At the end of the day, loving, caring for and admiring each other is all we have. To deny something as wonderful as connection is to wilfully deny potential and possibility.

If you focus on the negative, then you are diminishing your experience. Learn to see the gifts, the lesson that something (or someone) taught you.

Rose B. Simpson (b. 1983) is a mixed media artist who lives and works in Santa Clara Pueblo, New Mexico, and is from a long lineage of women working in ceramics in her tribe.

Source: The Great Women Artists Podcast, *2024*

Embrace the world

'You have to realize that the artist is the instrument. I'm the instrument that the art has to come through. [. . .] That's how it is. It goes through you. And it has a lot of you in there. Everybody's art – either what you think or what you feel – it's like a fingerprint.' —Vija Celmins

I love how Celmins includes thinking and feeling as part of art. Her words help us focus on the uniqueness of everyone: everybody's art is like a fingerprint. It is always going to be unique, because it can only come from you. If you are ever worried about creating the same thing as someone else – or that someone else is creating the same thing as you – remind yourself that you are a single entity with thoughts, feelings, experiences that are entirely specific, and sacred, to you.

Take Celmins: she draws meticulously crafted oceans and night skies (overleaf). So many people have depicted these subjects before her. Yet hers are different: from the scale of the work to the mono-chromatic colours she uses, and the all-over angle she takes, devoid of horizon lines.

Vija Celmins (b. 1938) was born in Latvia and moved to Indianapolis, USA, aged ten. As a young girl, she collected comic books and picture playing cards ('because I couldn't speak English'), and looked to images as a form of language. Eventually, photographs, and later scientific images, would become the source material for her art.

Source: Oral history interview with Vija Celmins, Archives of American Art, Smithsonian Institution, 11 February–15 October 2009

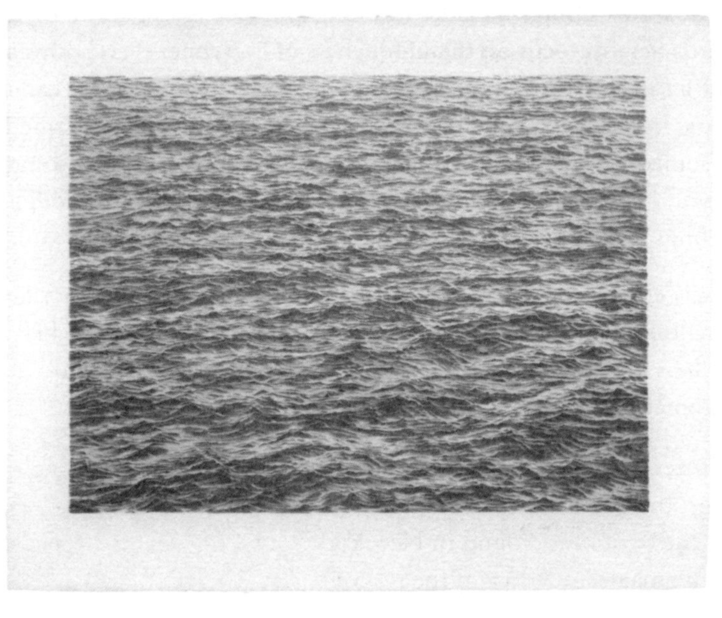

Vija Celmins, *Untitled Portfolio: Ocean,* 1975. Lithograph on Twinrocker Handmade Rag. Each: 12 ⅜ x 16 ⅜ inches; 31 x 42 cm © Vija Celmins, Courtesy Matthew Marks Gallery

Marvel at beauty

'My attitude is one of Love
is all adoration
for all the fringes
all the color
all tinsel creation.'
—Florine Stettheimer

It's Christmas Eve, and who better than Florine Stettheimer to be our guide for this shimmering season?

A poet, painter, performer and salon host, Stettheimer – working between the First and Second World Wars – captured glittering scenes of Manhattan life, elegant self-portraits and portraits of friends, outdoor picnics and 'spring sales' at Bendel's, in her signature palette of blazing oranges, yellows, greens and pinks.

But my favourite painting by her remains that of a yellow Christmas tree – as if constructed solely from light or a gold tinsel – adorned with colourful ornaments (see overleaf). Standing in the middle of a frozen lake and set against a dusky pink sky (with a gleaming red sun), the tree is surrounded by figure-skaters, sledges and skyscrapers evocative of those found in New York City. It's as if it is steeped both in the magical world and the real one, just like today.

On the night before Christmas, can you find some enchantment, marvel at the beauty of what people have created, and mark a time that feels like magic has descended on our world?

Florine Stettheimer (1871–1944) was an American artist and visionary working in a number of fields including painting, poetry, furniture-making, costume and set design.

Source: Stettheimer, Florine, Crystal Flowers, *New York, 1949 (published after her death by her sister, Ettie Stettheimer)*

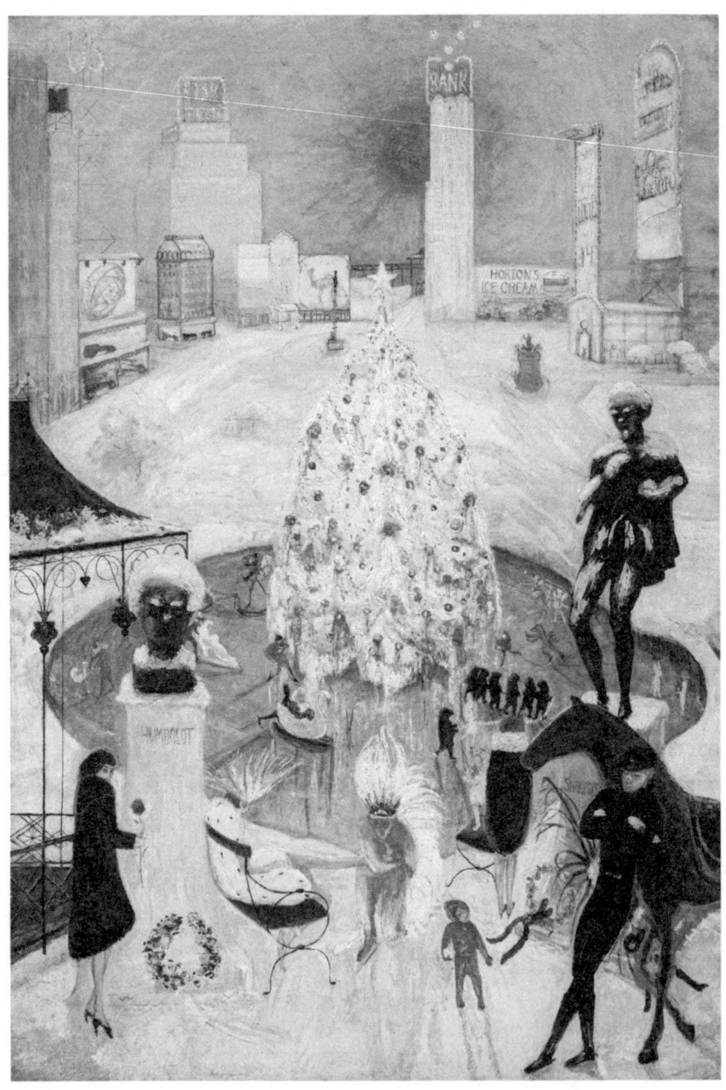

Florine Stettheimer, *Christmas*, c. 1930–40

Make the best out of life with the Queen of Christmas

'I have written my life in small sketches, a little today, a little yesterday . . . I look back on my life as a good day's work, it was done and I feel satisfied with it. I made the best out of what life offered.' —Grandma Moses

'Queen of Christmas' Anna Mary Robertson Moses – also known as 'Grandma Moses' – took up painting in the 1930s when she was in her seventies. (She once said, 'I just didn't have time.') She produced over 1,500 works, twenty-five of which were made after she turned 100 – not forgetting the 16 million Hallmark cards featuring her paintings that were sold in 1947!

Working from her vivid imagination, Moses painted simple folk scenes of people hanging up their colourful laundry, playing in the fields and making apple butter. She drew on the joyous memories of her long life and the simple beauty of the landscape that surrounded her in upstate New York, working without an easel, and using her bedroom or kitchen as a studio.

My favourites are her snow-filled scenes, sprinkled with glitter so they glisten (see overleaf). They evoke the delights of winter, with their powder-lined roofs, smoking chimneys, white speckled trees, and children in mismatched hats and scarves, sledging or helping to carry logs.

While the Christmas season may be filled with cheer, loved ones, family and festivities, for me the magic of Christmas Day lies in its stillness – as the only day in the Christian calendar when everything pauses, from the trains to the shops. It might be hectic for those with small children (or any age, for that matter), but if there's one day that you can save up to use for reflection, it's a day like today.

How can you, like Grandma Moses, take a moment to feel satisfied with what you've achieved? Notice how you've made the best out of what life offered, one day or one sketch at a time.

Grandma Moses (1860–1961) was an American artist famed for her joyous and simple depictions of landscapes in all different seasons.

Source: Grandma Moses: My Life's History, *Harper, 1952*

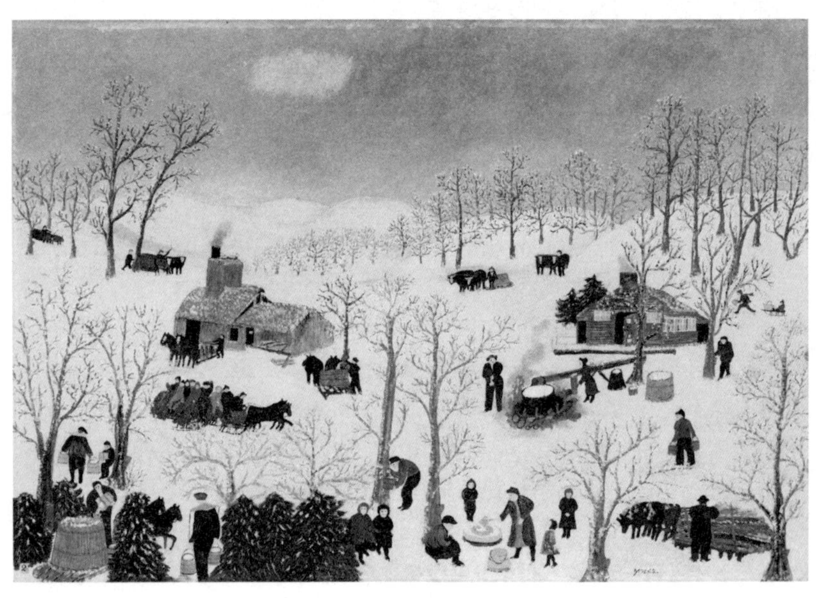

Grandma Moses, *Sugaring Off*, 1944

Be as honest as you can

'I like to be a glass house. There is no mask in my work. Therefore, as an artist, all I can share with other people is this transparency.' —*Louise Bourgeois*

As we edge towards the end of the year, take a great lesson from the French-American artist Louise Bourgeois, known for her prints, paintings, fabric works, sculptures and monumental installations that take the form of or draw on spiders, spirals, the body and more. She was born on Christmas Day 1911.

Think of all the artists who have come before you, all those you admire, the ways they've exposed themselves. Ask yourself, why is it that you admire them? Why are you drawn to their work? Is it because they dug deep, showed you something new, had the guts to speak about it in one way or another, and were, ultimately, honest? As humans, we are searching for honesty and transparency. We don't want to be lied to, or hidden from.

When you are making, or being in the world, how can you try to be like a glass house? Your viewer, lover or friend goes to you because they want to be let in. How joyful to connect to others.

The French-American artist **Louise Bourgeois** (1911–2010) was best known for her sculptures, prints, installations and fabric works, featuring motifs such as the spiral and the spider.

Source: 'Paulo Herkenhoff in conversation with Louise Bourgeois', in Louise Bourgeois, *Phaidon, 2003*

Embrace vulnerability

'All art is exposing. All art is about feeling, and pain, and everything. I think the thing to do always is not to let embarrassment put you off.' —Celia Paul

Whenever we put ourselves out there, we risk being embarrassed.

As we learnt yesterday, we go to artists because we want them to be honest with us. All art is exposing because it comes from a place of vulnerability, or putting yourself out there. The same is true of living: if we want to live honestly, we might expose ourselves. Take heart from all these great artists who have gone before us, who have not hidden behind embarrassment. Don't let anything put you off from joy!

Celia Paul (b. 1959) is a British artist, born in India. She paints intimate portrayals of those close to her, from her sisters to past lovers, whom she cloaks in a hazy glow.

Source: Celia Paul and Edmund de Waal in conversation with Katy Hessel, London Library, February 2023

Embrace your feelings

'Being an artist, [you] are so lucky because you can deal with inner feelings that you might not even be able to access with an analyst but it comes out in your art . . .' —*Audrey Flack*

What are you unable to communicate in words? How can you use art as a way to access and work out your feelings? Could it be through drawing what is in your mind; writing, without conscious thought; expressing yourself through music or dance; using a camera to capture how you feel (look up Tracey Emin's set of fifty selfies, titled *The Insomnia Room*)?

When we externalise our inner feelings through making, and give ourselves to the act of creation, we might just work out something that words couldn't give us the passkey for.

And remember: art doesn't have to be shared. You can use it just for yourself. Perhaps you'll be able to then work your emotions out in words. There is joy to be found in embracing your feelings, and confronting them with something that will be beautiful.

Audrey Flack (1931–2024) was an American sculptor of divine goddesses and Biblical characters as well as a pioneer of photorealist paintings. Never limiting herself, Flack was also a published author, and for many years, led vocals and banjo in her Audrey Flack and the History of Art Band.

Source: The Great Women Artists Podcast, *2024*

Stay interested

'It is simply this: do not tire, never lose interest, never grow indifferent – lose your invaluable curiosity and you let yourself die. It's as simple as that.' —Tove Jansson

What is the one thing that has united all those we've met over this year? A great curiosity, a thirst for learning, a desire to never lose interest, an urgent need to carry on looking and making; to be attuned and never grow indifferent; to know that all creative avenues are possible (no matter how big or small); and to know that beauty can always be present, whatever conditions you might find yourself in.

The Finnish writer and artist Tove Jansson lived through the horrors of both World Wars, but it was in the Second World War that she conceived of and began publishing stories about the wonderful world of the Moomins. As she once said: 'When I was feeling depressed and scared of the bombing and wanted to get away from my gloomy thoughts to something else entirely . . . I crept into an unbelievable world where everything was natural and benign – and possible.'

Using stories, colours and fantastical dreamlands to send her to faraway places in the depths of her imagination, Jansson made a world of warm, imaginative, open-minded creatures to remind us that whatever trenches we might find ourselves in, there can always be hope. What do you hope for in the year to come; what gives you hope in the life you live now? Take a moment, and write it down.

Tove Jansson (1914–2001) was a Swedish-speaking Finnish writer, artist, painter, cartoonist, novelist, illustrator and children's book author, best known for creating the wondrous world of the Moomins: the tales of Moominmamma, Moominpappa, and Moomintroll, and their adventures in Moominvalley.

Source: Jansson, Tove, Fair Play, *Sort of Books, 1989*

Recommit to your commitments

'Anyone can fly, all you gotta do is try.' —*Faith Ringgold*

Today is the penultimate day of the year. Whenever you joined us in this journey, celebrate what you've done, the wisdom you've learnt, the sense of possibility that can be found in living artfully. And remember, it's never too late to start anything up again. The most joyous thing you can do, as Ringgold says, is try.

Faith Ringgold (1930–2024) was a pioneering American artist known for her paintings, sculptures, story-quilts and children's books. Instrumental as an activist in the civil rights and feminist movements – and beyond – Ringgold, through her art, constantly challenged gender and racial inequalities and gave voice to the stories hidden by the media at the time.

Source: Ringgold said this many times. I heard her say it in conversation with her daughter, writer and critic Michele Wallace, at the Tate Modern, 2018

See in the New Year

'31st December 1947, 2.30 a.m.

My New Year's Toast: to all the devils, lusts, passions, greeds, envys, loves, hates, strange desires, enemies ghostly and real, the army of memories, with which I do battle – may they never give me peace.' —Patricia Highsmith

In the early hours of New Year's Eve 1947, the writer Patricia Highsmith was up toasting her battles. To feel deeply, to be imaginative and to apply that feeling to creative work, is a superpower that every human on the planet has been given, and that machines and AI cannot replace. It may feel relentless, even terrifying, to 'feel', but to have 'greeds', 'loves', 'memories' or 'strange desires' is part of being alive. Because if all those feelings gave you peace: what would be left of you?

To what will you toast tonight?

Patricia Highsmith (1921–95) was an American author of novels and short stories, famously known for creating the character Tom Ripley.

Source: Diary entry, 31 December 1947, Patricia Highsmith: Her Diaries and Notebooks, *Orion, 2021*

Acknowledgements

Thank you to my brilliant editor, Helen Conford, and literary agent, Karolina Sutton. Both have been the most incredible support over the last few years, continuously championing my work, and allowing me to write about artists and art history. Thank you to Izzy Redfern and the wider team at CAA. To everyone at Cornerstone and Penguin Random House: Venetia Butterfield, Laura Brooke, Najma Finlay, Joanna Taylor, Francisca Monteiro, Lydia Wiegel, Rebecca Ikin, Nicky Nevin, Peter Pawsey, Viki Ottewill, Ceara Elliott, Tim Bainbridge, Kirsten Greenwood, Alice Gomer, Emily Harvey, Phoenix Curland, Tineke Mollemans, Anjali Nathani, Lindsay Davies. Thank you to my US editor, Virginia Smith, and her fantastic team at Penguin Press. It is such an honour to work with you all.

Thank you to all the artists and artist estates included in this book, who gave me permission to feature your words and works. It is you who allow people like me to see the world in a better, hopeful and more joyous way. Thank you to everyone who approved, fact-checked and assisted in making this book possible, I am so grateful:

Alison Jacques, Fiona Amitai, and Isabel Mackenzie of Alison Jacques; Nick Willing and the Paula Rego team; Simon Prosser, Ruby Fatimilehin; Christine McMonagle and Sarah Knight at Hauser & Wirth; Maggie Wright at the Easton Foundation; Annabelle Birchenough, Ali MacGalip, Sibahle Daniel at Frith Street Gallery; Tucker Smith, Grace Taylor at the Wylie Agency; Caroline Hinnant, Lauren Gioia and Gabrielle Farina at Gagosian; Sara Chan, Niamh Brogan and Gabe Melson at David Zwirner; Virginia Sirena, Erin Manns, Bea Bradley at Victoria Miro; Leslie Tonkonow; Wendi Norris and Melanie Cameron; Marisa de Lempicka; Chrislan Fuller Manuel; Katarina Jerinic and The Woodman Family Foundation; Sara Fox at Pace; Phoebe Kong at

Marina Abramović studio; Harry Weller and Tracey Emin; Brandon Foushee; Nicolas Ochart and Andrew Blackley at Salon 94; Gemma Colgan; Carolyn Forrester at Jenna Gribbon studio; Frankie Rossi; Jana Nier Mooneyhan at the Niki de Saint Phalle Charitable Art Foundation; Emily Florido and Cecily Brown; Alison Lewis; Aya Satoh; Natalie Oleksy-Piekarski at Thomas Dane Gallery; Hannah Frieser at Carrie Mae Weems studio; Maria Davison; Sophie Bowness; Amy Hale; Ming Tiampo; Pamela Bannos; Peter K. Steinberg; Lavinia Singer; Lucy Howarth; Ben Berlow at Canada, NY; Andrea Provost; Veronica Levitt and Kaytlin Nodine at Casey Kaplan Gallery; Emma Vooght and Agata Rutkowska at White Cube; Lucy Price; Grace Storey; Ben Loveless; Riet Timmerman and Sam Will at Sadie Coles; Grace Hong and Rita Edwards at Galerie Lelong; Tilde Fredholm at Lévy Gorvy Dayan; Jessica Simas and Hannes Schroeder-Finckh at Sprüth Magers; Julie Niemi; Giulia Theodoli at Shirin Neshat studio; Tom Overton; Temitayo Shonibare and Es Devlin; Nellie Scott and Olivian Cha at Corita Art Center; Megan Schultz at Judy Chicago studio; Jonathan Horrocks, Yuka Lou, Amelia Good and Holly Stone at Stephen Friedman Gallery; Connor Monahan at Yoko Ono studio; Norah Perkins; Carlotta Dennis-Lovaglio; Liz O'Brien and Bonnie Steward at the Georgia O'Keeffe Museum; Ami Bouhassane and Kerry Negahban; Johanna Ortner at Maria Lassnig Foundation; Eleanor Johnson; Haani at Shahzia Sikander studio; Etsuko Sakurai; Judith Alexander at Judith Alexander Foundation; William T. Carson and Lisa Le Feuvre at the Holt Smithson Foundation; Sarah Shields and Ciara Derkenne at Art Gallery of New South Wales; Marika Lucas-Edwards and Tracey Dall at the National Gallery of Australia; Matthias Koddenberg at the Jeanne-Claude and Christo Foundation; Pam Johnson at the Dorothea Tanning Foundation; Astrid Meek at Wangechi Mutu studio; Kelsey Day; Shigeko Kubota and the Guerrilla Girls; Josh Milani; Georgia Lurie; Jamie Mackinnon; Ben Hunter; Sophia Jansson and Kira Schroeder; Lisa Wenger; Sofia Smith-Laing; Olivia Fraser; Monica

Truong; Virginia Nicholson; Sophie Partridge; Sarah Baxter at The Society of Authors; Maria Nevelson; Natasha Fairweather; Emma McKee; Maximillian William; Bridget Donahue; Molly Taylor at Kasmin Gallery; Kathleen Nugent Mangan at Lenore G. Tawney Foundation; Isabella Vitti at Ryan Lee Gallery; Emily Miraglia at Yancey Richardson; Agate Bortolussi; Macaella Gray at Ortuzar Projects; Claude Lewis; Daisy Murray Holman; Phil Alexandre; Hales Gallery; Michael Hoppen; Alexandra Truitt; Marc-Christoph Wagner at the Louisiana Museum; Mara Gans at Lisson Gallery; Arielle Stanger at Galerie St. Etienne; Severin Delfs at Hollis Taggart Gallery; Jurrell Lewis at Art21; Sally Mann; Raquel Mendieta; Junette Teng; Viva Ruggi.

Thank you to Ruth Chatto and Gilda Williams for your expert eagle eyes; Molly LaFosse for your hard work, brilliance, and heroic job organising permissions; Chantal Joffe for the conversations; Alex Needham for editing me at *The Guardian*; Holly Bott and Kate Cooper for your support; the London Library for welcoming me, and the Charleston team, too.

My brilliant friends – Alice, Gracie, Elle, Derya, Joel, Ruby, Amber, Flo, Ed Cumming, Lamorna Ash, Antonia Showering . . . and many more. You all know who you are. My wonderful family: Sarah, Felix, Michael, Katie, Victoria, Louisa (Jesse, Phoebe, Thea, Cleo), and especially to my kind (and very patient) parents, in particular my mum for always letting me read my work aloud to her again and again. This book is dedicated to you, for teaching me how to live an artful life!

Image Credits

p. 8: Paula Rego, *The Dance*, 1988 © Paula Rego Estate

p. 16: Luchita Hurtado, *Untitled*, 1969. Oil on canvas. 35 ¾ × 48 inches (90.8 × 121.9 cm). Signed and dated on verso. LH.180. © The Estate of Luchita Hurtado. Courtesy The Estate of Luchita Hurtado and Hauser & Wirth. Photo credit: Jeff McLane

p. 22: Ruth Asawa, *Untitled* (S.237, Hanging Six-Lobed, Interlocking Continuous Form), *c.* 1958. Hanging sculpture—enameled copper and brass wire. 72 x 15 x 15 inches. 182.9 x 38.1 x 38.1 cm. Artwork © 2025 Ruth Asawa Lanier, Inc. Courtesy David Zwirner

p. 28: Cornelia Parker. Installation view at Chisenhale Gallery for *Cold Dark Matter: An Exploded View*, 1991. Image courtesy the artist and Frith Street Gallery, London. Photo: Hugo Glendinning © the artist

p. 30: Agnes Denes, *Wheatfield – A Confrontation: Battery Park Landfill, Downtown Manhattan – With New York Financial Center*, 1982. Copyright Agnes Denes, courtesy Leslie Tonkonow Artworks + Projects

p. 47: Mary Husted, *Luke at 10 Days Old, Born 28 January 1963*, 1963, pencil on paper. Courtesy Mary Husted

p. 56: Leonora Carrington, *The Giantess (The Guardian of the Egg)*, *c.* 1947 © Estate of Leonora Carrington / ARS, NY and DACS, London 2025

p. 64: Celia Paul, *Plane Tree Shadow on my Wall*, 2013. Oil on canvas. 35.2 × 17.8 × 2 cm, 13 ⅞ × 7 ⅛ × ¾ in © Celia Paul, courtesy the artist

and Victoria Miro. Photography by Stephen White & Co., London

p. 76: Felix Gonzalez-Torres, *"Untitled" (Perfect Lovers)*, 1987–1990. Wall clocks. Two parts; ideally installed above head height. Original clocks: 13 ½ inches diameter each. Edition of 3, 1 AP. Installation view: Felix Gonzalez-Torres: The Politics of Relation. Museu d'Art Contemporani de Barcelona (MACBA), Barcelona, Spain. 26 Mar. – 19 Sep. 2021. Cur. Tanya Barson. Photo: Robert Ruiz © Estate Felix Gonzalez-Torres, courtesy of Felix Gonzalez-Torres Foundation

p. 81: Meta Vaux Warrick Fuller, *Ethiopia*, *c.* 1921, paint on plaster. H × W × D: 13 × 3 ½ × 3 ⅞ in. (33 × 8.9 × 9.8 cm). Collections of the Smithsonian National Museum of African American History and Culture, Gift of the Fuller Family, © Meta Vaux Warrick Fuller

p. 89: Artemisia Gentileschi, *Judith Slaying Holofernes*, 1620 ca, inv. 1890 n. 1567. Gallerie degli Uffizi. Gabinetto Fotografico delle Gallerie degli Uffizi – photo Roberto Palermo

p. 98: Francesca Woodman, *Self-Deceit #1*, 1978, from the *Self-Deceit* series. Gelatin silver print, 3 ⅝ × 3 9/16 in. (9.21 × 9.05 cm) © Woodman Family Foundation / DACS, London

p. 100: Frida Orupabo, *Untitled*, 2018. Collage: pigment print on acid-free cotton paper, mounting tape, split pins. 90.5 × 56.9 cm. 35 19/16 × 22 9/16 in. Unique. Courtesy Galerie Nordenhake. Photo: Carl Henrik Tillberg

p. 103: Sarah Lucas, *COOL CHICK BABY*, 2020, tights, wire, wool, shoes, acrylic paint, vinyl and metal chair. Sculpture: 96.5 × 77.5 × 90 cm / 38 × 30 × 35 ⅜ in plinth: 20.3 × 121.9 × 121.9 cm / 8 × 48 × 48 in © Sarah Lucas. Courtesy Sadie Coles HQ, London. Photo: Robert Glowacki

p. 119: Mary Delany, *Chrysanthemum Serotinum*, from an album (Vol. X, 17); Creeping Ox-Eye Daisy. 1781. Collage of coloured papers, with bodycolour and watercolour, on black ink background. British Museum, London. © The Trustees of the British Museum

p. 125: Senga Nengudi, *R.S.V.P. Reverie "Scribe"*, 2014, nylon mesh, sand and found metals, 231 × 137 × 170 cm | 91 × 54 × 67 inches © Senga Nengudi 2025, courtesy Sprüth Magers and Thomas Erben Gallery. Photo: Timo Ohler

p. 135: Es Devlin, *Come Home Again*, outside Tate Modern, 2022. Photo by Daniel Devlin

p. 138: Judy Chicago, *The Dinner Party*, 1974–79. Ceramic, porcelain, textile 576 × 576 in. (1463 × 1463 cm). Brooklyn Museum, gift of the Elizabeth A. Sackler Foundation, 2002.10 © Chicago Woodman LLC, Judy Chicago/Artists Rights Society (ARS), New York Photo © Chicago Woodman LLC, Donald Woodman/ ARS, New York

p. 143: Catherine Opie, *Matt and Jo*, 1993. C-print 20 × 16 in. 50.8 × 40.64 cm. © Catherine Opie. Courtesy the artist, Regen Projects, Los Angeles and Thomas Dane Gallery

p. 149: Leilah Babirye, *Senga Muzanganda (Auntie Muzanganda)*, 2020. Glazed ceramic, wire and found objects, 139.7 × 57.1 × 43.2 cm (55 × 22 ½ × 17 ⅛ in). Collection of Fotene Demoulas and Tom Coté. Copyright Leilah Babirye. Courtesy the artist; Stephen Friedman Gallery, London and New York; Gordon Robichaux, New York and Galerie Max Hetzler, Berlin | Paris | London | Marfa. Photo by Gregory Carideo

p. 161: Eva Hesse, *No title*. 1969– 70. Latex, rope, string, and wire. Dimensions variable. Purchase, with funds from Eli and Edythe L. Broad, the Mrs. Percy Uris Purchase Fund, and the Painting and Sculpture Committee. Inv. N.: 88.17a-b. Whitney Museum of American Art, New York, USA. © The Estate of Eva Hesse. Courtesy Hauser & Wirth. Photo: © 2025 Whitney Museum of American Art / Photo Scala, Florence

p. 164: Deborah Roberts, *Man[ly]*, 2019. Mixed media and collage on canvas, 165 × 114.3 cm (65 × 45 in). Private Collection. Copyright Deborah Roberts. Courtesy the artist and Stephen Friedman Gallery, London and New York. Photo by Paul Bardagjy

p. 169: Ayesha Singh, *Skewed Histories and Site Lines*, 2025, work-in-progress fragment of a digital print for the IAF façade of 468 × 40 ft, with images of Bega Begum's commissioned building named Humayun's Tomb, New Delhi, India. Image courtesy India Art Fair and Ayesha Singh

p. 173: Hannah Hoch, *Modenschau*, 1925–35 © DACS 2025, Grisebach GmbH. Photo: Kai-Annett Becker/ Berlinische Galerie

p. 178: Jenny Holzer, from *Survival* (1983–85), 1985. Installation: *Selection from the Survival Series*, Times Square, New York, 1985 © 2025 Jenny Holzer, ARS. Photo: John Marchael

p. 180: Howardena Pindell, *Untitled #49*, 2010, mixed media on board, 10 ¾ × 12 ½". Courtesy of the artist, Garth Greenan Gallery, New York, and White Cube

p. 192: Vivian Maier, *Self Portrait*, 1953 © Estate of Vivian Maier, Courtesy Maloof Collection and Howard Greenberg Gallery, New York

p. 196: Anna Maria Maiolino, *Entrevidas (Between Lives)*, from *Fotopoemação (Photopoemaction)* series, 1981, printed in 2014 Digital Print 122 × 78 cm / 48 × 30 ¾ in © Anna Maria Maiolino. Courtesy the artist and Hauser & Wirth. Photo: Stefan Altenburger Photography Zürich

p. 199: *Guerrilla Girls*, photo George Lange, 1991. Courtesy of Guerrilla Girls

p. 202: Rebecca Horn, *White Body Fan*, 1972, printed 2000. Gelatin silver photograph 58.5 × 42 cm. Art Gallery of New South Wales, purchased with funds provided by the Mervyn Horton Bequest 2003 © Estate of Rebecca Horn/Bild-Kunst. Copyright Agency Image © Art Gallery of New South Wales 12.2003

p. 205: Suzanne Valadon, *The Blue Room*, 1923. Oil on canvas, 90 × 116 cm. Artwork Location: Musée des Beaux-Arts, Limoges, France. Credit: RMN-Grand Palais / Bertrand Prévost / Dist. Foto SCALA, Florence 2025 © Photo Scala, Florence

p. 208: Doris Salcedo, *Act of Mourning, Plaza de Bolívar, Bogotá*, 2007, 25,000 candles (approx) © Doris Salcedo. Photo © Sergio Clavijo. Courtesy White Cube

p. 213: Mona Hatoum, *Current Disturbance*, 1996. © Mona Hatoum. Courtesy the artist. Photographer: Ben Blackwell. 2025

p. 217: Barbara Walker, *Vanishing Point 7 (Titian)*, 2018 © Barbara Walker. All rights reserved, DACS/Artimage. Photo: Chris Keenan

p. 222: Małgorzata Mirga-Tas, *Untitled (After Gentile da Fabriano)*, 2023. © Małgorzata Mirga-Tas. From the Collection of Kiran Nadar Museum of Art, New Delhi, India. Image courtesy the artist and Frith Street Gallery, London. Photo: Marek Gardulski

p. 225: Nancy Holt, *Sun Tunnels* (1973–76), Great Basin Desert, Utah. Concrete, steel, earth. Overall dimensions: 9 ft. 2-½ in. × 68 ft. 6in. × 53 ft. (2.8 × 20.8 × 16.2 m); length on the diagonal: 86 ft. (26.2 m). Photograph: Nancy Holt Collection Dia Art Foundation with support from Holt/Smithson Foundation © Holt/Smithson Foundation and Dia Art Foundation. Licensed by ARS, New York, and DACS, London

p. 235: Frida Kahlo, *Hammer and Sickle (and unborn baby)*, c. 1950. Dry plaster and mixed media (orthopedic corset). 41.28 x 33.02 x 15.4 cm. The Levett Collection / FAMM Museum, Mougins France. Photo: Jérôme Kelagopian

p. 242: Romaine Brooks, *Peter (A Young English Girl)*, 1923–24. Oil on canvas,

36 ⅛ × 24 ½ in. (91.9 × 62.3 cm), Smithsonian American Art Museum, Gift of the artist, 1970.70. Photo: © 2025 Smithsonian American Art Museum/Art Resource/Scala, Florence

p. 250: Tamara de Lempicka, *Portrait of Mrs. Rufus Bush*, 1929. Private Collection © 2025 Tamara de Lempicka Estate, LLC/ Adagp, Paris

p. 257: Loie Hollowell, *Standing in Blue*, 2018, oil paint, acrylic medium, sawdust, and high-density foam on linen mounted on panel, 72" × 54" × 3-½" (182.9 cm × 137.2 cm × 8.9 cm), #68878 © Loie Hollowell, courtesy Pace Gallery

p. 259: Kudzanai-Violet Hwami, *You are killing my spirit*, 2021. Oil on canvas 153 × 259.5 cm, 60 ¼ × 102 ⅛ in © Kudzanai-Violet Hwami, courtesy the artist and Victoria Miro. Photography by Jack Hems

p. 263: Lisa Yuskavage, *The Fuck You Painting*, 2020. Oil on linen, 12 × 11 ½ inches (30.5 × 29.2 cm) © Lisa Yuskavage. Courtesy the artist and David Zwirner

p. 266: Paula Rego, *Snow White and Her Stepmother*, 1995 © Paula Rego Estate

p. 289: Maggi Hambling, *April Wave Breaking*, oil on canvas, 2009, 153 × 244 cm © Maggi Hambling / Frankie Rossi Art Projects. Photographer: Doug Atfield

p. 291: Joy Hester, *Lovers [II]*, 1956, drawing in brush and ink and watercolour, image 75.3 (h) × 55.5 (w) cm, sheet 75.3 (h) × 55.5 (w) cm. National Gallery of Australia, Canberra. Purchased 1973 © 2025 Estate of Joy Hester/Copyright Agency. Licensed by DACS

p. 303: Karon Davis, *Echo & Narcissus: The Embrace*, 2023. Plaster, steel, glass eyes, tulle, and chicken wire, 70 × 35 × 40 inches (177.8 × 88.9 × 101.6 cm). Courtesy the artist and Salon 94. Photo by Elon Schoenholz. © Karon Davis

p. 306: Christo and Jeanne-Claude, *Surrounded Islands, Biscayne Bay, Greater Miami, Florida*, 1980–83. Photo: Wolfgang Volz © Christo and Jeanne-Claude Foundation

p. 317: Lina Bo Bardi, interior view at MASP, São Paolo. Photo: © Romullo Baratto

p. 326: Nicole Eisenman, *From Success to Obscurity*, 2004. Oil on canvas 129.5 × 101.6 cm / 51 × 40 in © Nicole Eisenman. Courtesy the artist and Hauser & Wirth

p. 340: Loretta Pettway, *Log Cabin – Single Block 'Courthouse Steps' variation (Local Name: 'Bricklayer')*, 1959, Cotton, 213.4 x 177.8 cm (84 x 70 in). Courtesy Souls Grown Deep Foundation and Alison Jacques © Loretta Pettway / Artists Rights Society (ARS), New York and DACS, London; photo: Stephen Pitkin/Pitkin Studio, Rockford, IL / Art Resource, NY

p. 352: Agnes Pelton, *Departure*, 1952 (oil on canvas). Private Collection Peter Palladino/The Agnes Pelton Society/ Bridgeman Images

p. 356: Barbara Hepworth, *The Family of Man*. Bronze, cast, and patinated. 1970. Allocated to the Fitzwilliam following acceptance in lieu by the Department for Culture, Media and Sport, from the Estate of Barbara Hepworth. Barbara Hepworth © Bowness. Photo © The Fitzwilliam

Museum, University of
Cambridge

p. 360: Clementine Keith-Roach, *Tide*,
2023, terracotta, plaster, wood and
steel armature, resin clay, acrylic
paint, 17 ¾ × 24 ⅜ × 22 ⅞ in. | 45 ×
62 × 58 cm. Courtesy the artist and
Ben Hunter, London. Photographer:
Damian Griffiths

p. 369: Magdalena Abakanowicz,
retrospective exhibition at the
Museum of Contemporary Art (Musée
d'art contemporain) Montreal, 1983.
Photo: Artur Starewicz/AACCF/
East News

p. 384: Lois Dodd, *Back of Men's Hotel
(from My Window)*, 2016, oil on linen,
42 × 30 inches. © Lois Dodd, courtesy
Alexandre Gallery, New York

p. 398: Marlene Dumas, *Oscar Wilde*,
2016. Image courtesy the artist and
Frith Street Gallery, London. Photo:
Marcus Leith © the artist

p. 400: Maggi Hambling, *Cedric,
February 8th 1982*. Charcoal on paper,
1982, 27 × 59.9 cm, British Museum,
London

p. 405: Installation view of Karon Davis,
No Good Deed Goes Unpunished at
Jeffrey Deitch, New York, 2021. Photo
by Cooper Dodds; courtesy of the
artist and Jeffrey Deitch, New York
and Los Angeles

p. 407: Ishiuchi Miyako, *Mother's #19*,
2001 © Ishiuchi Miyako, courtesy of
The Third Gallery Aya

p. 407: Ishiuchi Miyako, *Mother's #49*,
2002 © Ishiuchi Miyako, courtesy of
The Third Gallery Aya

p. 411: Julia Margaret Cameron, *The
Dream*, photo. Isle of Wight, 1869.

© Victoria and Albert Museum,
London

p. 415: Doris Salcedo, *Sumando Ausencias,
Plaza de Bolívar, Bogotá, Colombia*,
11 October 2016 © Doris Salcedo.
Photo © Oscar Monsalve. Courtesy
White Cube

p. 418: Installation view of Louise
Bourgeois's *Maman*, 1999 during
the exhibition *Louise Bourgeois:
The Eternal Thread*, Long Museum,
Shanghai, China (1½/18-2/24/19).
Photo: JJYPHOTO © The Easton
Foundation/Licensed by VAGA at
ARS, NY and DACS, London 2025

p. 424: Danielle Mckinney, *Hold your
Breath*, 2024. Oil on linen 24 × 18
inches, 61 × 45.7 cm. Framed: 24
⅞ × 18 ⅞ inches, 63.2 × 47.9 cm ©
Danielle Mckinney

p. 434: Lois Dodd, *Front Door Cushing*,
1982, oil on linen, 60 × 32 inches. ©
Lois Dodd, courtesy Alexandre Gallery,
New York

p. 436: Yoko Ono, *My Mommy Is
Beautiful*, 2004. Installation view,
Kunsthaus Zürich, 2022. Photo by
Franca Candrian © Kunsthaus
Zürich

p. 445: Augusta Savage, *Lift Every Voice
and Sing*, New York World's Fair, 1939.
Art & Artifacts Division, Schomburg
Center for Research in Black Culture,
The New York Public Library

p. 448: Dorothea Tanning, *Birthday*,
1942 © ADAGP, Paris and DACS,
London 2025

p. 454: Katherine Bradford, *Couples Swim*,
2015. Acrylic on canvas, 20 × 17 ⅛
inches (50.80 × 43.50 cm), courtesy the
artist and CANADA, New York

January

06/01: Courtesy of Louisiana Channel, 2023

07/01: Interview from *The Great Women Artists Podcast* by Deborah Levy. Copyright © 2021, Deborah Levy, used by permission of The Wylie Agency (UK) Limited

10/01: © 2025 The Josef and Anni Albers Foundation / Artists Rights Society (ARS), New York. Courtesy The Josef and Anni Albers Foundation and David Zwirner

14/01: © 2025 Ruth Asawa Lanier, Inc. Courtesy David Zwirner

15/01: *The Great Women Artists Podcast*, 2023. Copyright © Hilton Als, used by permission of The Wylie Agency LLC

20/01: © Agnes Denes

February

05/02: © 2025 Banco de México Diego Rivera Frida Kahlo Museums Trust, Mexico, D.F. / Artists Rights Society (ARS), New York

15/02: Campt, Tina M., *A Black Gaze*, p. 27, © 2021 Massachusetts Institute of Technology, by permission of The MIT Press

16/02: © Magdalene A.N. Odundo

20/02: Excerpted from 'Carrie Mae Weems: On Photography', published on Art21.org in September 2018. Original interview conducted by Susan Sollins in November 2008

23/02: Barbara Hepworth © Bowness

28/02: Nikki Giovanni , from the *On Being with Krista Tippett* episode 'Remembering Nikki Giovanni — ' "We Go Forward With a Sanity and a Love" ', first broadcast 17 March 2016. Reprinted with permission. Hear the full episode at onbeing.org

March

04/03: © Magdalene A.N. Odundo.

07/03: © 1963 Meredith Operations Corporation. All rights reserved. Reprinted/Translated from LIFE and published with permission of Meredith Operations Corporation. Reproduction in any manner in any language in whole or in part without written permission is prohibited. LIFE and the LIFE logo are registered trademarks of Meredith Operations Corporation. Used under license

11/03: *The Great Women Artists Podcast*, 2023. Copyright © Hilton Als, used by permission of The Wylie Agency LLC

15/03: Barbara Hepworth © Bowness

16/03: Interview from *The Great Women Artists Podcast* by Deborah Levy. Copyright © 2021, Deborah Levy, used by permission of The Wylie Agency (UK) Limited

17/03: Copyright © Binyam, Maya, 'Stealing It Back: A Conversation with Frida Orupabo', *The Paris Review*, 25 April 2022, used by permission of The Wylie Agency (UK) Limited

25/03: Courtesy of Louisiana
Channel, 2024

29/03: Copyright © Adler, Laure,
'Beginning with Color: An Interview
with Etel Adnan', *The Paris Review*, 4
October 2023, used by permission of
The Wylie Agency (UK) Limited

April

07/04: © 2025 Ruth Asawa Lanier, Inc.
Courtesy David Zwirner

21/04: © Catherine Opie. Courtesy the
artist, Regen Projects, Los Angeles and
Thomas Dane Gallery

28/04: Reproduced with permission of
the Curtis Brown Group Ltd

May

16/05: Copyright © Aitken, Will, 'Anne
Carson, The Art of Poetry No. 88', *The
Paris Review*, Issue 171, Fall 2004, used
by permission of The Wylie Agency
(UK) Limited and by permission of
Anne Carson and Aragi Inc. All rights
reserved

18/05: Excerpted from 'Jenny Holzer:
"For 7 World Trade" and "Redaction
Paintings"', published on Art21.org
in October 2016. Original interview
conducted by Susan Sollins in
December 2006

June

03/06: Barbara Hepworth © Bowness

24/06: Excerpted from 'Tania Bruguera:
Defining an Artist', published on
Art21.org in September 2019. Original

interview conducted by Susan Sollins
in March 2014

26/06: Quote by Helen Frankenthaler
© 2025 Helen Frankenthaler
Foundation, Inc.

30/06: © 2025 Banco de México Diego
Rivera Frida Kahlo Museums Trust,
Mexico, D.F. / Artists Rights Society
(ARS), New York

July

12/07: Reproduced with permission of the
Curtis Brown Group Ltd

August

Beauty: Copyright © Babbitt, Natalie,
Tuck Everlasting, Farrar, Straus and
Giroux, 1975

02/08: Ithell Colquhoun, *Goose of
Hermogenes*, first published in 1961
by Peter Owen, London. Extract
reproduced courtesy of Pushkin Press

07/08: Copyright © Hirsch, Edward,
'Susan Sontag, The Art of Fiction',
The Paris Review, Issue 143, Winter
1995, used by permission of The Wylie
Agency (UK) Limited

29/08: Barbara Hepworth © Bowness

31/08: Published in Great Britain by
Granta Books, 2023

September

05/09: Courtesy of Louisiana
Channel, 2022

12/09: © 2025 Banco de México Diego
Rivera Frida Kahlo Museums Trust,

Mexico, D.F. / Artists Rights Society (ARS), New York

13/09: By permission of Nick Laird and Faber and Faber Ltd

19/09: Excerpted from 'In the Studio: Lynn Hershman Leeson', published on Art21.org in October 2023. Original interview conducted by Christine Turner in December 2017

22/09: Loretta Pettway, *Log Cabin – Single Block 'Courthouse Steps' variation (Local Name: 'Bricklayer')*, 1959, Cotton, 213.4 x 177.8 cm (84 x 70 in). Courtesy Souls Grown Deep Foundation and Alison Jacques © Loretta Pettway / Artists Rights Society (ARS), New York and DACS, London; photo: Stephen Pitkin / Pitkin Studio, Rockford, IL / Art Resource, NY

25/09: Copyright © Dwyer, Kate, 'Throwing Yourself into the Dark: A Conversation with Anne Carson', *The Paris Review*, 17 April 2024, used by permission of The Wylie Agency (UK) Limited and by permission of Anne Carson and Aragi Inc. All rights reserved

October

02/10: Published in Great Britain by Granta Books, 2023

03/10: Barbara Hepworth © Bowness

November

04/11: By permission of The Society of Authors as the Literary Representative of the Estate of Virginia Woolf

14/11: Courtesy of Louisiana Channel, 2020

20/11: Quotation from Doris Salcedo in the Art21 television series *Art in the Twenty-First Century*, Season 5 'Compassion', 2009

25/11: Excerpted from 'In the Studio: Lynn Hershman Leeson', published on Art21.org in October 2023. Original interview conducted by Christine Turner in December 2017

December

01/12: Courtesy of Louisiana Channel, 2016

14/12: Excerpt from 'Projecting Fictions: Insurrection! Our Tools Were Rudimentary, Yet We Pressed On', published on Art21.org in October 2016. Original interview conducted by Susan Sollins in December 2002

16/12: *The Journals of Sylvia Plath* by Sylvia Plath, reproduced with permission of Faber and Faber Ltd

17/12: Copyright © Pinckney, Darryl, 'Elizabeth Hardwick, The Art of Fiction No. 87', *The Paris Review*, Issue 96, Summer 1985, used by permission of The Wylie Agency (UK) Limited

25/12: Copyright © 1952 (renewed 1980) Grandma Moses Properties Co. New York